Big Book of Quick Crosswords

300 puzzles

Book 3

Published by Richardson Publishing Limited.
www.richardsonpublishing.com

10 9 8 7 6 5 4 3 2 1

All puzzles supplied by Clarity Media Ltd.

Cover design by Junior London Ltd.

ISBN 978-1-913602-28-4

Printed and bound by CPI Group (UK) Ltd, Croydon CR0 4YY.

A catalogue record for this book is available from the British Library.

If you would like to comment on any aspect of this book, please contact us at:

E-mail: puzzles@richardsonpublishing.com

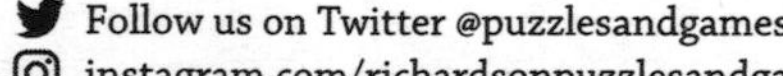
Follow us on Twitter @puzzlesandgames
instagram.com/richardsonpuzzlesandgames
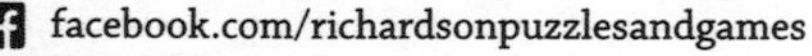
facebook.com/richardsonpuzzlesandgames

Contents

How to play

Write the answers to each of the clues in the grid to complete the crossword puzzle.

No. 1

Across

1 Game of chance (8)
5 Leave out (4)
9 Hidden storage space (5)
10 Provokes (7)
11 Put in the ground (7)
12 Courage; boldness (5)
13 Make worse (6)
14 Number of Apostles (6)
17 All (5)
19 Mournful poems (7)
20 Short trips on another's behalf (7)
21 Measuring instrument (5)
22 Locate or place (4)
23 Unnecessary (8)

Down

1 Open-mindedness (13)
2 Unfasten (7)
3 Very exciting (12)
4 Groups of three (6)
6 A thing that measures (5)
7 Blandness (13)
8 Generally accepted (12)
15 Time off (7)
16 Person to whom a lease is granted (6)
18 White heron (5)

No. 2

Across

1 Speaks publicly (6)
7 Shared (8)
8 Dry and mocking (3)
9 Bean (6)
10 Trees that bear acorns (4)
11 Ditches (5)
13 Competition (7)
15 Rich sweet roll (7)
17 Natural underground chambers (5)
21 Unpleasant monster (4)
22 Column (6)
23 Lad (3)
24 Temple dedicated to all the gods (8)
25 Named (6)

Down

1 Ahead (6)
2 Shelter; place of refuge (6)
3 Make a search (5)
4 Endanger (7)
5 Machines (8)
6 Not as light (6)
12 Shields from (8)
14 Helicopter (7)
16 Style of popular music (6)
18 Oral (6)
19 Steady (anag.) (6)
20 Hard rock (5)

No. 3

Across

1 Took temporary possession of (8)
5 Upper part of the body (4)
8 Former name of the Democratic Republic of Congo (5)
9 Precludes (7)
10 Nuclear ___ : device that generates energy (7)
12 Conspicuous (7)
14 One who breaks the rules (7)
16 Persistent problem (7)
18 Witty saying (7)
19 Stagger (5)
20 Blades for rowing a boat (4)
21 Frankly (8)

Down

1 Low humming sound (4)
2 Nasal (6)
3 Compliance (9)
4 Exertion (6)
6 Has objective reality (6)
7 Chaos (8)
11 Grouped together (9)
12 Straw hat (8)
13 Less attractive (6)
14 Black Sea peninsula (6)
15 Routed (anag.) (6)
17 Watery part of milk (4)

No. 4

Across

1 Large underground chamber (4)
3 Insincere and dishonest (3-5)
9 Not tense (7)
10 Red cosmetic powder (5)
11 An idea that is added later (12)
14 Item for catching fish (3)
16 Go to see (5)
17 Ground condensation (3)
18 Pay tribute to another (12)
21 Red-chested bird (5)
22 Oval (7)
23 Uses a piece of machinery (8)
24 Belonging to a woman (4)

Down

1 Window furnishings (8)
2 Personal attendant (5)
4 Roll of bank notes (3)
5 Luckily (12)
6 Defeated heavily (7)
7 Fixed costs (4)
8 Lavish event (12)
12 Plantain lily (5)
13 Small pincers (8)
15 Distress (7)
19 Plentiful (5)
20 A group of three people (4)
22 Make a living with difficulty (3)

No. 5

Across

1 Mocking (8)
5 Mischievous sprites (4)
9 Advised; encouraged (5)
10 Hot wind blowing from North Africa (7)
11 Malice (5)
12 Small social insect (3)
13 Locates or places (5)
15 Asserts (5)
17 Mountain pass (3)
19 Walk heavily and firmly (5)
20 Aims or purposes (7)
21 Command (5)
22 Clothing (4)
23 Climbed (8)

Down

1 Deep consideration of oneself (4-9)
2 Kind of music (7)
3 First part of the Bible (3,9)
4 Place inside something else (6)
6 Variety of strong coffee (5)
7 Easily angered (5-8)
8 Swimming technique (12)
14 Stashed away (7)
16 Deletes (6)
18 Coming after (5)

No. 6

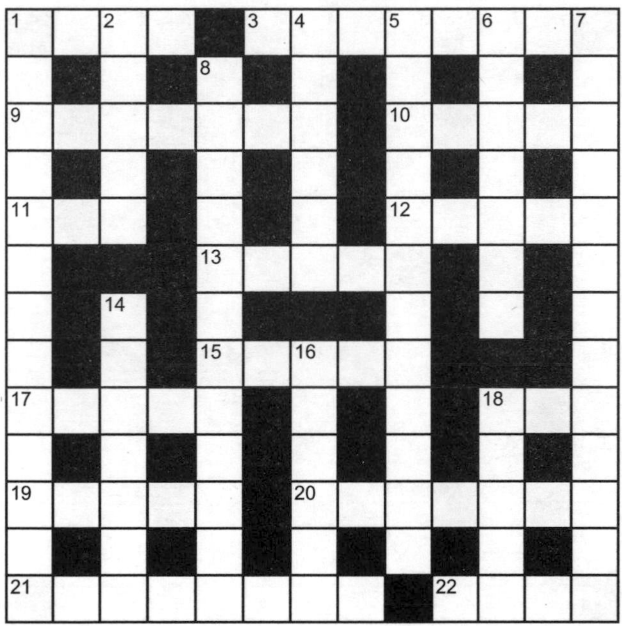

Across

1 Part of a sleeve (4)
3 Diabolical (8)
9 Uncertain (7)
10 Waterlogged ground (5)
11 Exclamation of contempt (3)
12 Member of a Catholic religious order (5)
13 Finely cut straw (5)
15 Big cat (5)
17 Hackneyed (5)
18 Use a chair (3)
19 Goodbye (Spanish) (5)
20 Strong verbal attack (7)
21 Enthusiasm (8)
22 Drop (4)

Down

1 Respond aggressively to military action (7-6)
2 One side of a gem (5)
4 Archimedes' famous cry (6)
5 Intolerable (12)
6 Meaninglessness (7)
7 Excessively negative about (13)
8 Food shop (12)
14 Unintelligent (7)
16 Diagrams (6)
18 Brazilian dance (5)

No. 7

Across

1 Fearful of open spaces (11)
9 Bustle (3)
10 Got up (5)
11 Relating to country life (5)
12 Corrodes (5)
13 Teacher (8)
16 Unorthodox person (8)
18 Darken (5)
20 Folds close together (5)
21 Tiny crustaceans (5)
22 Secret retreat (3)
23 Ghost (11)

Down

2 Fun activities (5)
3 Highways (5)
4 Showed to be true (6)
5 Perform in an exaggerated manner (7)
6 Granite (anag.) (7)
7 Very charming (11)
8 Expansion (11)
14 Pear-shaped fruit native to Mexico (7)
15 Cut of meat (7)
17 Roe of sturgeon (6)
18 Give a false notion of (5)
19 Extinct birds (5)

No. 8

Across

1 Upsetting (11)
9 Arose from slumber (5)
10 Damage (3)
11 Leaves out (5)
12 Large spoon with a long handle (5)
13 Proof of something (8)
16 Strong type of coffee (8)
18 Raucous (5)
21 Metal spikes (5)
22 Seed of an apple (3)
23 Respond to (5)
24 Positives and negatives (4,3,4)

Down

2 Restrain (7)
3 Discarded; binned (7)
4 Excitingly strange (6)
5 Iron alloy (5)
6 Wanderer (5)
7 Compose a dance routine (11)
8 Glass buildings (11)
14 Frenzied (7)
15 Drug that relieves pain (7)
17 Wrench an ankle (6)
19 Device that clears a car windscreen (5)
20 Linear measures of three feet (5)

No. 9

Across

1 Shelter for pigeons (8)
5 Effigy (4)
9 Swagger (5)
10 State of the USA (7)
11 In a carefree manner (12)
14 Born (3)
15 Lift up (5)
16 Long narrow inlet (3)
17 Highly abstract (12)
20 Pestering constantly (7)
22 Horse's cry (5)
23 Money in notes or coins (4)
24 Cartoon character who can fly (8)

Down

1 Portion of medicine (4)
2 Wordy (7)
3 Extremely harmful (12)
4 Popular beverage (3)
6 Worthless material (5)
7 A period of 366 days (4,4)
8 Insubordination (12)
12 Enlighten; educate morally (5)
13 Assisting the memory (8)
16 Philosophical theory (7)
18 Roman robes (5)
19 Protruding part of the lower jaw (4)
21 Antelope (3)

No. 10

Across

1 Theoretical (8)
5 Make beer or ale (4)
9 Fabric used to make jeans (5)
10 Rich fish soup (7)
11 State of the USA (12)
13 Applauds (6)
14 Yearly (6)
17 Strengthen; confirm (12)
20 Not outside (7)
21 The Norwegian language (5)
22 Negative votes (4)
23 Blows up (8)

Down

1 Totals (4)
2 Genuine (7)
3 Money paid for work (12)
4 Triangular bone at the base of the spinal column (6)
6 Noble gas (5)
7 Practicable (8)
8 In accordance with general custom (12)
12 A division between people (8)
15 Spoke (7)
16 Designed for male and female use (6)
18 Move out of the way (5)
19 Clarets (4)

No. 11

Across

1 State of the USA (4)
3 Creative (8)
9 Severe (7)
10 Path to follow (5)
11 Cuban dance (5)
12 Sign of the zodiac (7)
13 Heavy food (6)
15 Writing desk (6)
17 Reluctance to change (7)
18 Leg bone (5)
20 Softly radiant (5)
21 Type of cocktail (7)
22 Evacuating (8)
23 Cheese coated with red wax (4)

Down

1 Value too lowly (13)
2 Warning of danger (5)
4 Alcove (6)
5 Preliminary (12)
6 Crush underfoot (7)
7 Informal expression (13)
8 Immediately (12)
14 Coincide partially (7)
16 Fish with pink flesh (6)
19 Construct (5)

No. 12

Across

1 Abilities (6)
7 Impartial parties (8)
8 Hog (3)
9 Excessively (6)
10 Touch (4)
11 Ascends (5)
13 People of noble birth (7)
15 Irritating (7)
17 A sum owed (5)
21 Spiciness (4)
22 Device for removing impurities (6)
23 Depression (3)
24 Not pleasing to listen to (8)
25 Absorbent material (6)

Down

1 Pungent condiment (6)
2 Horse-drawn vehicles (6)
3 Growl with bare teeth (5)
4 Hiding underground (7)
5 Three-sided figure (8)
6 Flout (6)
12 Individual things (8)
14 Breathed in sharply (7)
16 Sorrowful (6)
18 Heavy load (6)
19 Multiply by three (6)
20 Surface shine (5)

No. 13

Across

1 One overly concerned with minor details (6)
4 Easily identifiable (6)
9 Remove a difficulty (7)
10 Caused by motion (7)
11 Narrow roads (5)
12 Joining together with cord (5)
14 Speculate (5)
17 Annoying insects (5)
19 Make wavy (5)
21 Finished (3,4)
23 Termite (anag.) (7)
24 Irritates (6)
25 Loves greatly (6)

Down

1 Pouch (6)
2 Opposite of up (4)
3 One's savings for the future (4,3)
5 Polite and courteous (5)
6 Closeness (8)
7 Dairy product (6)
8 Factual TV program (11)
13 Cut (8)
15 Tumbled from a horse (7)
16 Synopsis; diagram (6)
18 Sequence (6)
20 Concise and full of meaning (5)
22 Change course (4)

No. 14

Across

1 Unskilled; amateur (8)
5 Shaft on which a wheel rotates (4)
9 Less common (5)
10 Pamphlet (7)
11 Doctrine; system of beliefs (5)
12 Gang (3)
13 Country in the Middle East (5)
15 Group of birds (5)
17 Relieve or free from (3)
19 Planet on which we live (5)
20 Thief (7)
21 Unit of weight (5)
22 Level and regular (4)
23 Invariable (8)

Down

1 Irretrievable (13)
2 Sincere (7)
3 Resolutely (12)
4 Long swelling wave (6)
6 Vascular tissue in plants (5)
7 Institution (13)
8 Quarrelsome and uncooperative (12)
14 Predatory fish (7)
16 Exaggerate (6)
18 Mournful song (5)

No. 15

Across

1 Inventiveness (11)
9 Killer whales (5)
10 Cry of disapproval (3)
11 Rejuvenate (5)
12 Stomach exercise (3-2)
13 Compassion; benevolence (8)
16 Extremely happy (8)
18 e.g. beef and lamb (5)
21 Distinguishing characteristic (5)
22 Piece of cloth (3)
23 Rule (5)
24 Respectful (11)

Down

2 Large wine bottles (7)
3 Getting bigger (7)
4 Most pleasant (6)
5 Long pointed teeth (5)
6 Circle a planet (5)
7 Additionally (11)
8 Difficult and intricate (11)
14 Stand for small objects (7)
15 Sheer dress fabric (7)
17 Bearlike (6)
19 Debate in a heated manner (5)
20 Shopping binge (5)

No. 16

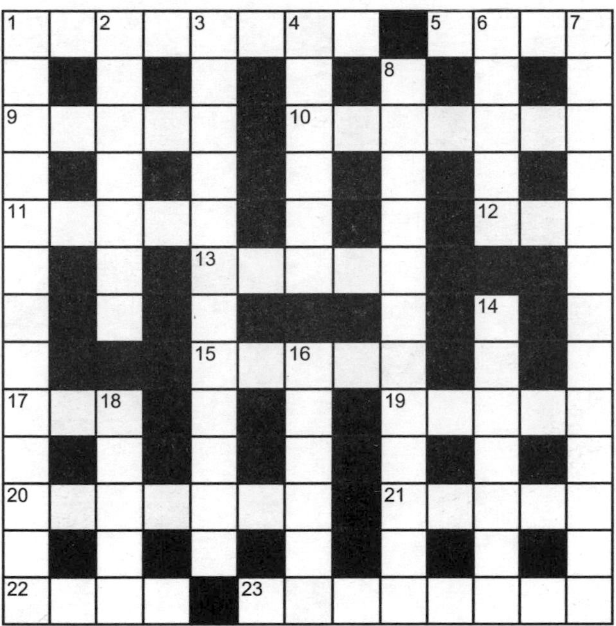

Across

1 Hand clapping (8)
5 Entrance corridor (4)
9 Camera image (5)
10 Jumping (7)
11 Dramatic musical work (5)
12 Louse egg (3)
13 South American dance (5)
15 English homework assignment (5)
17 Ancient boat (3)
19 Performing a deed (5)
20 Something showing a general rule (7)
21 Foresee or predict (5)
22 Wooden crosspiece attached to animals (4)
23 Deferrer (anag.) (8)

Down

1 Roughly (13)
2 Shore birds (7)
3 Therapeutic use of plant extracts (12)
4 Morose (6)
6 Horror film directed by Ridley Scott (5)
7 Given to thievery (5-8)
8 Major type of food nutrient (12)
14 Sharp painful blow (7)
16 Ball-shaped object (6)
18 Natural talent (5)

No. 17

Across

1 Crazy person (6)
4 Bleach (6)
9 Suitor (7)
10 Tumult (7)
11 Shoot with great precision (5)
12 God of love (5)
14 Mopes (5)
17 Sandy wasteland (5)
19 Large pile of something (5)
21 Imparts knowledge (7)
23 Ban on publication (7)
24 Broken fragments of glass (6)
25 Grinding tool (6)

Down

1 Believer in the occult (6)
2 Sullen (4)
3 Yields a supply of (7)
5 Rounded protuberances on camels (5)
6 Mexican pancake (8)
7 Hospital carers (6)
8 Computation (11)
13 Region of a shadow (8)
15 Mix a deck of cards (7)
16 Urges to act (6)
18 Jostle or push roughly (6)
20 Challenged (5)
22 A flat float (4)

No. 18

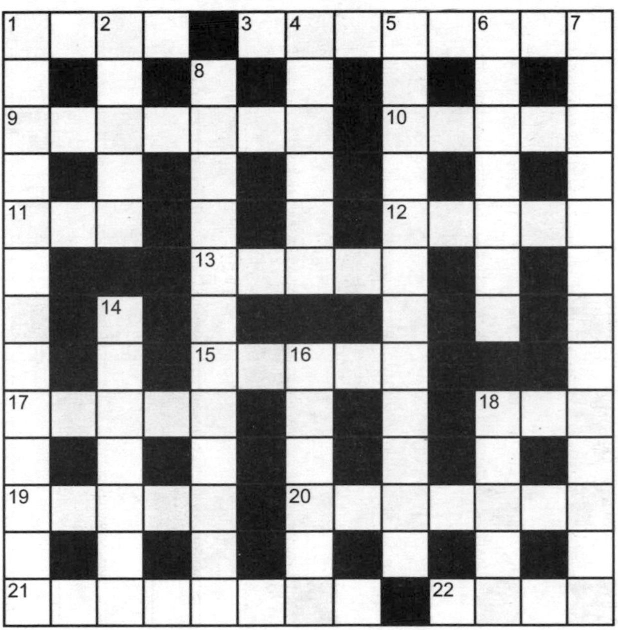

Across

1 Doubtful (4)
3 Person who repairs cars (8)
9 Nationalist (7)
10 Crustacean like a shrimp (5)
11 Bristle-like appendage (3)
12 Money (5)
13 Levy (5)
15 e.g. arms and legs (5)
17 Ship's load (5)
18 Sense of self-esteem (3)
19 Group (5)
20 Remains (7)
21 Releasing from a duty (8)
22 Military force (4)

Down

1 Unfeasible (13)
2 Japanese mattress (5)
4 Scope (6)
5 Despair (12)
6 Subtleties (7)
7 Sweets (13)
8 Garments worn in bed (12)
14 Nonconformist (7)
16 Woman in charge of nursing (6)
18 Senior figure in a tribe (5)

No. 19

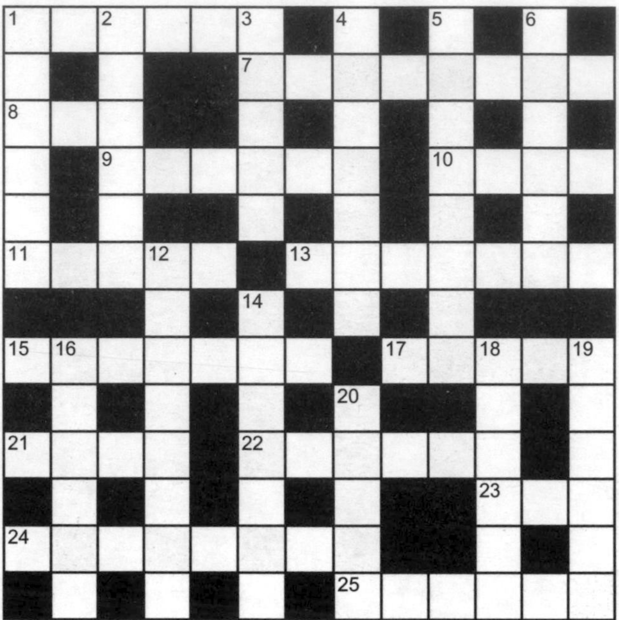

Across

1 Vivacious (6)
7 Twist together (8)
8 Solemn pledge (3)
9 Liveliness (6)
10 Snooker players use these (4)
11 Hoarse (5)
13 Rendered senseless (7)
15 Country that borders Libya (7)
17 Inner circle (5)
21 Insects that make honey (4)
22 Particles of sand (6)
23 Cuddle (3)
24 Rucksack (8)
25 Shouted out (6)

Down

1 Princely (6)
2 Letters like 'a' and 'e' (6)
3 Resay (anag.) (5)
4 Written law (7)
5 Large snake (8)
6 Sheepskin (6)
12 Memento (8)
14 Cotton fabric (7)
16 Margin of safety (6)
18 Imperial capacity measure (6)
19 Yearned for (6)
20 Tall and thin (5)

No. 20

Across

1 Daring (11)
9 Singing voice (5)
10 Sound of a dove (3)
11 Music with a recurrent theme (5)
12 Mistaken (5)
13 Offered (8)
16 Small loudspeakers (8)
18 Undo (5)
21 Deprive of weapons (5)
22 Animal fodder (3)
23 Sprites (5)
24 Temporary inability to remember something (6,5)

Down

2 Distinguished (7)
3 Taught (7)
4 Fester (6)
5 Insectivorous mammal (5)
6 Very masculine (5)
7 Consideration of the future (11)
8 US politician (11)
14 Rebuttal (7)
15 Made of clay hardened by heat (7)
17 Beetle that damages grain (6)
19 Herb (5)
20 Happening (5)

No. 21

Across

1 Formal agreement (8)
5 Pass (anag.) (4)
9 Country in the Himalayas (5)
10 Type of alcohol (7)
11 Harsh; corrosive (7)
12 Oarsman (5)
13 State of the USA (6)
14 Requesting (6)
17 Draws into the mouth (5)
19 Type of handicraft (7)
20 Building (7)
21 Musical pace (5)
22 Emit a breath of sadness (4)
23 Competition participants (8)

Down

1 Awareness (13)
2 One of the planets (7)
3 Connection or association (12)
4 Compel by intimidation (6)
6 Tough fibrous tissue (5)
7 Sanctimonious (4-9)
8 Marksman (12)
15 Brutal; cruel (7)
16 Television surface (6)
18 Hold on to tightly (5)

No. 22

Across

1 Makes wider (8)
5 Protective crust over a wound (4)
9 Cooks slowly in liquid (5)
10 Coming from the south (7)
11 Unpredictably (12)
13 Single-celled organism (6)
14 Emperor of Japan (6)
17 Atmospheric layer (12)
20 Sanction something reluctantly (7)
21 Implant (5)
22 Perfume ingredient (4)
23 Written laws (8)

Down

1 Having a lot to do (4)
2 Aromatic herb (7)
3 The dispersal of goods (12)
4 Subtle variation (6)
6 Races (anag.) (5)
7 Extravagant fuss (8)
8 Amazement (12)
12 Pepper plant (8)
15 Agile circus performer (7)
16 State with confidence (6)
18 Steps of a ladder (5)
19 Lyric poems (4)

No. 23

Across

1 Exterior of a motor vehicle (8)
5 Falls back (4)
9 Brief burst of bright light (5)
10 French dance (7)
11 Hostile aggressiveness (12)
14 Very cold; slippery (3)
15 Not quite right (5)
16 Pasture; meadow (3)
17 Middleman (12)
20 Give authority to (7)
22 Assists in a crime (5)
23 Team (4)
24 Spurned (8)

Down

1 Shine (4)
2 Group of parishes (7)
3 Small garden carts (12)
4 Floor mat (3)
6 Relay device (5)
7 Emaciated (8)
8 Make a guess that is too high (12)
12 Dirt (5)
13 Natives of a state (8)
16 Biggest (7)
18 Recorded (5)
19 Sued (anag.) (4)
21 Fish eggs eaten as food (3)

No. 24

Across

1 Internet meeting place (4,4)
5 Insect stage (4)
8 Bring together (5)
9 African country (7)
10 Receptacle for cigarette residue (7)
12 Blissful state (7)
14 Earnest (7)
16 Small ornament (7)
18 Ricochet (7)
19 Section of a long poem (5)
20 Ship's complement (4)
21 Anticlimax (8)

Down

1 Successful move (4)
2 Self-evident truths (6)
3 Capital of Iceland (9)
4 Expenditure (6)
6 Uncertain (6)
7 Rigorous investigation (8)
11 Anguish (9)
12 Abstruse (8)
13 Feasible (6)
14 Workplace for an artist (6)
15 Juicy citrus fruit (6)
17 Attic (4)

No. 25

Across

1 Changed (8)
5 Boyfriend or male admirer (4)
9 Sycophant (5)
10 Walked quickly (7)
11 Begrudges (7)
12 Dissenting religious groups (5)
13 Absence of passion (6)
14 Large prawns (6)
17 Relation by marriage (2-3)
19 Advocate (7)
20 A child beginning to walk (7)
21 Mortise insert (5)
22 Masticate (4)
23 Naive or sentimental (4-4)

Down

1 Desiring worldly possessions (13)
2 Salt lake in the Jordan valley (4,3)
3 Unseen observer (3,2,3,4)
4 Entangle (6)
6 Principle of morality (5)
7 Lacking in control (13)
8 Long athletics race (5-7)
15 Stonework (7)
16 Rare (6)
18 Ridge (5)

No. 26

Across

1 Feeling of hatred (11)
9 Animal foot (3)
10 Hardy agile ruminants (5)
11 Entice to do something (5)
12 Regal (5)
13 Mesmerism (8)
16 Merciless (8)
18 Strong lightweight wood (5)
20 Mature human (5)
21 Two times (5)
22 Intentionally so written (3)
23 Specialist in care for the feet (11)

Down

2 Minor road (5)
3 Tycoon (5)
4 Almost (6)
5 Challenging (7)
6 Furthest away (7)
7 Fitting (11)
8 Satisfactory (2,2,7)
14 Steadfast (7)
15 Compliment unduly (7)
17 Small crustacean (6)
18 Let air escape from a valve (5)
19 Slips (anag.) (5)

No. 27

Across

1 Consumes (4)
3 Great difficulty (8)
9 Leopard (7)
10 Religious table (5)
11 Go inside (5)
12 Upstart; one who has recently gained wealth (7)
13 Stomach crunches (3-3)
15 Strikes firmly (6)
17 Taken as a whole (7)
18 The reproduction of sound (5)
20 One image within another (5)
21 Kenya's capital (7)
22 Government by a king or queen (8)
23 Price (4)

Down

1 Art movement (13)
2 Principle or belief (5)
4 Sudden (6)
5 Graphical (12)
6 Warmest (7)
7 Musician (13)
8 Chair proctor (anag.) (12)
14 Treachery (7)
16 Settle decisively (6)
19 Italian cathedral (5)

No. 28

Across

1 Causing difficulties (11)
9 Bird claw (5)
10 One and one (3)
11 At that place; not here (5)
12 Establish (3-2)
13 Wrapper for a letter (8)
16 Concise (8)
18 Singing voices (5)
21 Wears well (5)
22 Make less bright (3)
23 Venerate; worship (5)
24 Youth (11)

Down

2 Be given (7)
3 Totally (7)
4 Move with a bounding motion (6)
5 Makes musical sounds (5)
6 Short choral composition (5)
7 Holland (11)
8 Neutral (11)
14 Triangle with three unequal sides (7)
15 Costing (anag.) (7)
17 Unfastens (6)
19 Shy (5)
20 Stable compartment (5)

No. 29

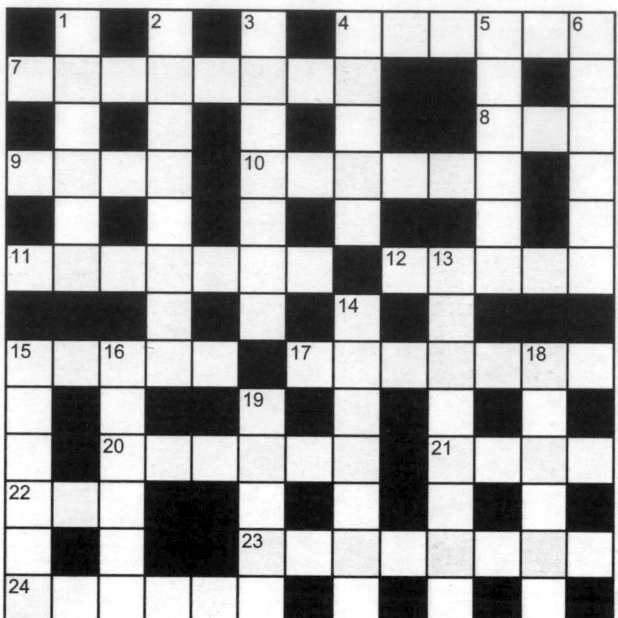

Across

4 Season (6)
7 Summary (8)
8 Item that unlocks a door (3)
9 Flightless bird (4)
10 Obstruct (6)
11 Attack (7)
12 Upper coverings of buildings (5)
15 Impudent; cheeky (5)
17 Astronomical units (7)
20 Establish by calculation (6)
21 Unpleasantly moist (4)
22 Female deer (3)
23 Imitator (8)
24 Colliers (6)

Down

1 Egg-shaped solids (6)
2 Opposite of departures (8)
3 Primarily (7)
4 Rocks back and forth (5)
5 Get by with what is available (4,2)
6 Poems; sounds alike (6)
13 Glass-like volcanic rock (8)
14 Hurtful (7)
15 Rarely (6)
16 Scattered about untidily (6)
18 Very large vulture (6)
19 Hits high up in the air (5)

No. 30

Across

1 Eat like a bird (4)
3 Lightest chemical element (8)
9 Bows (7)
10 Schemes (5)
11 Excessive response (12)
14 Silent (3)
16 Thin mortar (5)
17 Pay (anag.) (3)
18 Not excusable (12)
21 Bodies of water (5)
22 Weakened a solution (7)
23 Irritating (8)
24 Garden outbuilding (4)

Down

1 Acts in a play (8)
2 Strong thick rope (5)
4 Opposite of no (3)
5 Monotonously (12)
6 Study of rocks (7)
7 Overly curious (4)
8 Bravely (12)
12 In the company of (5)
13 Magnificent (8)
15 Model of the body (7)
19 Bungle (5)
20 Simple non-flowering plant (4)
22 Loud noise (3)

No. 31

Across

1 Yearly celebration (11)
9 Put in position (5)
10 Writing instrument (3)
11 Tortoise carapace (5)
12 Entrance hallway (5)
13 Grasslands (8)
16 Expression of praise (8)
18 Concave roofs (5)
21 Cook meat in the oven (5)
22 Bed for a baby (3)
23 SI unit of luminous flux (5)
24 Pertaining to office workers (5-6)

Down

2 Collection of sheets of paper (7)
3 Beseech (7)
4 Make possible (6)
5 Projecting horizontal ledge (5)
6 Response (5)
7 Make in bulk (4-7)
8 Increasing gradually by degrees (11)
14 Periodical (7)
15 Disease carried by mosquitoes (7)
17 Of the universe (6)
19 Contest (5)
20 Flatten on impact (5)

No. 32

Across

1 Hackneyed statement (6)
7 Fervently (8)
8 Frying pan (3)
9 Country in the Middle East (6)
10 Dice (anag.) (4)
11 This date (5)
13 Unity (7)
15 Insubstantial (7)
17 Timepiece (5)
21 Having no money (4)
22 Extremely courageous (6)
23 One's family (3)
24 Dismiss as unimportant (5,3)
25 Roofing material made of straw (6)

Down

1 Oppose a plan successfully (6)
2 Mean (6)
3 Polite address for a woman (5)
4 Confusing (7)
5 Distinguishing mark (8)
6 Extraterrestrials (6)
12 Tank for keeping fish (8)
14 Soften the effect of (7)
16 Periods of history (6)
18 Entry pass (6)
19 Side of an arch (6)
20 Rough version of a document (5)

No. 33

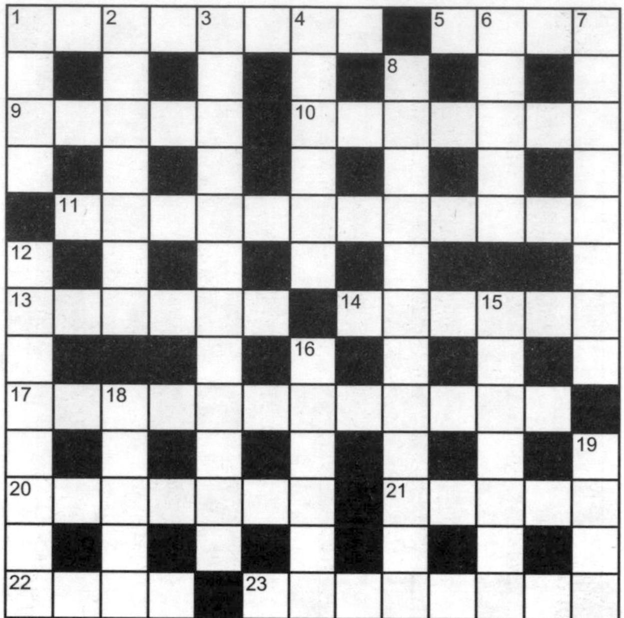

Across

1 Large rocks (8)
5 Lied (anag.) (4)
9 Style of Greek architecture (5)
10 Green with vegetation (7)
11 Drawback (12)
13 Dog-like mammals (6)
14 Ghost (6)
17 Narcissism (4-8)
20 Make a substantial profit (5,2)
21 Crazy (5)
22 Not knowing where one is (4)
23 Infancy (8)

Down

1 Areas of ground for growing plants (4)
2 Country whose capital is Kyiv (7)
3 Formal announcements (12)
4 Bring back to life (6)
6 Stage play (5)
7 Supplication (8)
8 Clearness (12)
12 Pertaining to the body (8)
15 Italian rice dish (7)
16 Ideally perfect state (6)
18 Vegetables related to onions (5)
19 Saw; observed (4)

No. 34

Across

1 Fraudulently (11)
9 Wild dog of Australia (5)
10 Edible nut (3)
11 Carer (anag.) (5)
12 Military trainee (5)
13 Act of removal (8)
16 Relating to courts of law (8)
18 Escapade (5)
21 Destiny; fate (5)
22 Zero (3)
23 Fast (5)
24 Plant-eating insect (11)

Down

2 Freezing (3-4)
3 Cause to absorb water (7)
4 Papal representative (6)
5 Unemotional (5)
6 Expressed clearly (5)
7 Greenish (11)
8 Style of painting (8,3)
14 Type of computer (7)
15 Assign (7)
17 Aloof (6)
19 Directly opposite in character (5)
20 Exposes to danger (5)

No. 35

Across

1 Visage (4)
3 Aspiration (8)
9 Deep gorges (7)
10 Garden tools (5)
11 Shyness (12)
13 Painter (6)
15 Harsh (6)
17 Spanish adventurer (12)
20 Foot joint (5)
21 Lively festivities (7)
22 Innate ability (8)
23 Care for or look after (4)

Down

1 Absurd (8)
2 Crave; desire (5)
4 Failed to hit the target (6)
5 Regardless of (12)
6 Annoying (7)
7 Facial feature (4)
8 Irrelevant (12)
12 Informed upon (8)
14 Box of useful equipment (7)
16 Set in layers (6)
18 Research deeply (5)
19 Heroic tale (4)

No. 36

Across

1 Small bottle (4)
3 Reverie (8)
9 Harmonious relationship (7)
10 Rescues (5)
11 By chance (12)
14 Pouch; enclosed space (3)
16 Pick out; choose (5)
17 Level golf score (3)
18 Occult (12)
21 Similar (5)
22 Expressed disapproval facially (7)
23 Fence of stakes (8)
24 Unfortunately (4)

Down

1 Person highly skilled in music (8)
2 Fruit (5)
4 Division of a play (3)
5 Long essay (12)
6 Surround completely (7)
7 Source of inspiration (4)
8 Entirety (12)
12 Free from dirt (5)
13 Introductory pieces of music (8)
15 Critical (7)
19 Relating to the kidneys (5)
20 Part of a door fastening (4)
22 Gave a meal to (3)

No. 37

Across

1 Hair-cleansing preparations (8)
5 Injure (4)
8 Brace (5)
9 Part of a church near the altar (7)
10 Trailblazer (7)
12 Depict in a particular way (7)
14 Split (7)
16 Island in the West Indies (7)
18 Pragmatist (7)
19 Genuflected (5)
20 Tiny specks (4)
21 Pristine (5-3)

Down

1 Unwell (4)
2 Forum icon (6)
3 Spicy sausage (9)
4 Hold a position or job (6)
6 Male relatives (6)
7 Put up with (8)
11 Unreserved in speech (9)
12 Lied under oath (8)
13 Marked effect (6)
14 Speak hesitantly (6)
15 Not noticed (6)
17 Cook slowly in liquid (4)

No. 38

Across

1 Capital of Bahrain (6)
4 Thought; supposed (6)
9 Live longer than (7)
10 Spruce up (7)
11 Therefore (5)
12 Domesticated (5)
14 Nasal passageway (5)
17 Seed cases (5)
19 Knocks into (5)
21 Expressive (of music) (7)
23 Writing fluid holder (7)
24 Leave a place (6)
25 Six-legged arthropod (6)

Down

1 Outsider (6)
2 Longest river (4)
3 Ways of doing things (7)
5 Piece of land (5)
6 Tidiness (8)
7 Obligations (6)
8 All the time (11)
13 Cartographer (8)
15 Heighten (7)
16 Constrain or compel (6)
18 Soundless (6)
20 Ladder rungs (5)
22 Sweet dessert (4)

No. 39

Across

1 The West (8)
5 Freezes over (4)
8 Lingers furtively (5)
9 Porch (7)
10 Discharge from a hole in a pipe (7)
12 Primates (7)
14 Become husky (7)
16 Act of going back in (2-5)
18 Mountaineer (7)
19 Indian monetary unit (5)
20 Capital of Peru (4)
21 Adjoining (8)

Down

1 Greasy (4)
2 Opera by Bizet (6)
3 Harm the reputation of (9)
4 Books (6)
6 Strong cloth used to make sails (6)
7 Male astronaut (8)
11 Ridge of the Himalayas (9)
12 Pertaining to measurement (8)
13 Inert gaseous element (6)
14 Composite of different species (6)
15 Flexible (6)
17 Temporary outside shelter (4)

No. 40

Across

1 Animal feet (4)
3 Raised road (8)
9 A number defining position (7)
10 Come with (5)
11 Antique; not modern (3-9)
14 Eccentric (3)
16 Ellipses (5)
17 That vessel (3)
18 Reallocate (12)
21 Confess to be true (5)
22 Design of fashionable clothes (7)
23 Paper printout of data (4,4)
24 Strong beers (4)

Down

1 Etiquette (8)
2 Trudged through water (5)
4 Pointed tool (3)
5 Part of the mind (12)
6 Table servers (7)
7 System of contemplation (4)
8 Unfriendly (12)
12 Vital organ (5)
13 Young hares (8)
15 Visionary (7)
19 Normal (5)
20 Solemn promise (4)
22 Container for a drink (3)

No. 41

Across

1 Shade of blue (11)
9 Diving bird (3)
10 Sudden sharp pains (5)
11 Ice cream is often served in these (5)
12 Toy bear (5)
13 Having no worries (8)
16 Cosmos (8)
18 Large intestine (5)
20 Japanese form of fencing (5)
21 Old-fashioned (5)
22 Item used in cricket (3)
23 Well-known sentence (11)

Down

2 Found agreeable (5)
3 Make good on a debt (5)
4 Sacred phrase (6)
5 Salvaged (7)
6 Convent (7)
7 Great upheavals (11)
8 Scatter widely (11)
14 Mechanical keyboard (7)
15 Tuneful (7)
17 Stop talking (4,2)
18 Programmer (5)
19 Parts of the cerebrum (5)

No. 42

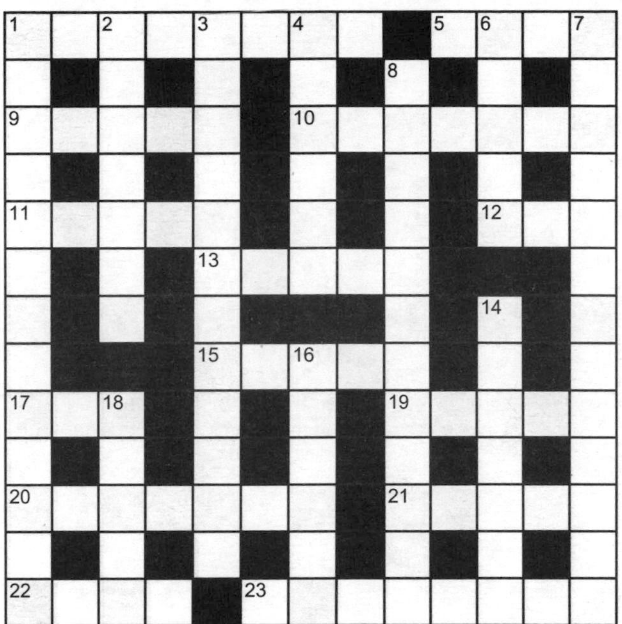

Across

1 Assigns a job to (8)
5 South Asian garment (4)
9 Relating to a city (5)
10 Drinking vessel (7)
11 Warning noise from an emergency vehicle (5)
12 Small sprite (3)
13 Play a guitar (5)
15 Bottoms of shoes (5)
17 Anger (3)
19 Wound from a wasp (5)
20 Plans to do something (7)
21 Promotional wording (5)
22 Yellow part of an egg (4)
23 Come before in time (8)

Down

1 Ease of use or entry (13)
2 State of being very poor (7)
3 Not staying the same throughout (12)
4 Unsteady gait (6)
6 Saying (5)
7 Untiring (13)
8 Not allowable (12)
14 Connoisseur; gourmet (7)
16 Diminish (6)
18 Praise enthusiastically (5)

No. 43

Across

4 Trite remark (6)
7 Sport popular in America (8)
8 Swish (of an animal's tail) (3)
9 Luxurious; stylish (4)
10 Soak up (6)
11 Surprise (7)
12 Sculptured symbol (5)
15 Groups of animals (5)
17 Platform (7)
20 Capital of Germany (6)
21 Argues (4)
22 Chatter (3)
23 Predict the future (8)
24 Expert in a particular subject (6)

Down

1 Prance around (6)
2 Tied up (8)
3 Shackle (7)
4 Nearby (5)
5 Cattle herder (6)
6 Next after seventh (6)
13 Able to read and write (8)
14 Nation (7)
15 Finish a telephone call (4,2)
16 Decorative strip of fabric (6)
18 Ill (6)
19 High up (5)

No. 44

Across

1 Depart suddenly (6)
4 Get hold of (6)
9 Continuing (7)
10 Herb related to parsley (7)
11 Tennis stroke (5)
12 Small seat (5)
14 Divide; separate (5)
17 Irritable (5)
19 Ancient harps (5)
21 Certificate (7)
23 Quarrel or haggle (7)
24 Hate (6)
25 Knitted pullover (6)

Down

1 Dancing clubs (6)
2 Arrive (4)
3 Astonishing things (7)
5 Counterfeit (5)
6 Beekeeper (8)
7 Gold lump (6)
8 Deliberately cruel (4-7)
13 Cloudy (8)
15 Circus apparatus (7)
16 Decreased one's speed (6)
18 Annually (6)
20 Road information boards (5)
22 Cereal grains used as food (4)

No. 45

Across

1 Founded (11)
9 Auction offer (3)
10 Aimed (anag.) (5)
11 Train tracks (5)
12 Poetic verse (5)
13 Boring into (8)
16 Unfairness (8)
18 Religious book (5)
20 Sets of players (5)
21 Acoustic detection system (5)
22 Lipid (3)
23 Spookiness (11)

Down

2 Regrettably (5)
3 Pure love (5)
4 Linger aimlessly (6)
5 Germ-free (7)
6 Show (7)
7 Shortened (11)
8 Homework tasks (11)
14 Corrupt (7)
15 Estimates (7)
17 Passageway through rock (6)
18 Element with atomic number 5 (5)
19 Polishes (5)

No. 46

Across

1 Headland (4)
3 Hazardous (8)
9 Inclination (7)
10 Colossus (5)
11 Small venomous snake (5)
12 Kettledrums (7)
13 Resistant to something (6)
15 Stick to (6)
17 Beginning to exist (7)
18 Short treatise (5)
20 Lift with effort (5)
21 Containerful (7)
22 Apparition (8)
23 Disgust with an excess of sweetness (4)

Down

1 Friendship (13)
2 Yearned for (5)
4 Distinct being (6)
5 Menacing (12)
6 Strong reaction of anger (7)
7 Mawkishly (13)
8 Separation; alienation (12)
14 Eyelash cosmetic (7)
16 Expresses one's opinion (6)
19 Dreadful (5)

No. 47

Across

1 Support (6)
7 Comical (8)
8 Not on (3)
9 Avoiding waste; thrifty (6)
10 Song by two people (4)
11 Cabs (5)
13 Word opposite in meaning to another (7)
15 Speak to (7)
17 Be sparing with (5)
21 Dagger handle (4)
22 Shape (6)
23 Nay (anag.) (3)
24 Cheerily (8)
25 Protect from danger (6)

Down

1 Quantity (6)
2 Element added to the end of a word (6)
3 Part of the leg (5)
4 Grinning (7)
5 Severe traffic congestion (8)
6 Certainly (6)
12 Source of annoyance (8)
14 Able to read minds (7)
16 Stage plays (6)
18 Time of widespread glaciation (3,3)
19 Made a victim of (6)
20 Becomes worn at the edges (5)

No. 48

Across

1 Causes pain or suffering (8)
5 Coniferous trees (4)
8 Tread heavily (5)
9 Cornmeal (7)
10 Restricted in use (7)
12 Period of conflict (7)
14 Showed something briefly (7)
16 Needleworker (7)
18 Urgent (7)
19 Join together (5)
20 Wise; herb (4)
21 Large Eurasian maple (8)

Down

1 Peas (anag.) (4)
2 Bloom (6)
3 Lacking tolerance (9)
4 Push over (6)
6 Set on fire (6)
7 Reference point; norm (8)
11 Tree known for the nut it produces (9)
12 Frailty (8)
13 Assisting (6)
14 Foamy (6)
15 Coiffure (6)
17 Your current location (4)

No. 49

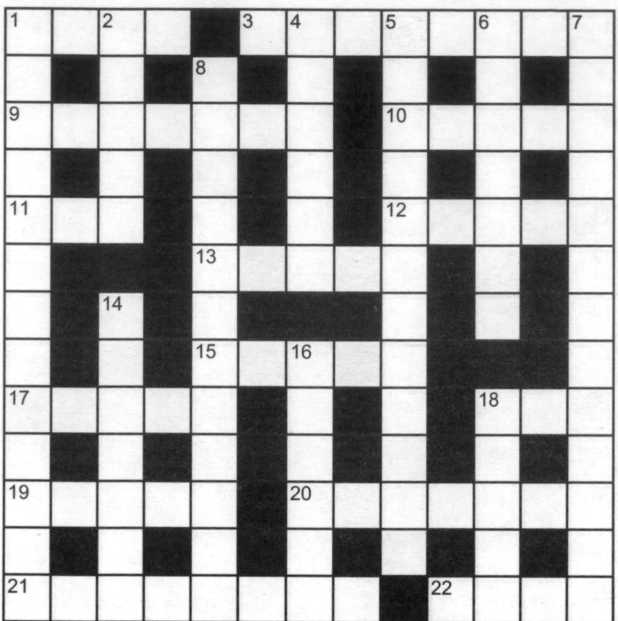

Across

1 Strongbox (4)
3 Highly seasoned smoked beef (8)
9 Person who keeps watch (7)
10 Anxiety (5)
11 Popular edible fish (3)
12 Latin American dance (5)
13 Public meeting for open discussion (5)
15 Moves back and forth (5)
17 Major African river (5)
18 Annoy constantly (3)
19 Gemstones (5)
20 Impresario (7)
21 Showering with liquid (8)
22 Item of footwear (4)

Down

1 Embarrassed (4-9)
2 Narrow sea inlet (5)
4 Part of a stamen (6)
5 Act of sending a message (12)
6 A Roman Catholic devotion (7)
7 Inflexibility (13)
8 Vehemently (12)
14 Mythical being (7)
16 Selected (6)
18 Insect larva (5)

No. 50

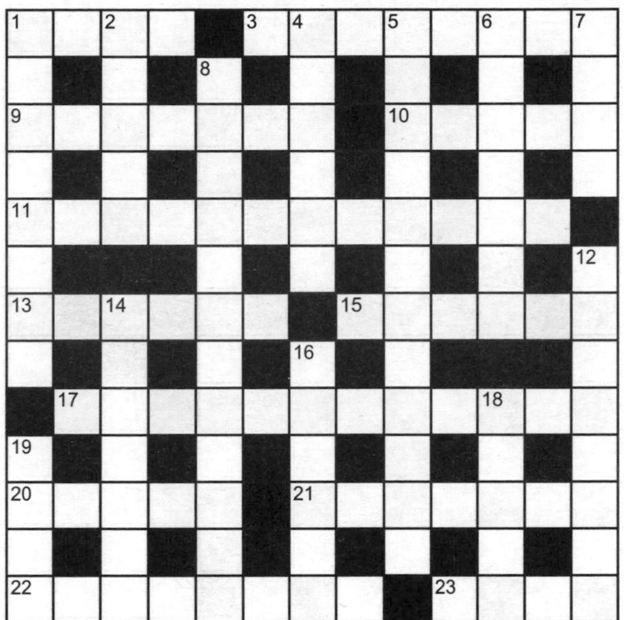

Across

1 Sharp nail as on a cat (4)
3 Awkwardly (8)
9 Identifying outfit (7)
10 Unfasten (5)
11 Person's physical state (12)
13 Cause to fall from a horse (6)
15 Type of engine (6)
17 Having a tendency to become liquid (12)
20 Detailed assessment of accounts (5)
21 Within earshot (7)
22 Imitations; satires (8)
23 Askew (4)

Down

1 North African semolina (8)
2 Relating to bees (5)
4 Extremes (6)
5 Hillside (12)
6 Irreligious (7)
7 Pull abruptly (4)
8 Showed not to be true (12)
12 Insincere praise (8)
14 Slim (7)
16 Gas with formula C4H10 (6)
18 Arm joint (5)
19 Complain unreasonably; fish (4)

No. 51

Across

1 Border (6)
7 Terraced (anag.) (8)
8 Wily (3)
9 Claw (6)
10 Flat-bottomed boat (4)
11 Strong currents of air (5)
13 Flexible (7)
15 Understanding of another (7)
17 School of fish (5)
21 So be it (4)
22 Enclosed recess (6)
23 Container (3)
24 Aromatic herb (8)
25 Steers (6)

Down

1 Relaxing (6)
2 Sculptured symbols (6)
3 Elegance; class (5)
4 Severely (7)
5 Adverse reaction (8)
6 Breakfast food (6)
12 Coaches (8)
14 The Windy City (7)
16 e.g. monkey or whale (6)
18 Make a larger offer at auction (6)
19 Wildcats (6)
20 Departing (5)

No. 52

Across

1 Unites (8)
5 Corner (4)
9 Soft fruit (5)
10 Large cushion for sitting on (7)
11 Building (12)
13 Descend down a cliff (6)
14 Split along a natural line (6)
17 Untimely (12)
20 Written language for blind people (7)
21 Nationality of Oscar Wilde (5)
22 Snake-like fish (4)
23 Pessimistic (8)

Down

1 Hats (4)
2 Grassland areas (7)
3 Unfriendly (12)
4 Set out on a journey (6)
6 One of the United Arab Emirates (5)
7 Person who maintains machines (8)
8 Annulment (12)
12 Having considerable worth (8)
15 Unsurpassed (3-4)
16 Lively Spanish dance (6)
18 Will (5)
19 Gossip (4)

No. 53

Across

4 Long thin line or band (6)
7 Fragrant (8)
8 Your (poetic) (3)
9 Method; fashion (4)
10 Capital of the Philippines (6)
11 Redecorate (7)
12 Plied (anag.) (5)
15 Elevators (5)
17 Knoll (7)
20 Wildcat (6)
21 Small pointed missile (4)
22 Lay seed in the ground (3)
23 Disappears (8)
24 Seat on the back of a horse (6)

Down

1 Opposite of after (6)
2 Forbearing (8)
3 Appearing to be (7)
4 Large pebble (5)
5 Impose or require (6)
6 Data input device (6)
13 Lacking humility (8)
14 Sprinkling (7)
15 Rents out (6)
16 Moved steadily (of a river) (6)
18 Part of a flower (6)
19 Aromatic spice (5)

No. 54

Across

1 Citing as evidence (8)
5 Long poem (4)
9 Tough problem (5)
10 Lock of curly hair (7)
11 Made (12)
13 Least polite (6)
14 Call off (6)
17 Happiness (12)
20 Animal fat (7)
21 Redden (5)
22 Skirt worn by ballet dancers (4)
23 People who clean with brooms (8)

Down

1 Mountain system in Europe (4)
2 Throw away (7)
3 Restrict within limits (12)
4 Standard; usual (6)
6 Lighter (5)
7 Strongholds (8)
8 Impossible to achieve (12)
12 Highly critical remark (8)
15 Outfit (7)
16 Narrow trench (6)
18 Eject lava (5)
19 Resistance unit (pl.) (4)

No. 55

Across

1 Atop (4)
3 Muttered (8)
9 Sharp tooth (7)
10 Position or point (5)
11 Smooth cream of vegetables (5)
12 Gave a description of (7)
13 Changes; modifies (6)
15 Quick sleep (6)
17 Natural environment (7)
18 Work hard (5)
20 Game of chance (5)
21 Departing (7)
22 Passing (of time) (8)
23 Regretted (4)

Down

1 Totally trustworthy (13)
2 Academy Award (5)
4 Not ready to eat (of fruit) (6)
5 Knowing more than one language (12)
6 Repeats from memory (7)
7 Deprived (13)
8 Intended to attract notice (12)
14 European country (7)
16 Taken illegally (6)
19 Word of farewell (5)

No. 56

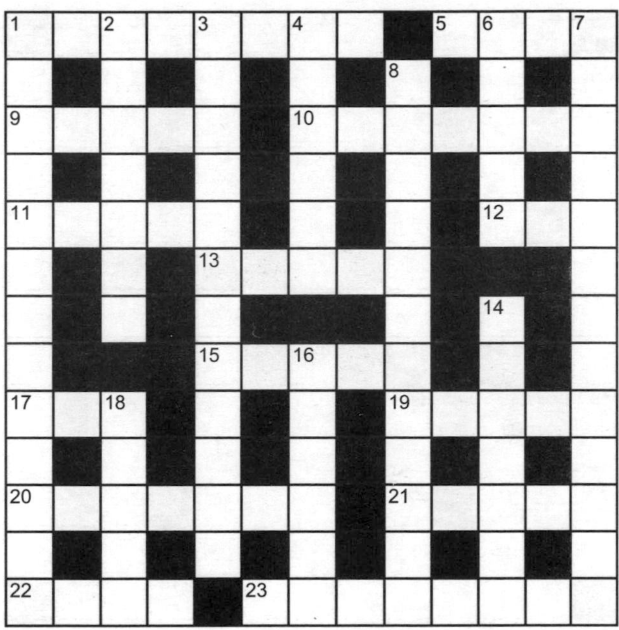

Across

1 Cunning; contrivance (8)
5 Creative thought (4)
9 Social division in some societies (5)
10 Agitate (7)
11 Grade (anag.) (5)
12 Female sheep (3)
13 Young females (5)
15 Continuing in existence (5)
17 Pub that may provide accommodation (3)
19 Settle for sleep (of birds) (5)
20 Exceptional; not usual (7)
21 Stringed instrument (5)
22 University in Connecticut (4)
23 Tries (8)

Down

1 As another option (13)
2 Part of a gun (7)
3 Binoculars (5,7)
4 Duplicating machine (6)
6 Wet thoroughly (5)
7 Shortened forms of words (13)
8 Capable of being moved (12)
14 Adult (5-2)
16 Contaminate (6)
18 Pertaining to birth (5)

No. 57

Across

1 Excellent (11)
9 Particle that holds quarks together (5)
10 Plaything (3)
11 Ethical (5)
12 Greeting (5)
13 Household implements (8)
16 Recurring at intervals (8)
18 Loud metallic sound (5)
21 Headdress of a monarch (5)
22 Pull at (3)
23 Shout of appreciation (5)
24 Going on and on (5-6)

Down

2 Not carrying weapons (7)
3 e.g. from London (7)
4 Shrub with glossy leaves (6)
5 Freshwater food fish (5)
6 Essential (5)
7 e.g. share news (11)
8 Relating to fireworks (11)
14 Disagreement (7)
15 Postpone (7)
17 Get away from (6)
19 Simple aquatic plants (5)
20 Triangular wall part (5)

No. 58

Across

1 Area of a church (4)
3 Fierce contest (8)
9 Biting (7)
10 Form of oxygen found in the atmosphere (5)
11 Germicide (12)
14 Sphere or globe (3)
16 Individual things (5)
17 Large salt water body (3)
18 Smooth and easy progress (5,7)
21 Sailing ship (5)
22 Preserves in vinegar (7)
23 Representative example (8)
24 Stringed instrument (4)

Down

1 Refer to famous people one knows (4-4)
2 Action words (5)
4 Not in (3)
5 Illustration facing the title page of a book (12)
6 Reasons for thinking something (7)
7 Abound (4)
8 Poorly fed (12)
12 Modifies (5)
13 Gift of money (8)
15 Support (7)
19 Embed; type of filling (5)
20 Pass over (4)
22 Breed of dog (3)

No. 59

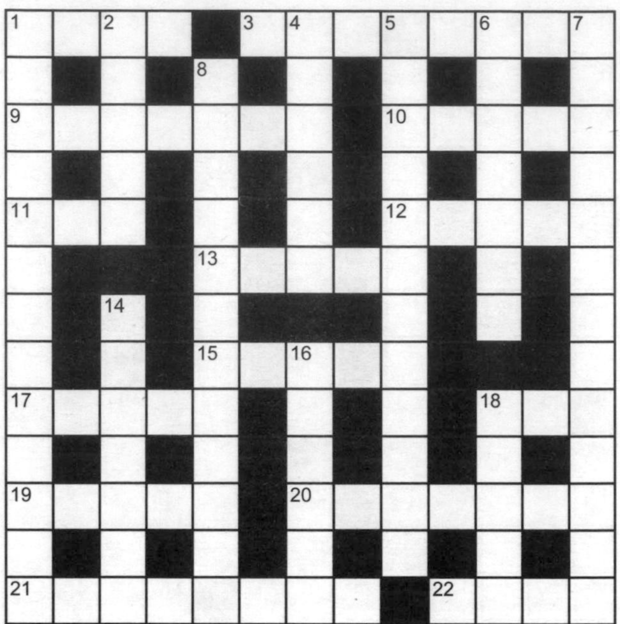

Across

1 Simpleton (4)
3 Fine soft wool (8)
9 Undoing a knot (7)
10 Distinctive design (5)
11 SI unit of illuminance (3)
12 Passenger ship (5)
13 Stare at fiercely (5)
15 Borders (5)
17 Join together; merge (5)
18 Part of a curve (3)
19 Skewered meat (5)
20 Stronghold (7)
21 Intensified (8)
22 Ewer (anag.) (4)

Down

1 Verified again (6-7)
2 Milky plant fluid (5)
4 Long-haired variety of cat (6)
5 Vagrancy (12)
6 Increases a deadline (7)
7 Fizz (13)
8 Unpleasant (12)
14 Trickle (7)
16 Bet (6)
18 Stand up (5)

No. 60

Across

1 Most pleased (8)
5 Surrounding glow (4)
8 Show off (5)
9 Penetrates (7)
10 More fortunate (7)
12 Old (7)
14 Forgive (7)
16 Combined metals (7)
18 Separated; remote (7)
19 Financial incentive (5)
20 Men (4)
21 Amicable (8)

Down

1 Possess (4)
2 Stopped temporarily (6)
3 Honesty; probity (9)
4 Provide (6)
6 Poorly dressed child (6)
7 Obscure (8)
11 Police officer (9)
12 Getting away from (8)
13 Stylish; high quality (6)
14 Worshipper (6)
15 Taxed (6)
17 Openly refuse to obey an order (4)

No. 61

Across

1 Small North American avian (8)
5 Finished; complete (4)
9 Beneath (5)
10 Capital of Nicaragua (7)
11 Orcas (6,6)
13 Omen (6)
14 Stage whispers (6)
17 Deceiver (6-6)
20 Raging fire (7)
21 Delicious (5)
22 Obtains (4)
23 Partially hidden (8)

Down

1 Smudge (4)
2 Eternal (7)
3 Electronic security device (7,5)
4 Comment (6)
6 Period of keeping awake to pray (5)
7 Re-evaluate (8)
8 Eager (12)
12 Dealing with (8)
15 Piece of furniture (7)
16 Boards (anag.) (6)
18 Not in good physical condition (5)
19 Stained (4)

No. 62

Across

1 Dreadful (4)
3 Assimilate again (8)
9 Be adequate (7)
10 First Greek letter (5)
11 Smells strongly (5)
12 Line that touches a curve (7)
13 Attributes (6)
15 Compact group of mountains (6)
17 Long wandering journey (7)
18 Type of poem (5)
20 Reason for innocence (5)
21 Touched (7)
22 Compliant; submissive (8)
23 Amaze (4)

Down

1 Tidier crayons (anag.) (13)
2 Firearm (5)
4 Votes into office (6)
5 Forcible indoctrination (12)
6 Weigh down (7)
7 Animal used for heavy work (5,2,6)
8 Displeased (12)
14 Whenever (7)
16 Punctuation mark (6)
19 Arm of a body of water (5)

No. 63

Across

1 Spherical objects (4)
3 Verifying (8)
9 Voter (7)
10 Requirements (5)
11 A grouping of states (12)
14 Soak up; wipe away (3)
16 Large waterbirds (5)
17 Thee (3)
18 In a creative manner (12)
21 Coral reef (5)
22 Blood relation (7)
23 Atmospheric moisture (8)
24 Change (4)

Down

1 Defeat (8)
2 Greenish-bronze fish (5)
4 Female pronoun (3)
5 Recovering from illness (of a person) (12)
6 Clumsily (7)
7 Breathe convulsively (4)
8 Determined (6-6)
12 Cereal plant (5)
13 Ability to float (8)
15 Carry out an action (7)
19 Subsidiary proposition (5)
20 Make a ___ of: bungle (4)
22 Clothing needed for an activity (3)

No. 64

Across

1 Devices that cause motion (6)
4 Greatly respect (6)
9 Alfresco (4-3)
10 Violent and lawless person (7)
11 Palm fruits (5)
12 Raised to the third power (5)
14 Have in common (5)
17 Strength (5)
19 Denim (anag.) (5)
21 High spirits (7)
23 Fabled monster (7)
24 Spreads out and apart (6)
25 On the beach; on land (6)

Down

1 A system of measurement (6)
2 Petty quarrel (4)
3 Makes one think of (7)
5 Pay out money (5)
6 Praising highly (8)
7 Bog (6)
8 Act of hiding something (11)
13 Happening every two years (8)
15 Sets out on a journey (7)
16 Pictorial representations (6)
18 Slight prickling sensation (6)
20 Silly (5)
22 After the beginning of (4)

No. 65

Across

1 Prickly plant with fragrant flowers (4)
3 Go beyond a limit (8)
9 Four-stringed guitar (7)
10 Mix up or confuse (5)
11 Conceals (5)
12 Burst violently (7)
13 Make tidier (6)
15 Most recent (6)
17 Actress (anag.) (7)
18 Friend (Spanish) (5)
20 Decrease; lessen (5)
21 Gets out (7)
22 Boating (8)
23 Remain (4)

Down

1 Crude but effective (5,3,5)
2 Players who form a team (5)
4 Watched (6)
5 Re-emergence (12)
6 Larval frog (7)
7 Affectedly (13)
8 Re-evaluation (12)
14 Antiquated (7)
16 Towards the rear of a ship (6)
19 Data entered into a system (5)

No. 66

Across

1 Wonderfully (11)
9 Less narrow (5)
10 Limb (3)
11 Oneness (5)
12 Doglike mammal (5)
13 Extremely tall (8)
16 Portable device to keep rain out (8)
18 Slopes (5)
21 Cuts slightly (5)
22 Did possess (3)
23 Long poems derived from ancient tradition (5)
24 Act of publishing in several places (11)

Down

2 Critiques (7)
3 Legal practitioners (7)
4 e.g. from New Delhi (6)
5 Opposite of south (5)
6 Exit (5)
7 Reliable (11)
8 Abashed (11)
14 Pass across or through (7)
15 Inactive pill (7)
17 Lunatic (6)
19 Dirty (5)
20 Rapidity of movement (5)

No. 67

Across

1 Nightclub employees (8)
5 Legendary story (4)
9 Magical incantation (5)
10 Widen (7)
11 And also (12)
13 Commands (6)
14 Obstruct (6)
17 Made in bulk (4-8)
20 Least remote (7)
21 Clumsy (5)
22 Ox-like mammals (4)
23 Cartoon artist (8)

Down

1 Shrub; uncultivated land (4)
2 Overturned (7)
3 Someone skilled in penmanship (12)
4 Set of instructions (6)
6 Ye old (anag.) (5)
7 Social insect (8)
8 Sleepwalking (12)
12 Typically; usually (8)
15 e.g. iron or oxygen (7)
16 Make less hard (6)
18 Predatory marine fish (5)
19 Celestial body (4)

No. 68

Across

1 Skippers (8)
5 This grows on your head (4)
8 Public disturbances (5)
9 Study of animals (7)
10 Rational; reasonable (7)
12 Build in a certain place (7)
14 Bring a law into effect again (2-5)
16 Educational establishment (7)
18 Amino acid (7)
19 Come into contact with (5)
20 Moved quickly (4)
21 Large fish (8)

Down

1 Thin rope (4)
2 On time (6)
3 Self-confidence (9)
4 Spout (6)
6 Admit openly (6)
7 Monarchist (8)
11 Device that makes electricity (9)
12 Slipcase (anag.) (8)
13 Region of France (6)
14 Feel sorrow for one's deeds (6)
15 Level a charge against (6)
17 Cut of beef from the leg (4)

No. 69

Across

1 Inn (8)
5 Country in West Africa (4)
9 Musical instrument (5)
10 Present for acceptance (7)
11 Bodies of writing (7)
12 Confusion (3-2)
13 Establish by law (6)
14 Provoke (6)
17 Principle laid down by an authority (5)
19 Turns red with embarrassment (7)
20 Sudden inclination to act (7)
21 Speak in public without preparation (2-3)
22 Wine container (4)
23 Participant in a meeting (8)

Down

1 Valetudinarian (13)
2 Featured in the leading role (7)
3 Thriftily (12)
4 Revoke (6)
6 Attach (5)
7 Not capable of being restrained (13)
8 Corresponding; proportionate (12)
15 Breathed in (7)
16 Showing utter resignation (6)
18 Stares with the mouth wide open (5)

No. 70

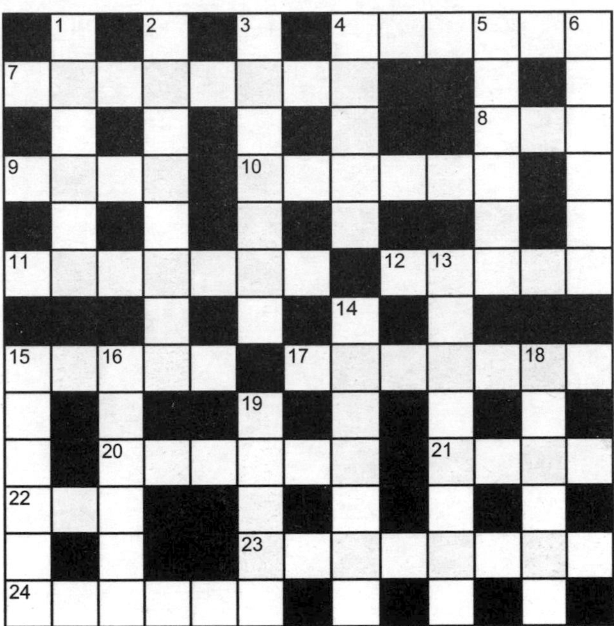

Across

4 Examine again (6)
7 Neutral particle with negligible mass (8)
8 Flat-topped cap with a tassel (3)
9 Big cat (4)
10 Gaming tile with pips in each half (6)
11 Cosmetic liquids (7)
12 Moist (of air) (5)
15 Group of students; category (5)
17 Cutting into pieces (7)
20 Capital of Greece (6)
21 Immense (4)
22 Cause friction (3)
23 Small falcons (8)
24 Slumbers (6)

Down

1 Sheep known for its wool (6)
2 Drawing templates (8)
3 Making an offer at auction (7)
4 Chambers (5)
5 Impart knowledge (6)
6 Magician (6)
13 Exposes (8)
14 Nearest (7)
15 Bird sounds (6)
16 Fit for cultivation (of land) (6)
18 Hold close (6)
19 Sudden movements (5)

No. 71

Across

1 e.g. Picasso or Braque (6)
4 Bustled about nervously (6)
9 Final parts of stories (7)
10 Pertaining to the liver (7)
11 Valleys (5)
12 Brief smell (5)
14 State of nervous excitement (5)
17 Person who goes on long walks (5)
19 One who steals (5)
21 Placed a bet (7)
23 Personal possession (7)
24 Surrenders (6)
25 Of practical benefit (6)

Down

1 Type of nut (6)
2 High-pitched noise (4)
3 Stem the flow of (4,3)
5 Unbuttoned (5)
6 Protective skin cream (8)
7 Cease (6)
8 Misleadingly (11)
13 Closely acquainted (8)
15 Equilateral parallelogram (7)
16 Muggy (6)
18 Arranged like rays (6)
20 Destined (5)
22 Quantity of bread (4)

No. 72

Across

1 Slingshot (8)
5 Building covering (4)
9 Health professional (5)
10 Sophisticated hair style (7)
11 Competitors in a sprint (7)
12 Major artery (5)
13 Plant with deep purple flowers (6)
14 Destroy (6)
17 This follows day (5)
19 Stupid (7)
20 Set apart (7)
21 Fishing net (5)
22 Snoozes (4)
23 Hard work (8)

Down

1 Violation (13)
2 Capital of Ontario (7)
3 Advantageous; superior (12)
4 Migratory grasshopper (6)
6 Possessor (5)
7 Tremendously (13)
8 Feeling let down (12)
15 Go faster than (7)
16 Long and very narrow (6)
18 Assembly (5)

No. 73

Across

1 Physical weakness (8)
5 Young sheep (4)
8 Maritime (5)
9 Mexican spirit (7)
10 Plundering (7)
12 Quiver (7)
14 Aerial rescue (7)
16 Prepared for an exam (7)
18 Prodding with the elbow (7)
19 Put up with (5)
20 Froth of soap and water (4)
21 Extreme reproach (8)

Down

1 Sand hill (4)
2 Relating to cattle (6)
3 Songs for babies (9)
4 Gossip (6)
6 Excuses of any kind (6)
7 Boastful person (8)
11 Deficit in a bank account (9)
12 Streams of rain (8)
13 Avoided (6)
14 In slow tempo (of music) (6)
15 Weak through age or illness (6)
17 Main body of a book (4)

No. 74

Across

1 Roadside board showing directions (8)
5 Gain deservedly (4)
9 Twilled cotton fabric (5)
10 Deferring action (7)
11 Ability to acquire and apply knowledge (12)
14 Help; assist (3)
15 From that time (5)
16 Took an exam (3)
17 Caused by disease (12)
20 Nattier (anag.) (7)
22 Evade (5)
23 Light beams from the sun (4)
24 Scholarly (8)

Down

1 Draw into the mouth using a straw (4)
2 Smiled broadly (7)
3 Opposite of amateur (12)
4 Fasten with stitches (3)
6 Negative ion (5)
7 Disregards (8)
8 Very determined (6-6)
12 Foreign language (informal) (5)
13 Device that reduces vibrations (8)
16 A placeholder name (2-3-2)
18 Tawdry (5)
19 Allows to happen (4)
21 Juvenile newt (3)

No. 75

Across

1 Not hard (4)
3 Suppressing (8)
9 Bring up; rear (7)
10 Regions (5)
11 What p.m. stands for (4,8)
14 Mischievous sprite (3)
16 Speak in a slow manner (5)
17 Cohere (3)
18 Unending (12)
21 Once more (5)
22 Bird of prey (7)
23 Narrow street or passage (8)
24 Swollen mark (4)

Down

1 Brief summary (8)
2 Military constructions (5)
4 Definite article (3)
5 Deceitfully (12)
6 Floating mass of frozen water (7)
7 Core meaning (4)
8 Brusque and surly (12)
12 Domain (5)
13 Wild flower (8)
15 Game played on a sloping board (7)
19 Beast (5)
20 Mother (4)
22 By way of (3)

No. 76

Across

1 Extinct bird (4)
3 Roman building (8)
9 Pursues (7)
10 Furnishings of a room (5)
11 Supply with new weapons (5)
12 Income (7)
13 Roll of parchment (6)
15 Word that qualifies another (6)
17 Completely enveloping (7)
18 Not asleep (5)
20 Creamy-white substance (5)
21 Fall back (7)
22 Gibberish (8)
23 Sight organs (4)

Down

1 Removal of trees from an area (13)
2 Triangular river mouth (5)
4 Ridiculous (6)
5 Separately (12)
6 Fragrant compound (7)
7 Pleasantness (13)
8 Preservative (12)
14 e.g. use a towel after showering (3-4)
16 Begins (6)
19 Be relevant (5)

No. 77

Across

1 Obstacle; barrier (11)
9 Uncooked (of meat) (3)
10 Alert (5)
11 Powerful forward movement (5)
12 Destitute (5)
13 Type of pasta often eaten with cheese (8)
16 Wealth (8)
18 Threshold (5)
20 Filthy (5)
21 Cloaked (5)
22 Speck (3)
23 Act of staying away from work (11)

Down

2 Large hunting knife (5)
3 Sorrowful (5)
4 Country once ruled by Idi Amin (6)
5 Day of the week (7)
6 Elate (7)
7 Changed completely (11)
8 Cause to happen unexpectedly (11)
14 Yield (7)
15 Use again (7)
17 Floor covering (6)
18 Small house (5)
19 Fashions; styles (5)

No. 78

Across

1 Rigidly; sternly (8)
5 Chemical salt (4)
8 Broaden (5)
9 Regain strength (7)
10 Rousing songs (7)
12 Adolescent (7)
14 Divisions of a group (7)
16 Exclusion from the workplace (7)
18 Enticed (7)
19 Excessively mean (5)
20 Small horse (4)
21 Unit of pronunciation (8)

Down

1 Stitches (4)
2 Lower (6)
3 Lowest female singing voice (9)
4 Immature insects (6)
6 Taxes (6)
7 Bogs or marshes (8)
11 Catchline (anag.) (9)
12 Work surface (8)
13 Discernment (6)
14 Hard to digest (6)
15 Residential district (6)
17 Hint (4)

No. 79

Across

1 Stargazers (11)
9 Showered with love (5)
10 Pro (3)
11 Referred to (5)
12 Enclosed (5)
13 They compete in the Olympic Games (8)
16 Arduous (8)
18 Take great satisfaction in (5)
21 Legendary stories (5)
22 Carry a heavy object (3)
23 Not true (5)
24 Result of a person losing a lot of water (11)

Down

2 Not thorough (7)
3 Enigmas (7)
4 Indigenous (6)
5 Doctor (5)
6 Fissures (5)
7 Type of music (4,3,4)
8 One who held a job previously (11)
14 Lenient (7)
15 Type of porch (7)
17 Of the eye (6)
19 Not clearly stated (5)
20 Towering (5)

No. 80

Across

1 Swindle (4)
3 Fans (8)
9 Young tree (7)
10 Public square (5)
11 Organic compound (5)
12 Elevate (7)
13 Solemn promise (6)
15 Spring back (6)
17 Continue (5,2)
18 Pains (5)
20 Complete trust (5)
21 Passionate (7)
22 Writer of the words to a song (8)
23 Fastens a knot (4)

Down

1 Rude (13)
2 Songbird (5)
4 Type of canoe (6)
5 Imitator (12)
6 Avoidance (7)
7 Brazenness (13)
8 Written in pictorial symbols (12)
14 Prior (7)
16 Except when (6)
19 Port-au-Prince's location (5)

No. 81

Across

4 Remove weapons (6)
7 Capital of Chile (8)
8 Bland soft food (3)
9 Ale (4)
10 Arise from (6)
11 Small bone (7)
12 Renown (5)
15 Dubious (5)
17 Liberty (7)
20 Elaborately adorned (6)
21 Attack at speed (4)
22 Helpful hint (3)
23 Orderliness (8)
24 Marsh plants (6)

Down

1 Stroke lightly (6)
2 Marine echinoderm (8)
3 Light shoes (7)
4 Workers (5)
5 Attach (6)
6 Sample (anag.) (6)
13 Infallible (8)
14 Pals (7)
15 Religions (6)
16 Inclined (6)
18 Serving no functional purpose (6)
19 Vertical spars for sails (5)

No. 82

Across

1 Measure of effectiveness (8)
5 Singe; burn (4)
9 Number of deadly sins (5)
10 Spiny anteater (7)
11 Productivity (12)
14 Additionally (3)
15 Chocolate powder (5)
16 Periodic publication (abbrev.) (3)
17 Firm rebuke (12)
20 Bright red (7)
22 Mother-of-pearl (5)
23 Creative disciplines (4)
24 Earthenware (8)

Down

1 Simple (4)
2 Highly excited (7)
3 In a persuasive manner (12)
4 Signal for action (3)
6 Row of bushes (5)
7 Redeploy (8)
8 Devoted to music (12)
12 Concentrate on (5)
13 SE Asian country (8)
16 Single eyeglass (7)
18 Intended (5)
19 Extremely (4)
21 Bitumen (3)

No. 83

Across

1 In unbroken sequence (11)
9 Humiliate (5)
10 Cheek (slang) (3)
11 Sticky (5)
12 Military blockade (5)
13 Exemption (8)
16 Unyielding (8)
18 Bewildered (5)
21 Living thing (5)
22 Young bear (3)
23 Amide (anag.) (5)
24 Done with great care (11)

Down

2 End result (7)
3 Remaining (7)
4 Wooden house (6)
5 Levels; ranks (5)
6 One-way flow structure (5)
7 Easy target (7,4)
8 Stretch out completely (11)
14 Prune (3,4)
15 Residence of the Pope (7)
17 Outlaw (6)
19 Striped animal (5)
20 Evil spirit (5)

No. 84

Across

1 Clear (8)
5 Repetition of a sound (4)
9 Understand (5)
10 Changes gradually (7)
11 Environment (12)
13 Sloping (of a typeface) (6)
14 Free from danger (6)
17 The management of a home (12)
20 Small booth (7)
21 Staggers (5)
22 Vegetable matter used as fuel (4)
23 School pupils (8)

Down

1 Excavates (4)
2 Kitchen implement (7)
3 Impudence (12)
4 Winged child (6)
6 Assembly of witches (5)
7 Completely preoccupied with (8)
8 Easy-going (4-8)
12 Drink consumed before bed (8)
15 Restaurant in a workplace (7)
16 Soften; become less severe (6)
18 Shadow (5)
19 Potential applications (4)

No. 85

Across

1 Light volcanic rock (6)
4 Fashioned (6)
9 Day trips (7)
10 Walked upon (7)
11 Equine animal (5)
12 Electronic device one clicks (5)
14 Wards (anag.) (5)
17 Work at a loom (5)
19 Dog leashes (5)
21 Young children (7)
23 Take a seat (3,4)
24 Transmitter (6)
25 Turn to ice (6)

Down

1 For the time being (3,3)
2 Short note or reminder (4)
3 Hugged (7)
5 Tie; snag (5)
6 All-round view (8)
7 Sprints (6)
8 Strikingly different (11)
13 Undo; loosen (8)
15 Faster (7)
16 Advantages (6)
18 Make certain of (6)
20 Range (5)
22 Back of the neck (4)

No. 86

Across

4 Shovels (6)
7 Unthinking (of a response) (4-4)
8 Blend together (3)
9 Succulent (4)
10 Coarse cloth (6)
11 Renews membership (7)
12 Used up; exhausted (5)
15 Uncertain; risky (5)
17 Cook in hot fat (4-3)
20 Going out with (6)
21 Vein of metal ore (4)
22 Collection of paper (3)
23 Force of resistance; abrasion (8)
24 Showy (6)

Down

1 Steep in liquid (6)
2 Remove a monarch (8)
3 Revoke (7)
4 Move sneakily (5)
5 Reduce to a lower grade (6)
6 Group of six (6)
13 Fill (with data) (8)
14 Flightless seabird (7)
15 Got rid of (6)
16 Treat indulgently (6)
18 Extremely fashionable; scalding (3-3)
19 A moment (5)

No. 87

Across

1 Labels (4)
3 Moral instructions (8)
9 Piece of research (7)
10 Tree with an edible nut (5)
11 Difficulty (12)
14 Cry (3)
16 Holy chalice (5)
17 Clumsy person (3)
18 Discreditable (12)
21 Heavily loaded (5)
22 Drifted about on water (7)
23 Putting into practice (8)
24 Lids (anag.) (4)

Down

1 Always in a similar role (of an actor) (8)
2 Murkiness (5)
4 Decay (3)
5 Surrender (12)
6 High-pitched flute (7)
7 Having a sound mind (4)
8 Hostility (12)
12 Muscular contraction (5)
13 Upset; hurt (8)
15 Form or accumulate steadily (5-2)
19 Asian pepper plant (5)
20 Prayer (4)
22 Cooling tool (3)

No. 88

Across

1 Unit of type-size (4)
3 20th century art movement (8)
9 Friendly (7)
10 Performed on stage (5)
11 Avoided by social custom (5)
12 Cover with a hard surface layer (7)
13 Succulent plant (6)
15 Seem (6)
17 Slackens (7)
18 Hawaiian greeting (5)
20 Corpulent (5)
21 Let out (7)
22 Publicity (8)
23 Incline (4)

Down

1 Playful trick (9,4)
2 Scale (5)
4 Not level (6)
5 Intolerable (12)
6 Trespass (7)
7 Large sea (13)
8 Completeness (12)
14 Tightly framed camera shot (5-2)
16 Loan shark (6)
19 Egg-shaped (5)

No. 89

Across

1 Going up on foot (8)
5 Move fast in a straight line (4)
9 Record on tape (5)
10 Platform projecting from a wall (7)
11 Device for putting out fires (12)
14 Increase in amount (3)
15 Cry of excitement (5)
16 Fluffy scarf (3)
17 Absurd (12)
20 Boasting (7)
22 Hate (5)
23 Variety of chalcedony (4)
24 Discard; abandon (8)

Down

1 Bay (4)
2 Put in order (7)
3 Style of playing blues (6-6)
4 Arrest (3)
6 Fabric (5)
7 Dawn (8)
8 Crucial (3,9)
12 Phantasm (5)
13 Classic Spanish soup made from raw vegetables (8)
16 Sweeps (7)
18 Dark wood (5)
19 Smile broadly (4)
21 Command to a horse (3)

No. 90

Across

1 Piece of printed matter (8)
5 Stylish and fashionable (4)
8 Sing softly (5)
9 Impassive (7)
10 Look into (7)
12 Burdensome (7)
14 Groups together (7)
16 Follow a winding course (of a river) (7)
18 e.g. shrimp or crab (7)
19 Reluctant (5)
20 Aromatic herb (4)
21 Of many different kinds (8)

Down

1 e.g. a mallard (4)
2 Selection (6)
3 Made reference to (9)
4 Pokes gently (6)
6 Type of music (3-3)
7 Gives permission (8)
11 Case (9)
12 Antique; obsolete (8)
13 Scoundrel (6)
14 Classifies; sorts (6)
15 Still existing (6)
17 Dull heavy sound (4)

No. 91

Across

1 Frustrating (11)
9 One circuit of a track (3)
10 Rescuer (5)
11 Absolute (5)
12 Remains somewhere (5)
13 Opposite of a promotion (8)
16 Pear-shaped fruits native to Mexico (8)
18 Elector (5)
20 Not containing anything (5)
21 Removes the skin from (5)
22 Sap (anag.) (3)
23 Censure severely (11)

Down

2 Looked at open-mouthed (5)
3 Takes a break (5)
4 In a lively manner (6)
5 Twisting force (7)
6 Country whose capital is Abuja (7)
7 Intricately (11)
8 Accurate timer (11)
14 Master of ceremonies (7)
15 West Indian musical style (7)
17 Possessors (6)
18 Movable helmet part (5)
19 Browned bread (5)

No. 92

Across

1 Mislead (8)
5 Dull pain (4)
9 Australian marsupial (5)
10 Nerve impulses (7)
11 Uncertain (12)
13 Frightens; startles (6)
14 Line of latitude (6)
17 One who takes part in a protest (12)
20 Distribute illicitly (7)
21 Ring solemnly (5)
22 At any time (4)
23 Routine and ordinary (3-2-3)

Down

1 Create (4)
2 Shoulder blade (7)
3 Modestly (12)
4 Purify then condense (6)
6 Tiny piece of food (5)
7 Distinction (8)
8 Evening dress for men (6,6)
12 Lower jaw (8)
15 Continue (7)
16 Mark of disgrace (6)
18 Large deer (5)
19 Ruse (4)

No. 93

Across

1 Re-emerge (8)
5 Molten rock (4)
9 Third Greek letter (5)
10 Argues against (7)
11 Long locks of hair (7)
12 Armature of an electric motor (5)
13 Capital of Canada (6)
14 Sightseeing trip in Africa (6)
17 Track of an animal (5)
19 Skilled sportsman (7)
20 Terrestrial (7)
21 Ruined; rendered inoperable (5)
22 Mediocre (2-2)
23 Household cooling devices (8)

Down

1 Virtuousness (13)
2 Part of a chair (7)
3 Laudatory (12)
4 Evoke a feeling (6)
6 Valuable thing (5)
7 Aggressive self-assurance (13)
8 Easy to converse with (12)
15 Ingredient in nail polish remover (7)
16 Legal practitioner (6)
18 Unpleasant giants (5)

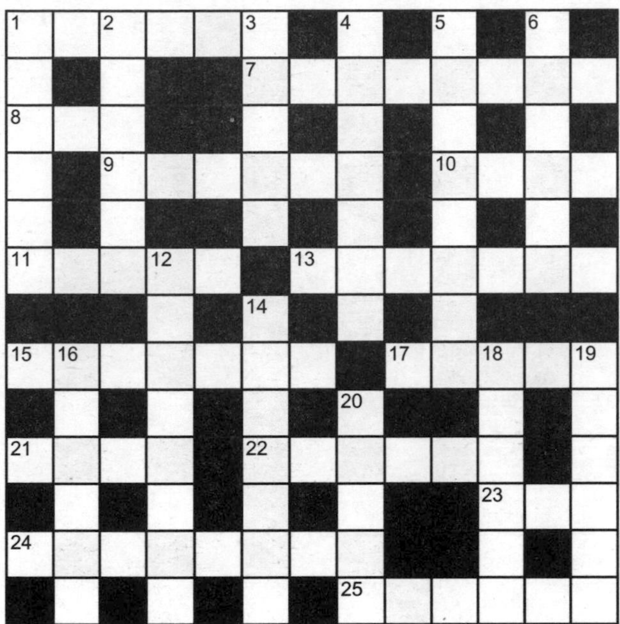

Across

1 Throes (anag.) (6)
7 Apparatus for hoisting loads (8)
8 Small amount of something (3)
9 Very crowded (of a place) (6)
10 Electrically charged particles (4)
11 Misplaces (5)
13 Developed (7)
15 More than enough (7)
17 Heats up (5)
21 Circle around the head of a saint (4)
22 Respite (6)
23 Craze (3)
24 Closure of a system or factory (8)
25 Mourn the loss of (6)

Down

1 Trying experience (6)
2 Excessive self-confidence (6)
3 Lines where fabric edges join (5)
4 Progress (7)
5 A Roman emperor (8)
6 Spring suddenly (6)
12 Canine (3,5)
14 Fame (7)
16 Fine; great (6)
18 Shuffle playing cards (6)
19 Thick wet mud (6)
20 Throw forcefully (5)

No. 95

Across

1 Sudden heavy rain shower (8)
5 Domesticated ox (4)
9 Type of leather (5)
10 Small beetles (7)
11 Finished (5)
12 Male turkey (3)
13 Spends time doing nothing (5)
15 Flaring stars (5)
17 Creative activity (3)
19 Store in a secret place (5)
20 First (7)
21 Not suitable in the circumstances (5)
22 Plant stem part from which a leaf emerges (4)
23 Inducing sleep (8)

Down

1 Opening of a subject to debate (13)
2 Held and used a tool (7)
3 A type of error in speech (8,4)
4 Legitimate (6)
6 Authoritative proclamation (5)
7 Uncaring (13)
8 Reclamation (12)
14 Inflexible and unyielding (7)
16 Depression between hills (6)
18 Bronze medal position (5)

No. 96

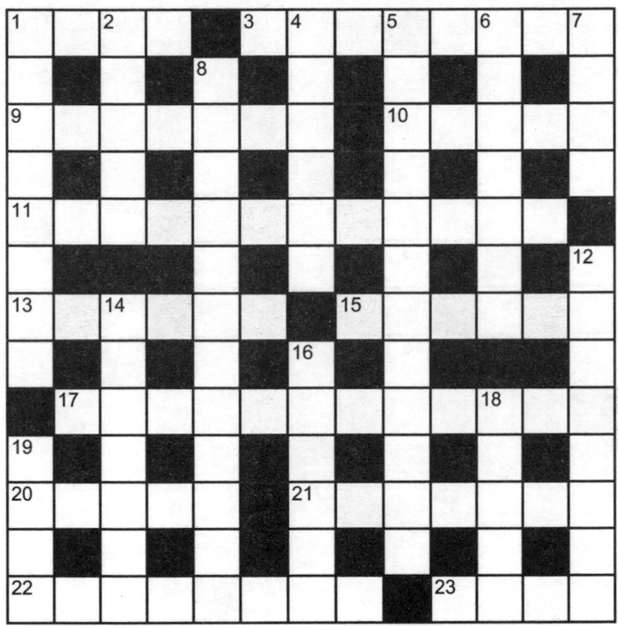

Across

1 Cries (4)
3 Hot and humid (8)
9 Refrain from (7)
10 Brings up (5)
11 Contests (12)
13 Moon of the planet Jupiter (6)
15 Central parts of cells (6)
17 Process of combining (12)
20 Camel-like animal (5)
21 Sturdy thickset canine (7)
22 Coerce into doing something (8)
23 Depart from (4)

Down

1 Stole; grabbed suddenly (8)
2 Broom made of twigs (5)
4 Rotten (of food) (6)
5 Especially (12)
6 Water passage (7)
7 Whip (4)
8 Butterfly larvae (12)
12 00:00 on a 24-hour clock (8)
14 Search through (7)
16 Male hairdresser (6)
18 Alphabetical list in a book (5)
19 A brief piece of film (4)

No. 97

Across

1 Raise to the third power (4)
3 Engravings (8)
9 Caring for (7)
10 Confound (5)
11 Ordinary dress (5,7)
14 Male sheep (3)
16 Comic dramatic work (5)
17 Vital plant juice (3)
18 Spotless (5-3-4)
21 Pertaining to birds (5)
22 Containing no water at all (4,3)
23 French bread stick (8)
24 Dressed (4)

Down

1 Plot (8)
2 Former name of Myanmar (5)
4 Label (3)
5 Very upsetting (5-7)
6 Tidies up (7)
7 Pace (4)
8 Importance (12)
12 Insect grub (5)
13 Fully aware (4-4)
15 Soaking up (7)
19 Foot-operated lever (5)
20 Sharp bristle (4)
22 Wager (3)

No. 98

Across

1 Spatters with liquid (8)
5 Loud noise (4)
8 Receded (5)
9 Finery (7)
10 Pasta strips (7)
12 Young goose (7)
14 Soft toffee (7)
16 Warship (7)
18 Creepiest (7)
19 Long for (5)
20 e.g. perform karaoke (4)
21 Foretells (8)

Down

1 Ooze (4)
2 Identifying tags (6)
3 Secondary occupations (9)
4 Ringer (anag.) (6)
6 Form of a gene (6)
7 Full measure of a drink (8)
11 Elated (9)
12 Huge ice masses (8)
13 Move faster than (6)
14 Depression from a meteor impact (6)
15 Picture produced from many small pieces (6)
17 Public houses (4)

No. 99

Across

1 Cosmetic treatment of the feet (8)
5 Flow copiously (4)
9 Run away (5)
10 Young chicken (7)
11 Dimly; not clearly (12)
14 Distress; misery (3)
15 Higher than (5)
16 Wetland (3)
17 A large number (12)
20 Relaxes (7)
22 In the lead (5)
23 Sharp or acid in taste (4)
24 Similarity between different things (8)

Down

1 Elapse (of time) (4)
2 Make insane (7)
3 Blends; mixtures (12)
4 Mock (3)
6 Not illuminated (5)
7 Moving at speed (8)
8 Comical tuner (anag.) (12)
12 Mythical monster (5)
13 Bathing costume (8)
16 Most healthy (7)
18 Less high (5)
19 In an inactive way; with no particular purpose (4)
21 Speak; state (3)

No. 100

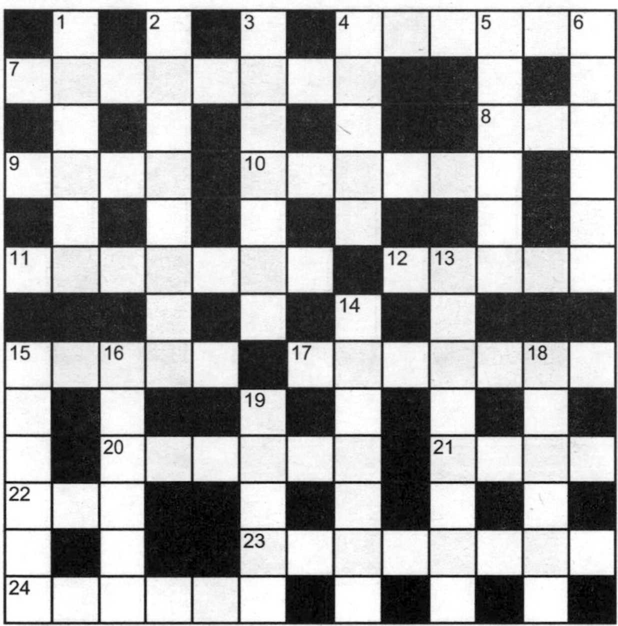

Across

4 Wreckage washed ashore (6)
7 e.g. from Tokyo (8)
8 Item of furniture one sleeps on (3)
9 Call to mind (4)
10 Belief in a god or gods (6)
11 Risky enterprise (7)
12 Simple song (5)
15 Solids with six equal square faces (5)
17 Insult (3-4)
20 Foam (6)
21 Solitary (4)
22 Cooking utensil (3)
23 Control (8)
24 Sailing vessels (6)

Down

1 Easily done (6)
2 Holder of invention rights (8)
3 Long-haired hunting dogs (7)
4 Precious stone (5)
5 Surrender (6)
6 Noon (6)
13 Habitually lazy (8)
14 Most important (7)
15 Rough (of water) (6)
16 Sea in northern Europe (6)
18 Licentious; deliberate (6)
19 Low dull sounds (5)

No. 101

Across

1 Official language of Pakistan (4)
3 Minced meat products (8)
9 Offend the modesty of (7)
10 Move on hands and knees (5)
11 Humming sound (5)
12 Enunciating (7)
13 Coronets (6)
15 History play by Shakespeare (5,1)
17 Items made from fired clay (7)
18 Become subject to (5)
20 Diacritical mark (5)
21 Type of natural disaster (7)
22 Non-functioning period (8)
23 Tailless amphibian (4)

Down

1 Unexpected (13)
2 Postpone (5)
4 Opposite of passive (6)
5 Blasphemous (12)
6 Slowly moving mass of ice (7)
7 Autonomous (4-9)
8 Beginning (12)
14 Effluence (7)
16 A complex whole (6)
19 Lead a discussion (5)

No. 102

Across

1 Title of a newspaper (8)
5 Musical or vocal sound (4)
9 Repeat something once more (5)
10 Reverberating (7)
11 Process of enlarging one's muscles (12)
13 Vibration (6)
14 Easy victory (4-2)
17 Bump (12)
20 Chirping insect (7)
21 Armistice (5)
22 Welsh emblem (4)
23 Short heavy club (8)

Down

1 Roman god of war (4)
2 Type of sugar (7)
3 Carefree (5-2-5)
4 Street (6)
6 Small antelope (5)
7 Pleasing and captivating (8)
8 Showing complete commitment (12)
12 Not usual (8)
15 Block (7)
16 Pertaining to the mind (6)
18 Expect; think that (5)
19 Eager (4)

No. 103

Across

1 Needless (11)
9 Flour dough used in cooking (5)
10 Deep hole in the ground (3)
11 Small container (5)
12 A leaf of paper (5)
13 Feigns (8)
16 War memorial (8)
18 Follows orders (5)
21 Surface upon which one walks (5)
22 Wonder (3)
23 Semiconductor (5)
24 Science of communications in living things and machines (11)

Down

2 Saunter (anag.) (7)
3 Made bare (7)
4 Came next (6)
5 Neck warmer (5)
6 Push back (5)
7 Extraordinary (11)
8 Creating an evocative mood (11)
14 Penalty (7)
15 Terse (7)
17 Urge to do something (6)
19 Foe (5)
20 Grasslike marsh plant (5)

No. 104

Across

1 Very dirty (6)
4 Scared (6)
9 Nasal opening (7)
10 Traversed (7)
11 Dank (5)
12 Increase in size (5)
14 Ten more than forty (5)
17 Pinch; squeeze (5)
19 Mix smoothly (5)
21 Livid (7)
23 Imaginary creature (7)
24 Judged (6)
25 Give a job to (6)

Down

1 Groups of birds (6)
2 Company symbol (4)
3 Flesher (anag.) (7)
5 Combines (5)
6 Annul or abolish (8)
7 Holds up (6)
8 Unconcerned (11)
13 Speed up (8)
15 Chemical element (7)
16 Exist in great numbers (6)
18 Organ (6)
20 Steered a car (5)
22 Female child (4)

No. 105

Across

1 Freed from an obligation (8)
5 Cease moving (4)
8 Person staying at a hotel (5)
9 Teller (7)
10 Stopping place for a train (7)
12 Debate (7)
14 Lubricates (7)
16 Spicy Spanish sausage (7)
18 Sudden increase (7)
19 Friendship (5)
20 Extremities of the feet (4)
21 Disturb (8)

Down

1 Therefore (Latin) (4)
2 Happenings (6)
3 Medley of dried petals (9)
4 More than is necessary (6)
6 Like vinegar (6)
7 Sharpness (of taste) (8)
11 Lessen (9)
12 Reduction in price (8)
13 Whipped cream dessert (6)
14 Rule with authority (6)
15 Rigid; stern (6)
17 Variety; sort (4)

No. 106

Across

1 The acting out of a particular part (4,4)
5 Slide; lose grip (4)
9 Talent; ability (5)
10 Zephyrs (7)
11 Without parallel (6,2,4)
13 Take as being true (6)
14 Upward slope (6)
17 Break up (12)
20 Mediterranean coastal region (7)
21 Unit of heat (5)
22 Part of a pedestal (4)
23 Official orders (8)

Down

1 Widespread (4)
2 Raises dough (using yeast) (7)
3 Renditions (12)
4 Measure of how strongly an object reflects light (6)
6 Musical toy (5)
7 Sweet food courses (8)
8 Showed (12)
12 Walked about (8)
15 Beg (7)
16 US state whose capital is Carson City (6)
18 Rescued (5)
19 Flightless birds (4)

No. 107

Across

1 Ending that leaves one in suspense (11)
9 Make a choice (3)
10 Wanderer (5)
11 Arm joint (5)
12 Mounds of loose sand (5)
13 Squid dish (8)
16 Truly (8)
18 Move sideways (5)
20 Resides (5)
21 Freedom from war (5)
22 Beer container (3)
23 Ongoing disagreement (11)

Down

2 Language of ancient Rome (5)
3 Areas of agricultural land (5)
4 Capital of Cuba (6)
5 Small Arctic whale (7)
6 Morally right (7)
7 Fantastically (11)
8 Innovative or pioneering (7,4)
14 Stipulation (7)
15 Active part of a fire (7)
17 Red salad fruit (6)
18 View; picture (5)
19 Fists (5)

No. 108

Across

1 Customs; settled tendencies (6)
4 Moved over ice (6)
9 Exceptionally large (7)
10 Dreamlike (7)
11 Of definite shape (5)
12 Rigid (5)
14 Clenched hands (5)
17 Grape (anag.) (5)
19 Friends (5)
21 Tiresome (7)
23 Direct or control a machine (7)
24 Hesitate (6)
25 Classify (6)

Down

1 Homes (6)
2 Male hog (4)
3 Become airborne (4,3)
5 Toys flown in the wind (5)
6 Multiplying by three (8)
7 Fears greatly (6)
8 Everything that orbits the sun (5,6)
13 Cheeky (8)
15 Arachnids (7)
16 Reverberated (6)
18 Outcome (6)
20 Charming and elegant (5)
22 Upon (4)

No. 109

Across

- **1** Water-resistant jacket (8)
- **5** Complacent (4)
- **9** Climbing spike (5)
- **10** Dark pigment in skin (7)
- **11** Coming between two things (12)
- **14** Don (anag.) (3)
- **15** Name of a book (5)
- **16** Unwell (3)
- **17** Fellow plotter (12)
- **20** Grotesque monster (7)
- **22** Damp (5)
- **23** In a tense state (4)
- **24** Personal magnetism (8)

Down

- **1** Thick cord (4)
- **2** Chanted (7)
- **3** Intense (12)
- **4** Goal (3)
- **6** Ray (5)
- **7** Warily (8)
- **8** Heavy long-handled tool (12)
- **12** Saying; slogan (5)
- **13** Vehicle with one wheel (8)
- **16** Traditional piano keys (7)
- **18** Reclining (5)
- **19** Volcano in Sicily (4)
- **21** Tree (3)

No. 110

Across

1 Five cent coin (US) (6)
7 Salve (8)
8 Listening device (3)
9 Wrestling hold (6)
10 Money given to the poor (4)
11 These keep your feet warm (5)
13 Terribly (7)
15 Examined hastily (7)
17 Type of lizard (5)
21 Prima donna (4)
22 Former female pupil (6)
23 Home for a pig (3)
24 Someone paddling a light boat (8)
25 Entertained (6)

Down

1 Royal people (6)
2 Brandy (6)
3 Very bad (5)
4 Unfamiliar (7)
5 Not ripe (of fruit) (8)
6 Hard tooth coating (6)
12 Large marsupial (8)
14 Protein found in hair (7)
16 Peak (6)
18 Pursues (6)
19 Complied with a command (6)
20 Small group ruling a country (5)

No. 111

Across

1 Deep ditches (8)
5 Ostrich-like bird (4)
9 Silk fabric (5)
10 Segmented worm (7)
11 Clothing such as a vest (12)
14 Small shelter (3)
15 Factual evidence (5)
16 How (anag.) (3)
17 Verification (12)
20 Kneecap (7)
22 Start (5)
23 Having pains (4)
24 With great haste (8)

Down

1 Mission (4)
2 No longer in existence (7)
3 Despicable (12)
4 Long period of time (3)
6 Divide by two (5)
7 Arithmetic operation (8)
8 Making no money (12)
12 Marrying man (5)
13 Yellowish edible seed (8)
16 Beaten by hammering (of metals) (7)
18 Indentation (5)
19 Solely (4)
21 What we breathe in (3)

No. 112

Across

1 Cause to remember (6)
7 Outlines in detail (8)
8 Deity (3)
9 Topics for debate (6)
10 Related by blood (4)
11 Model figures used as toys (5)
13 Respects (7)
15 Rowing or sailing for pleasure (7)
17 Short notes (5)
21 Platform leading out to sea (4)
22 Mineral form of silica (6)
23 Part of a coat (3)
24 Seal off a place (8)
25 Guard against (6)

Down

1 Having a rough surface (of terrain) (6)
2 Positioned in the middle (6)
3 First appearance (5)
4 Occurrence (7)
5 Organism that exploits another (8)
6 Different from (6)
12 Ability to read (8)
14 Not level (7)
16 Bird with yellow and black plumage (6)
18 Gag; silence (6)
19 Oozed (6)
20 Scraped at (5)

No. 113

Across

1 Of like kind (4)
3 Forbid (8)
9 Secret place (7)
10 Exposed (5)
11 Conflict of opinion (12)
14 Remove branches (3)
16 Expels from a position (5)
17 Burdensome charge (3)
18 Limitless (12)
21 Longest river in Europe (5)
22 Mode (7)
23 Heard (8)
24 Exchange for money (4)

Down

1 Timetable (8)
2 Ciphers (5)
4 Mud channel (3)
5 Female school boss (12)
6 Hereditary title (7)
7 Periodic movement of the sea (4)
8 Bring together into a mass (12)
12 Gets less difficult (5)
13 Outer (8)
15 Spots (7)
19 Woman getting married (5)
20 Wicked (4)
22 Sum charged (3)

No. 114

Across

1 Respectful (11)
9 Exclusive newspaper story (5)
10 Round bread roll (3)
11 Manor (anag.) (5)
12 Pertaining to the Netherlands (5)
13 Intrigue (8)
16 Liar (8)
18 Humble (5)
21 Tree of the birch family (5)
22 Chewy substance (3)
23 The body below the ribs and above the hips (5)
24 Incalculable (11)

Down

2 Frees from an obligation (7)
3 Entrap (7)
4 Wears away (6)
5 Used a computer keyboard (5)
6 Head monk of an abbey (5)
7 Phraseology (11)
8 Not having a written constitution (11)
14 Large island of Indonesia (7)
15 Attentive; conscious of (7)
17 Birthplace of St Francis (6)
19 Ladies (5)
20 Shows tiredness (5)

No. 115

Across

1 People who provide massages (8)
5 Belonging to us (4)
8 Spree (5)
9 Acted properly (7)
10 Tool that is useful for the Arctic (3,4)
12 Most tidy (7)
14 Novelty (7)
16 Cigarette constituent (7)
18 Stronghold (7)
19 Building add-on (5)
20 Covers; tops (4)
21 Planned (8)

Down

1 Gangs (4)
2 Spanish title for a married woman (6)
3 Vigorous (9)
4 Burrowing long-eared mammal (6)
6 Uncover (6)
7 Close associate (8)
11 Eradicate (9)
12 Maritime (8)
13 Diminished (6)
14 Bad-tempered mythical creature (6)
15 Pressed clothes (6)
17 Chopped (4)

No. 116

Across

4 Spirited horses (6)
7 Confused mixture (8)
8 Happiness (3)
9 Link a town with another (4)
10 A size of book page (6)
11 Hindered (7)
12 Flowers (5)
15 Small woodland (5)
17 Mythical creature active at night (7)
20 Comes up (6)
21 Settee (4)
22 Put down (3)
23 Finding (8)
24 Reactive metal (6)

Down

1 Conical tent (6)
2 TV stations (8)
3 Dinner party; feast (7)
4 Bundle of wheat (5)
5 Relishes (6)
6 Fashions (6)
13 Facing (8)
14 Plunder (7)
15 Hardened part of the skin (6)
16 Entreated; beseeched (6)
18 Pay back money (6)
19 Sacred song or hymn (5)

No. 117

Across

1 Comprehends (11)
9 The spirit of a people (5)
10 Came across (3)
11 Higher in place (5)
12 Moist stiff mixture (5)
13 Ancestral lines of descent (8)
16 Spanish dance (8)
18 Total disorder (5)
21 Calls out like a lion (5)
22 Argument against something (3)
23 Large fruit with pulpy flesh (5)
24 Diplomatic officials (11)

Down

2 Biting sharply (7)
3 Endless (7)
4 Plan of action (6)
5 Greek fabulist (5)
6 Meads (anag.) (5)
7 Verify again (6-5)
8 Energetically or vigorously (11)
14 Beautified (7)
15 Item used by asthma sufferers (7)
17 Mixes up or confuses (6)
19 Snake toxin (5)
20 Punctuation mark (5)

No. 118

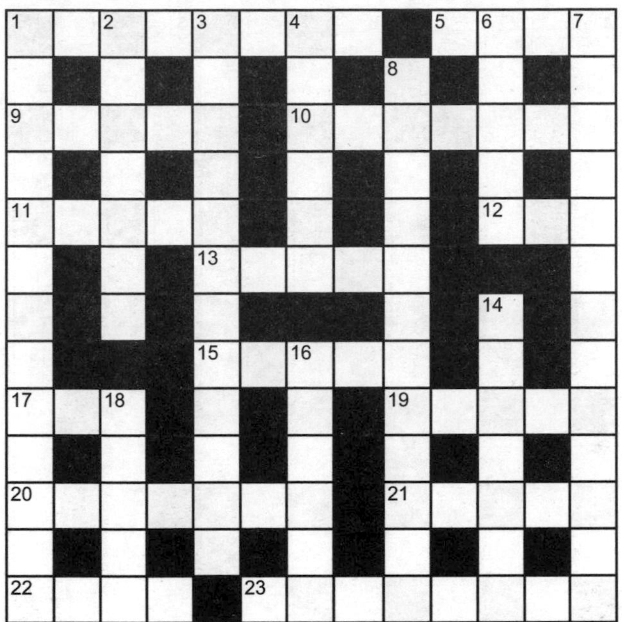

Across

1 Upper interior surfaces of rooms (8)
5 List of food items available (4)
9 Frenzied (5)
10 Powerful dog (7)
11 Performer (5)
12 Polite address for a man (3)
13 Imitative of the past (5)
15 Zest (5)
17 e.g. Hedwig in Harry Potter (3)
19 Pale orange tropical fruit (5)
20 Cherubic (7)
21 Core group; basic unit (5)
22 Goes wrong (4)
23 Unsporting activity (4,4)

Down

1 Sympathetic and merciful (13)
2 Caused to catch fire (7)
3 Incurably bad (12)
4 Ploy (6)
6 Makes (a sound) (5)
7 Regrettably (13)
8 Relating to horoscopes (12)
14 Thing causing outrage (7)
16 Plaster for coating walls (6)
18 Beer (5)

No. 119

Across

1 Water channel (6)
7 Choosing from various sources (8)
8 Cook in hot oil (3)
9 Fillings (6)
10 Fish-eating eagle (4)
11 Earnings (5)
13 Dig out of the ground (7)
15 Relating to current affairs (7)
17 Legend (5)
21 Logical division (4)
22 Observing (6)
23 Implore (3)
24 Stops temporarily (8)
25 Sharp pain (6)

Down

1 Laugh boisterously (6)
2 Attempting (6)
3 Receive and pass on a message (5)
4 Shutting (7)
5 Representations or descriptions of data (8)
6 Finch (6)
12 Engraved inscription (8)
14 Dried grapes (7)
16 Detestable (6)
18 Famous London clock (3,3)
19 Regime (anag.) (6)
20 Wild animal; monster (5)

No. 120

Across

1 Select; choose (4)
3 Went before (8)
9 Behave well (7)
10 Book (5)
11 Repetition of the same sound (12)
13 Wiped out (6)
15 Chase (6)
17 Thick-skinned herbivorous animal (12)
20 Ascended (5)
21 Reddening of the skin (7)
22 Stir dust (anag.) (8)
23 Landlocked country in Africa (4)

Down

1 Boxes (8)
2 Humped ruminant (5)
4 Sharp reply (6)
5 Building (12)
6 Sly (7)
7 As expected (4)
8 Metal device for removing tops (6,6)
12 Argued logically (8)
14 Assumed identities (7)
16 Musical works (6)
18 Maw (5)
19 Push; poke (4)

No. 121

Across

1 Advocate of representative government (8)
5 Large wading bird (4)
9 Crime of burning something (5)
10 Agreed or corresponded (7)
11 Amiability (12)
14 Shed tears (3)
15 Explore or examine (5)
16 Owed and payable (3)
17 Easily (12)
20 Non-pedigree dog (7)
22 Extremely happy period (5)
23 24 hour periods (4)
24 Additional book matter (8)

Down

1 Dull (4)
2 Stingy (7)
3 Characteristic of the present (12)
4 Era (anag.) (3)
6 Cleanse the body (5)
7 Move out the way of (8)
8 Having an efficient approach to one's work (12)
12 Witty (5)
13 Shouted very loudly (8)
16 Postponed (7)
18 Amusing (5)
19 Shut with force (4)
21 Boy (3)

No. 122

Across

1 Correct to the last detail (4-7)
9 Gamble (5)
10 17th Greek letter (3)
11 Change (5)
12 Topic (anag.) (5)
13 Anxious uncertainty (8)
16 Wedding (8)
18 Decapod crustaceans (5)
21 Memos (5)
22 The gist of the matter (3)
23 Strike repeatedly (5)
24 Energetically (11)

Down

2 Side of a coin bearing the head (7)
3 Wasted time (7)
4 Large birds of prey (6)
5 Relinquish (5)
6 Gold measure (5)
7 Semi-transparent (11)
8 Witches (11)
14 A parent's mother (7)
15 Incomplete (7)
17 Long-legged rodent (6)
19 Monastery church (5)
20 Dark reddish-brown pigment (5)

No. 123

Across

1 Wages (8)
5 Neat in appearance (4)
9 Implied without being stated (5)
10 Act of awakening from sleep (7)
11 Leading (anag.) (7)
12 Type of chemical bond (5)
13 Sell to the public (6)
14 Small summer-house (6)
17 Needing to be scratched (5)
19 Stands about idly (7)
20 Kind of abbreviation (7)
21 Female relation (5)
22 365 days (4)
23 Makes remote; cuts off (8)

Down

1 Noteworthy and rare (13)
2 Acknowledgement of payment (7)
3 Growing stronger (12)
4 Protects (6)
6 Sticky substance exuded by trees (5)
7 Spite (13)
8 Inspiring action (12)
15 Highest mountain (7)
16 Large feathers (6)
18 Papal court (5)

No. 124

Across

1 Deciduous trees (4)
3 Stressed (8)
9 Reindeer (7)
10 Panorama (5)
11 Law court official (5)
12 Made to individual order (7)
13 Recess (6)
15 Buyer and seller (6)
17 Meatier (anag.) (7)
18 Feeling of fear (5)
20 Boredom (5)
21 Relating to heat (7)
22 Follow another vehicle too closely (8)
23 Circular movement of water (4)

Down

1 Expression of approval (13)
2 Merriment (5)
4 Round and plump (6)
5 Person who listens into conversations (12)
6 Tuft of grass (7)
7 Completely (opposed) (13)
8 Shortening (12)
14 Dry red table wine of Italy (7)
16 Group of seven (6)
19 Titled (5)

No. 125

Across

1 Closing section of music (4)
3 Cutting instrument (8)
9 The first Gospel (7)
10 Lover of Juliet (5)
11 Edge of a cup (3)
12 Suggest (5)
13 The beginning of something (5)
15 Consumer of food (5)
17 Certain to end in failure (2-3)
18 Used to be (3)
19 Lazy person; layabout (5)
20 Japanese flower arranging (7)
21 Curiosity (8)
22 Reasons; explanations (4)

Down

1 Understanding (13)
2 Piece of information (5)
4 Escrow (anag.) (6)
5 Author of screenplays (12)
6 Diffusion of molecules through a membrane (7)
7 Meteors (8,5)
8 Evergreen shrub (12)
14 Dithers (7)
16 Themes (6)
18 Ire (5)

No. 126

Across

1 Imaginary (8)
5 One of the continents (4)
9 Remnant of a dying fire (5)
10 Learner (7)
11 Taking part in a game (7)
12 Small woody plant (5)
13 Sense of musical time (6)
14 Language (6)
17 Follow on (5)
19 Group of assistants (7)
20 Volcanic crater (7)
21 Capital of Vietnam (5)
22 Reduce one's food intake (4)
23 Banister (8)

Down

1 Wet behind the ears (13)
2 Public collection of books (7)
3 Uncurled (12)
4 Countenance (6)
6 Give a solemn oath (5)
7 Destroying microorganisms (13)
8 Fully extended (12)
15 A rich mine; big prize (7)
16 Mistakes in printed matter (6)
18 Medicinal ointment (5)

No. 127

Across

1 Blue precious stone (8)
5 Moat (anag.) (4)
9 Apprehended with certainty (5)
10 Good qualities (7)
11 Comprehensible (12)
14 A man's dinner jacket (abbrev.) (3)
15 Many times (5)
16 Support for a golf ball (3)
17 Irresistible (12)
20 Of the stomach (7)
22 Hurled away (5)
23 Travel by horse (4)
24 Two-wheeled vehicles (8)

Down

1 Japanese beverage (4)
2 Mythical bird (7)
3 From this time on (12)
4 Increase the running speed of an engine (3)
6 Part of the hand (5)
7 Overcame (8)
8 Mathematics of triangles (12)
12 Type of coffee (5)
13 More powerful (8)
16 Slender stemlike plant appendage (7)
18 Became less difficult (5)
19 Nocturnal birds of prey (4)
21 22nd Greek letter (3)

No. 128

Across

1 Catholic leader (4)
3 Playful (8)
9 Give too much money (7)
10 Avocet-like wader (5)
11 Detection technology (5)
12 Perfect happiness (7)
13 Not dense (6)
15 Taxonomic groupings (6)
17 Suggested but not stated explicitly (7)
18 Dry red wine (5)
20 Swiftly (5)
21 Wealthiest (7)
22 Author (8)
23 Undulating (4)

Down

1 Defer action (13)
2 Ask for earnestly (5)
4 Being nosy (6)
5 Minimum purchase cost at auction (7,5)
6 Emulate (7)
7 Wastefully; lavishly (13)
8 Brutally; harshly (12)
14 Seems (7)
16 Decorates (6)
19 24th Greek letter (5)

No. 129

Across

4 Adhesive putty (6)
7 Affluent (4-2-2)
8 Broad inlet of the sea (3)
9 Decant (4)
10 Largest South American country (6)
11 Christian ministers (7)
12 Ski run (5)
15 Irritates (5)
17 Mental strain (7)
20 Looked at menacingly (6)
21 Felines (4)
22 Large (3)
23 Awesome (8)
24 Saturated with liquid (6)

Down

1 Set of chromosomes (6)
2 Relating to office work (8)
3 Stealing (7)
4 Grinding tooth (5)
5 Pieces of furniture (6)
6 Wolflike wild dog (6)
13 Lacking confidence (8)
14 Sheets and blankets (7)
15 Spherical objects (6)
16 Carried with difficulty (6)
18 Yield (6)
19 Wrong (anag.) (5)

No. 130

Across

1 Believed to be true (8)
5 Rules of a country (4)
9 Organ (5)
10 Museum keeper (7)
11 UFO (6,6)
13 Haphazardly (6)
14 Narrow passage of water (6)
17 Lexicons (12)
20 Enhance a photo (7)
21 Take forcibly (5)
22 Uncommon (4)
23 Importance; stress (8)

Down

1 Having inherent ability (4)
2 Soldiers who fought on horseback (7)
3 Penny-pinching (12)
4 Coop up (6)
6 Loft (5)
7 Female students' society (8)
8 Productive insight (12)
12 Person walking aimlessly (8)
15 Streets (7)
16 Song of devotion (6)
18 Supply with food (5)
19 Musical work (4)

No. 131

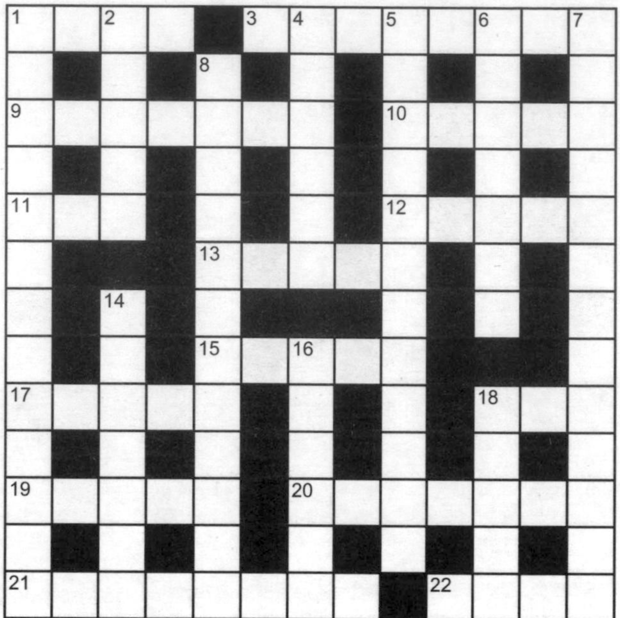

Across

1 Renown (4)
3 Food of the gods (8)
9 Incorporates into (7)
10 Sing like a bird (5)
11 Sewn edge (3)
12 Stage (5)
13 Send money (5)
15 Extremely small (prefix) (5)
17 Wipe (5)
18 Possesses (3)
19 The entire scale (5)
20 Move; agitate (7)
21 Children beginning to walk (8)
22 Relinquish (4)

Down

1 Boxing class division (13)
2 Musical note (5)
4 Building exhibiting objects (6)
5 Person who receives office visitors (12)
6 Winding shapes (7)
7 Capable of being understood (13)
8 Based on untested ideas (12)
14 Unusually lucky (of a person's life) (7)
16 Bit of partly burnt wood (6)
18 Dwelling (5)

No. 132

Across

1 More slothful (6)
4 Sample of cloth (6)
9 Uncovers; reveals (7)
10 Vivid (7)
11 Slithering animal (5)
12 Open disrespect (5)
14 e.g. oxygen and nitrogen (5)
17 Froglike amphibians (5)
19 Curbs (5)
21 Discard from memory (7)
23 Pertaining to plants (7)
24 Creepier (6)
25 Season of the Church year (6)

Down

1 Giggles (6)
2 Sixth Greek letter (4)
3 Engraving (7)
5 Totally erases (5)
6 State of Australia (8)
7 Move or travel hurriedly (6)
8 Dismantle (11)
13 Mileage tracker (8)
15 Played for time (7)
16 Fit for consumption (6)
18 Naturally illuminated (6)
20 e.g. taste or touch (5)
22 Helper (4)

No. 133

Across

1 Apex or peak (4)
3 Sailing swiftly (8)
9 Imitate (7)
10 Enclosed (of animals) (5)
11 Skilled joiner (12)
13 Inform (6)
15 Art of growing dwarfed trees (6)
17 Courtesy (12)
20 Connection; link (3-2)
21 Coarse beach gravel (7)
22 Decorative designs (8)
23 Metal fastener (4)

Down

1 Shape of the waxing moon (8)
2 Small firework (5)
4 Make (6)
5 Absolute authority in any sphere (12)
6 Act of entering (7)
7 Deities (4)
8 Grandeur (12)
12 Squander money (8)
14 Strong stream of water (7)
16 Make less tight (6)
18 Two cubed (5)
19 Finish (4)

No. 134

Across

1 Interpret the meaning of (8)
5 Contest between two people (4)
9 Customary practice (5)
10 Platform (7)
11 Chiefly (7)
12 Cloak (5)
13 Agree (6)
14 Cooking in hot oil (6)
17 Woodwind instruments (5)
19 Crisp plain fabric (7)
20 Japanese massage technique (7)
21 Covered with water (5)
22 Step on a ladder (4)
23 Troublemaker (8)

Down

1 Betrayer (6-7)
2 Feeling of vexation (7)
3 Precondition (12)
4 Opinion pieces (6)
6 Living in a city (5)
7 Compiler of a dictionary (13)
8 Unemotional and practical (6-2-4)
15 Imprecise (7)
16 Grunts (anag.) (6)
18 Aromatic vegetable (5)

No. 135

Across

1 Tunnel under a road for pedestrians (6)
7 Outmoded (8)
8 Longing (3)
9 Each (6)
10 Vases (4)
11 Midges (5)
13 Great bravery (7)
15 Mistake; blunder (4,3)
17 Content (5)
21 Adolescent (4)
22 Small hills (6)
23 Head covering (3)
24 Gives life to (8)
25 Exit; Bible book (6)

Down

1 Intelligence activity (6)
2 Yellow fruit (6)
3 Bonds of union (5)
4 Showed a person to their seat (7)
5 Eye disease (8)
6 Holds one's ground (6)
12 Science of classification (8)
14 Promotes commercially (7)
16 Getting older (6)
18 Shoved (6)
19 Young people (6)
20 Sowed (anag.) (5)

No. 136

Across

1 Gives strength to (8)
5 Slow (anag.) (4)
9 A line from a piece of music (5)
10 Belligerent (7)
11 Hassles; prickles (7)
12 Sticky sweet liquid (5)
13 Pay no attention to (6)
14 Pilot (6)
17 Upright (5)
19 Car motors (7)
20 River in South America (7)
21 Surpass (5)
22 Uses a stool (4)
23 Lengthen (8)

Down

1 Magnificent (13)
2 Operating doctor (7)
3 Rate of increase in speed (12)
4 Freshest (6)
6 Willow twig (5)
7 Any means of advancement (8,5)
8 Scolding (8-4)
15 The small details of something (7)
16 Pollute (6)
18 Kick out (5)

No. 137

Across

1 Helps; benefits (6)
7 Captives (8)
8 Water barrier (3)
9 Crazy (6)
10 Cultivated (4)
11 Wise men (5)
13 Become more precipitous (7)
15 Windpipe (7)
17 Bent; bandy (5)
21 Pull a sulky face (4)
22 Manly (6)
23 Not near (3)
24 Withdraws (8)
25 Elegant and slender (6)

Down

1 Venomous snakes (6)
2 Equipping with weapons (6)
3 Remove wool from sheep (5)
4 Upward slopes (7)
5 Hot pepper (8)
6 Insect of the order Coleoptera (6)
12 And so on (2,6)
14 Repair a vehicle (7)
16 Firmly established (6)
18 Wretched (6)
19 Decide with authority (6)
20 Very unpleasant (5)

No. 138

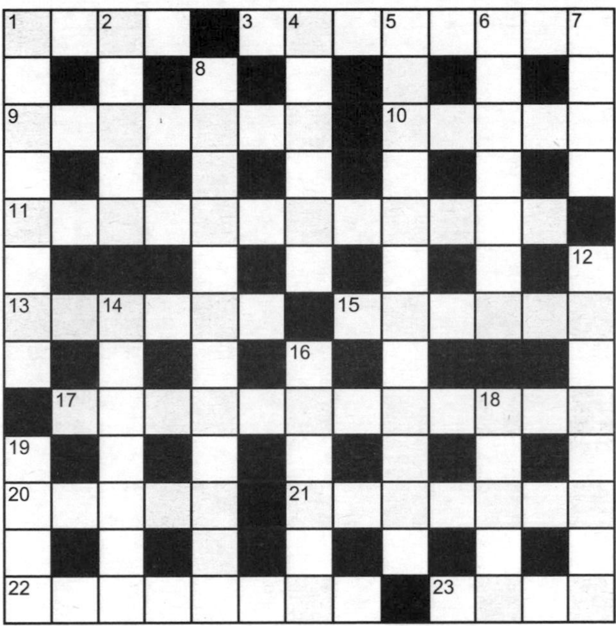

Across

1 Musical composition (4)
3 Unfit for consumption (of food) (8)
9 Player of an instrument that is low in pitch (7)
10 Indian lute (5)
11 International multi-sport event (7,5)
13 Line of equal pressure on a map (6)
15 Wild horse (6)
17 Resolvable (12)
20 Chunk (5)
21 Release (7)
22 A formal exposition (8)
23 Comedy sketch (4)

Down

1 Slower than sound (8)
2 Beastly (5)
4 See (6)
5 Hopelessly (12)
6 Among (7)
7 Book of the Bible (4)
8 Misplaced net (anag.) (12)
12 To a certain extent (8)
14 Late (7)
16 Love affairs (6)
18 Opposite of white (5)
19 Crush with a sharp blow (4)

No. 139

Across

1 Style and movement in art (6)
7 Exceptional (8)
8 Irritate (3)
9 Narrow sea inlets (6)
10 Tidy (4)
11 Speaks (5)
13 Bordeaux wines (7)
15 Moving back and forth (7)
17 Comedian (5)
21 Game played on horseback (4)
22 Money received (6)
23 Domestic animal (3)
24 In every respect (3-5)
25 Coders (anag.) (6)

Down

1 Warning (6)
2 Containerful (6)
3 Joyous and happy (5)
4 Letter (7)
5 Plot outline for a play (8)
6 Common volcanic rock (6)
12 Musical instrument (8)
14 Not modern (7)
16 Entirely (6)
18 Guardian (6)
19 Raved (6)
20 Rushes along (5)

No. 140

Across

1 Seven-sided polygon (8)
5 Audacity (4)
8 Bores (anag.) (5)
9 Secured against loss or damage (7)
10 Announcements (7)
12 Bodyguards (7)
14 Apart; into pieces (7)
16 Comes into view (7)
18 Thoroughly (2,5)
19 Small crude shelter (5)
20 Messy substance (4)
21 Made unhappy (8)

Down

1 Brave person; idol (4)
2 Communal (6)
3 Responding to (9)
4 Pungent edible bulbs (6)
6 Continent (6)
7 Guiding principle (8)
11 Conquered; was victorious (9)
12 Going inside (8)
13 Blush (6)
14 Respiratory condition (6)
15 Highly motivated (6)
17 Delighted (4)

No. 141

Across

1 Assists; holds up (8)
5 Group of countries in an alliance (4)
9 Exposes secret information (5)
10 Social gathering of old friends (7)
11 Winged angelic beings (7)
12 Swiftness or speed (5)
13 Type of confectionery (6)
14 Implant deeply (6)
17 Modify (5)
19 Ruled (7)
20 Greek goddess of retribution (7)
21 Stroll (5)
22 Fathers (4)
23 Judges; evaluates (8)

Down

1 Complete in itself (of a thing) (4-9)
2 Flat highland (7)
3 Obfuscation (12)
4 Songbird with a spotted breast (6)
6 Dens (5)
7 Satisfaction (13)
8 Establish as genuine (12)
15 Public transport vehicle (7)
16 Outer parts of bread loaves (6)
18 Targeted (5)

No. 142

Across

1 Structured set of information (8)
5 Main island of Indonesia (4)
8 Small boat (5)
9 Slanted characters (7)
10 Plausible; defensible (7)
12 Game participants (7)
14 Learned person (7)
16 Garden flower (7)
18 Tallier (anag.) (7)
19 Not tight (5)
20 Thoughtfulness (4)
21 Court of justice (8)

Down

1 Gaming cubes (4)
2 Frozen plain (6)
3 Have profits that equal costs (5,4)
4 Goes round the edge of; garments (6)
6 With hands on the hips (6)
7 Respondent (8)
11 Disco (9)
12 Booklet (8)
13 Not moving (6)
14 Mariner (6)
15 Isolated inlet of the sea (6)
17 Business agreement (4)

No. 143

Across

1 Woodland (6)
4 Book of the Bible (6)
9 Tapering stone pillar (7)
10 Choice cut of beef (7)
11 Furnaces (5)
12 Shoe ties (5)
14 Works hard (5)
17 Annoying (5)
19 Scope or extent (5)
21 Film directed by Stephen Gaghan (7)
23 Hide (7)
24 Swollen edible root (6)
25 Expressions (6)

Down

1 Remains preserved in rock (6)
2 Sound of a lion (4)
3 Unaccompanied musician (7)
5 Small spot (5)
6 Bald (8)
7 Having a jaunty appearance (6)
8 Intentionally (11)
13 Grouped together (8)
15 Stimulated; urged on (7)
16 Craned (anag.) (6)
18 Longs (for) (6)
20 Youngsters aged from 13 - 19 (5)
22 Adult male singing voice (4)

No. 144

Across

1 Domineering (11)
9 Long bench (3)
10 Slabs of peat for fuel (5)
11 Regular beat (5)
12 Container for storing items (5)
13 Grateful (8)
16 Orderly and logical (8)
18 Celestial body (5)
20 Young sheep (5)
21 Tease or pester (5)
22 Range of knowledge (3)
23 Ancestors (11)

Down

2 Promised (5)
3 Hear a court case anew (5)
4 Make better (6)
5 Reply (7)
6 Make ineffective (7)
7 Extremely impressive (11)
8 Eternal (11)
14 Hair-cleansing product (7)
15 Table support (7)
17 Cloud of dust and gas in space (6)
18 Receive a ball in one's hands (5)
19 Creator (5)

No. 145

Across

1 Tube (4)
3 Praising (anag.) (8)
9 Tallinn's country (7)
10 Floor of a building (5)
11 Slippery fish (3)
12 Find an answer to (5)
13 Seashore (5)
15 Capital of Bulgaria (5)
17 Active cause (5)
18 What a spider weaves (3)
19 Phrase that is not taken literally (5)
20 Breathing aid in water (7)
21 In these times (8)
22 A single time (4)

Down

1 Intent (13)
2 Floral leaf (5)
4 Sporting arenas (6)
5 Picture (12)
6 Concern; implicate (7)
7 50th anniversary of a major event (6,7)
8 Not familiar with or used to (12)
14 Trailer (7)
16 Gaudy (6)
18 Rouse from sleep (5)

No. 146

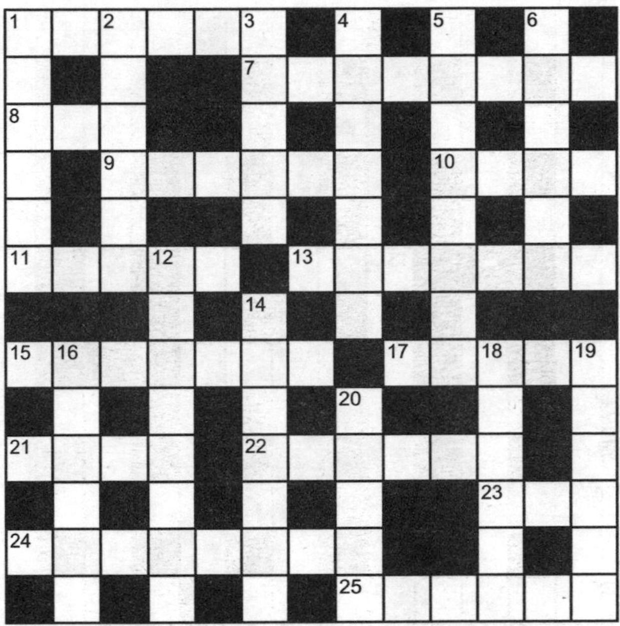

Across

1 Hurting (6)
7 Made better (8)
8 Achieved (3)
9 Lower someone's dignity (6)
10 Tartan skirt (4)
11 Reside (5)
13 Clowns (7)
15 Courageously (7)
17 Models for a photograph (5)
21 Rotate (4)
22 Parody (6)
23 Man's best friend (3)
24 Part of the brain (8)
25 Supplies sparingly (6)

Down

1 Mixed up or confused (6)
2 Nestle together (6)
3 Donor (5)
4 Aquatic invertebrates (7)
5 White crested parrot (8)
6 Basement (6)
12 Aromatic shrub (8)
14 Sense of resolution (7)
16 Computer networking device (6)
18 Country in North Europe (6)
19 Raised platforms (6)
20 Basic units of chemical elements (5)

No. 147

Across

1 Coal mine (8)
5 Gelatinous substance (4)
9 Deluge (5)
10 Harmful (7)
11 Wearing glasses (12)
14 Attempt to do (3)
15 Conventions (5)
16 Male child (3)
17 Relating to numbers (12)
20 Imitator (7)
22 Be the same as (5)
23 Large bag (4)
24 Speaking many languages (8)

Down

1 Face (anag.) (4)
2 In a relaxed manner (7)
3 Freedom from control (12)
4 Moved quickly on foot (3)
6 Snarl (5)
7 Living in (8)
8 Thoroughly (12)
12 About (5)
13 Puts up with something (8)
16 Aquatic bird (7)
18 Subject matter (5)
19 Overabundance (4)
21 Excessively (3)

No. 148

	1		2		3		4			5		6
7												
										8		
9					10							
11								12	13			
							14					
15		16				17					18	
					19							
		20							21			
22												
					23							
24												

Across

4 Small pit or cavity (6)
7 Expression of gratitude (5,3)
8 Athletic facility (3)
9 Near (4)
10 Strongly opposed (6)
11 Least attractive (7)
12 Computer memory units (5)
15 Gave away (5)
17 Need (7)
20 Lets up (6)
21 Unwieldy ship (4)
22 Soil; dirt (3)
23 Person skilled in languages (8)
24 Agile (6)

Down

1 Throwing at a target (6)
2 Preserve or hold sacred (8)
3 Junction between nerve cells (7)
4 Entices (5)
5 Imperative (6)
6 Military forces (6)
13 Young (8)
14 Explanations (7)
15 Widespread (6)
16 Crown (6)
18 Enjoy greatly (6)
19 Stagnant (5)

No. 149

Across

1 Enormous (11)
9 Tree of the genus Quercus (3)
10 Words that identify things (5)
11 Belonging to them (5)
12 Tripod for an artist (5)
13 Operatic texts (8)
16 Day of the week (8)
18 Tribe (anag.) (5)
20 Remove paint from a wall (5)
21 Two children born at the same time (5)
22 Close-fitting hat (3)
23 Brevity in expressing oneself (11)

Down

2 Finds agreeable (5)
3 Committee (5)
4 Former students (6)
5 Food samplers (7)
6 Originality (7)
7 Metabolic equilibrium (11)
8 Instrument for recording heart activity (11)
14 Tortilla rolled around a filling (7)
15 Sterile (7)
17 Keeps away from (6)
18 Subatomic particle (5)
19 Small nails (5)

No. 150

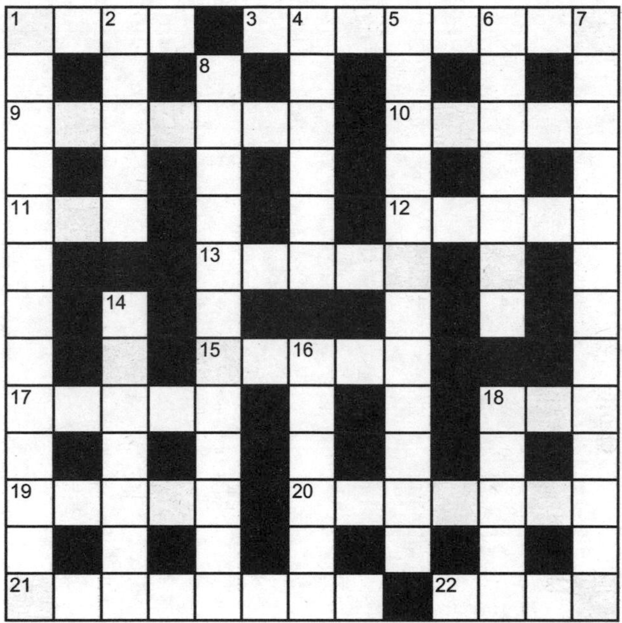

Across

1 Mimic (4)
3 Disease caused by a lack of thiamine (8)
9 Temporary measure (7)
10 Funny person (5)
11 First woman (3)
12 Craftsman who uses stone (5)
13 Faint bird cry (5)
15 Crowbar (5)
17 Make a map of (5)
18 21st Greek letter (3)
19 Conclude (5)
20 Criminal (7)
21 Increase (8)
22 Lies (anag.) (4)

Down

1 Economical (4-9)
2 Plain writing (5)
4 Reveal (6)
5 Without equal (12)
6 All together (2,5)
7 Put to trouble (13)
8 Relating to farming (12)
14 Movement of vehicles en masse (7)
16 Closely woven fabric (6)
18 Summits (5)

No. 151

Across

1 Piece of software (11)
9 Negligent (3)
10 Chessmen (5)
11 Indian garments (5)
12 Tablets (5)
13 Recurrent (8)
16 Shows (8)
18 Beads (anag.) (5)
20 Exhaust gases (5)
21 Boats (5)
22 Finish first (3)
23 Introductory (11)

Down

2 Component of a computer image (5)
3 Songbirds (5)
4 Indistinct (6)
5 Adornments of hanging threads (7)
6 Large flightless bird (7)
7 Omnipotent (3-8)
8 Radiant; sumptuous (11)
14 Glisten (7)
15 At the ocean floor (7)
17 Boredom (6)
18 Buffalo (5)
19 Effluent system (5)

No. 152

Across

1 Strain (4)
3 Paint-spraying device (8)
9 Love; genre of fiction (7)
10 Spiritual being (5)
11 Boolean operator (3)
12 Overly self-assertive (5)
13 Fairy (5)
15 Widespread dislike (5)
17 Insinuate (5)
18 Having a high temperature (3)
19 Rogue; scoundrel (5)
20 Wild (of an animal) (7)
21 Midday (8)
22 Jealousy (4)

Down

1 Young person (6,7)
2 Thigh bone (5)
4 Refrigerator compartment (6)
5 Gossip (12)
6 Improve equipment (7)
7 Unenthusiastically (4-9)
8 Joblessness (12)
14 Highest singing voice (7)
16 Sent out; distributed (6)
18 Mortal (5)

No. 153

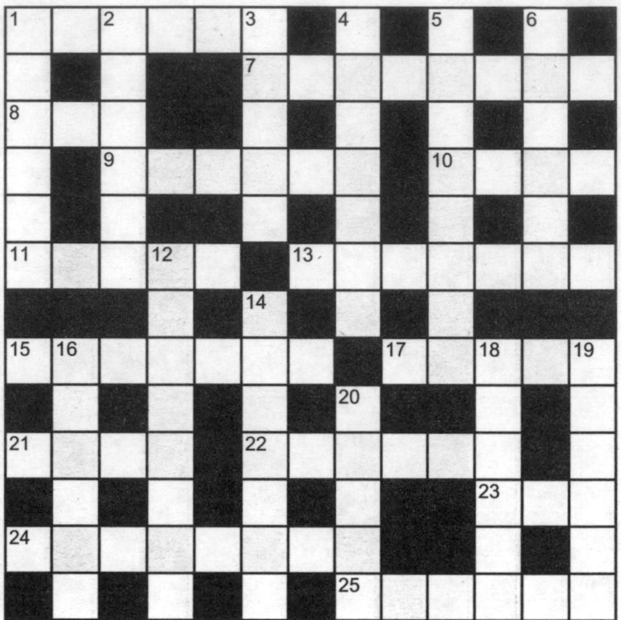

Across

1 Matures (of fruit) (6)
7 Relating to a topic (8)
8 Deviate off course (3)
9 Disagree (6)
10 Suggestion or tip (4)
11 Challenges (5)
13 Seed bid (anag.) (7)
15 Sauce made from tomatoes (7)
17 Planet (5)
21 Instrument that is plucked (4)
22 Dung beetle (6)
23 Mouthpiece attached to a bridle (3)
24 Base of a statue (8)
25 Flammable material (6)

Down

1 Had corresponding sounds (6)
2 Very fine substance (6)
3 Cram (5)
4 Small fruits (7)
5 Exaggerated masculinity (8)
6 Prevented from moving (6)
12 Fugitives (8)
14 Throb (7)
16 Overjoyed (6)
18 Stole from (6)
19 Person who owes money (6)
20 Defect (5)

No. 154

Across

1 Enter unlawfully (8)
5 Fish (4)
8 Moisten meat (5)
9 Subsiding (7)
10 Written additions (7)
12 Singer; type of bird (7)
14 Relating to what one eats (7)
16 Wanderer (7)
18 Commanded (7)
19 Lucky accident (5)
20 Cut (of grass) (4)
21 Recklessly determined (4-4)

Down

1 Bats (anag.) (4)
2 Christian festival (6)
3 Widespread (9)
4 Having only magnitude (6)
6 Workers' groups (6)
7 Debatably (8)
11 Dishonest (9)
12 Beetle larva that bores into timber (8)
13 Glass opening in a wall (6)
14 Work hard; toil (6)
15 Renounce an oath (6)
17 Greatest (4)

No. 155

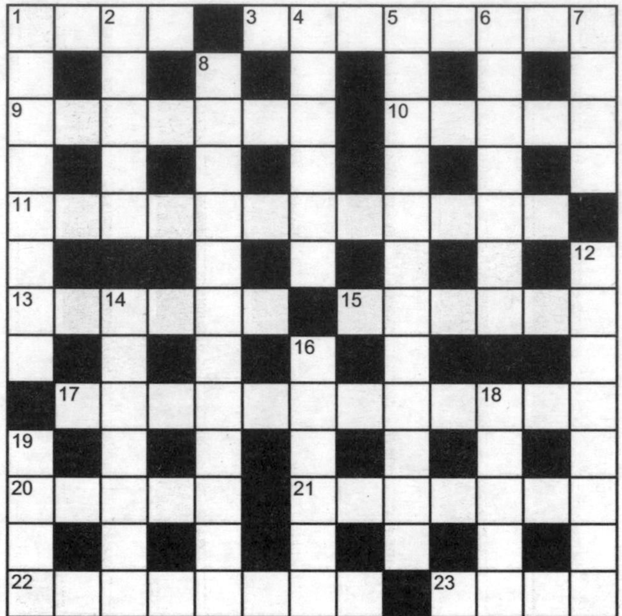

Across

1 Stone block (4)
3 African country (8)
9 Alfresco (7)
10 Artifice (5)
11 Provincialism (12)
13 Mineral used to make plaster of Paris (6)
15 Brandy distilled from cherries (6)
17 Relation by marriage (7-2-3)
20 Brief appearance (5)
21 Difficult choice (7)
22 Plan anew (8)
23 Poker stake (4)

Down

1 Obstruction in a passage (8)
2 Awake and out of bed (5)
4 Dissertation (6)
5 Understandably (12)
6 Clergymen (7)
7 Ancient boats (4)
8 Rude (12)
12 Glass container for displaying objects (8)
14 Monumental Egyptian structure (7)
16 Veteran sailor (3,3)
18 Citrus fruit (5)
19 Skin mark from a wound (4)

No. 156

Across

1 Astound (11)
9 Hairstyle (3)
10 Exhibited (5)
11 Sweeping implement (5)
12 Alleviate (5)
13 Merchant (8)
16 Minute aquatic plant (8)
18 Aromatic herb of the mint family (5)
20 Smudges (5)
21 One who puts in a lot of effort (5)
22 Tap (anag.) (3)
23 Measure of heat (11)

Down

2 Defamatory statement (5)
3 Growing thickly (of a beard) (5)
4 Develop gradually (6)
5 Small fast ship (7)
6 Learning institutions (7)
7 Word used by magicians (11)
8 Unending life (11)
14 Motivate (7)
15 Ballroom dance (3-4)
17 Simpler (6)
18 Rupture (5)
19 Wonderful (5)

No. 157

Across

1 Travel on water (4)
3 Small-scale musical drama (8)
9 Embodiment (7)
10 Worthiness (5)
11 Praise highly (5)
12 Pertaining to the heart (7)
13 Slender candles (6)
15 Third sign of the zodiac (6)
17 Succeed financially (7)
18 Extreme (5)
20 Logical and easy to understand (5)
21 Least tame (7)
22 Campaigner (8)
23 Mineral powder (4)

Down

1 Lacking originality (13)
2 Balearic party island (5)
4 Penetrate (6)
5 Regretfully (12)
6 End stations (7)
7 Not living up to expectations (13)
8 Repository for misplaced items (4,8)
14 Saying (7)
16 Large groups of people (6)
19 Eighth Greek letter (5)

No. 158

Across

1 Gloomily (8)
5 Scorch (4)
9 Poisonous (5)
10 Capital of China (7)
11 Main premises of a company (12)
14 Metal container; is able to (3)
15 Birds lay their eggs in these (5)
16 Draw (3)
17 Uncomplimentary (12)
20 Accumulation of uncompleted work (7)
22 Lose a contest intentionally (5)
23 Office table (4)
24 Is composed of (8)

Down

1 Be foolishly fond of (4)
2 A score less four (7)
3 Not on purpose (12)
4 Research place (abbrev.) (3)
6 Select group of people (5)
7 Official list of names (8)
8 Type of cloud (12)
12 Surprise result (5)
13 Cleansed thoroughly (8)
16 Tureens (anag.) (7)
18 Accurate pieces of information (5)
19 Pairs (4)
21 Sticky substance (3)

No. 159

Across

1 Pamper (11)
9 Fishing pole (3)
10 Chars (5)
11 Large crow (5)
12 Craftily (5)
13 Capital of Australia (8)
16 e.g. gels and emulsions (8)
18 Produce eggs (5)
20 Let (5)
21 Piece of code to automate a task (5)
22 Auction item (3)
23 Unintelligible (11)

Down

2 Weirdly (5)
3 Entrance hall (5)
4 Gaseous envelope of the sun (6)
5 Undress (7)
6 Reveals (anag.) (7)
7 Radically (11)
8 Link together (11)
14 Rid of something unpleasant (7)
15 Worker who supervises others (7)
17 Ordained minister (6)
18 Ruin (5)
19 Collection of maps (5)

No. 160

Across

1 Crises (11)
9 Soft paste (5)
10 Excellent serve (3)
11 Apart from (5)
12 Abominable snowmen (5)
13 Control (8)
16 Capable of being wrong (8)
18 More secure (5)
21 Scorch (5)
22 Cup (3)
23 Small bottles (5)
24 Act of harassing someone (11)

Down

2 Contemplations (7)
3 Revokes (7)
4 Obtain by coercion (6)
5 Shyly (5)
6 Make law (5)
7 Argumentative (11)
8 Quantification (11)
14 Mass of flowers (7)
15 Give up (7)
17 Opposite of an acid (6)
19 Contrapuntal composition (5)
20 Variety show (5)

No. 161

Across

4 Turn down (6)
7 Spanish dance (8)
8 Excavated soil (3)
9 Fastened; suspended (4)
10 Embarrassing mistake (3-3)
11 Sends back into custody (7)
12 Garden buildings (5)
15 Acknowledged; assumed (5)
17 Very distant (7)
20 Denial (anag.) (6)
21 Large trade show (4)
22 Seed vessel (3)
23 Thieves (8)
24 Mock (6)

Down

1 Entice or attract (6)
2 Move to another country (8)
3 A person in general (7)
4 Machine; automaton (5)
5 Unfastened (6)
6 Contrapuntal compositions (6)
13 Blissful (8)
14 Food pantries (7)
15 Swallowed quickly (6)
16 Seller (6)
18 Aim to achieve something (6)
19 Spherical body (5)

No. 162

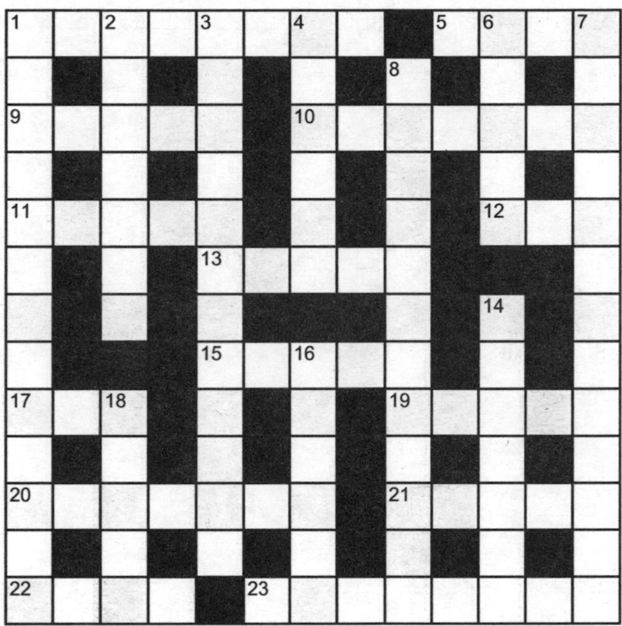

Across

1 Course of study (8)
5 Song for a solo voice (4)
9 Object on which a bird roosts (5)
10 Mobile phone (7)
11 Pass a rope through (5)
12 Key on a computer keyboard (3)
13 Strong alcoholic drink (5)
15 Juicy fruit (5)
17 Be in debt (3)
19 Lowest point (5)
20 Poured with rain (7)
21 Small airship (5)
22 Spool-like toy (4)
23 Calmly (8)

Down

1 In a manner that exceeds what is necessary (13)
2 Prowlers (7)
3 Accomplishments (12)
4 Confirmed or supported a decision (6)
6 Restore factory settings (5)
7 Account of one's own life (13)
8 Not guided by good sense (12)
14 Hour of going to sleep (7)
16 Pasta strip (6)
18 Mournful poem (5)

No. 163

Across

4 Quantity you can hold (6)
7 Speculative (8)
8 Put a question to (3)
9 Entice (4)
10 Moves very slowly (6)
11 Angered (7)
12 With a forward motion (5)
15 Dizzy (5)
17 Piecemeal and disjointed (7)
20 Long-tailed crow (6)
21 Close by (4)
22 Conciliatory gift (3)
23 Mammal that chews the cud (8)
24 Military blockades (6)

Down

1 Vertical pillar (6)
2 Timber for burning (8)
3 Device attached to a door (7)
4 Lane; passageway (5)
5 Complete failure (6)
6 Feeling of fondness (6)
13 Discovering; finding out (8)
14 Cries out loudly (7)
15 Hotel patrons (6)
16 Indentation (6)
18 Spinal (anag.) (6)
19 Urges on (5)

No. 164

Across

1 Gemstone (4)
3 Rodent (8)
9 Singer (7)
10 Natural yellow resin (5)
11 Excessively forward (12)
14 Opposite of old (3)
16 Picture border (5)
17 Pair of actors (3)
18 Unhappy (12)
21 Musical note (5)
22 Fighter (7)
23 Gives a right to (8)
24 Raps (anag.) (4)

Down

1 Resident (8)
2 Make amends (5)
4 Belonging to us (3)
5 Calculations of dimensions (12)
6 Not attached (7)
7 Currency of France and Germany (4)
8 Not enough (12)
12 Clear and apparent (5)
13 Reflective thinker (8)
15 Palest (7)
19 Spring flower (5)
20 Double-reed instrument (4)
22 Insect which collects pollen (3)

No. 165

Across

1 Round (8)
5 Unable to hear (4)
9 Knocks loudly (5)
10 Belief (7)
11 As a result (12)
14 Possess (3)
15 Run away with a lover (5)
16 North American nation (abbrev.) (3)
17 Military judicial body (5,7)
20 Fractional part (7)
22 Push gently (5)
23 Emperor of Rome 54-68 AD (4)
24 Relied on (8)

Down

1 Young lions (4)
2 Summary of results (7)
3 Completely unaware of (12)
4 Ruction (3)
6 Be alive; be real (5)
7 Male comedian (8)
8 Jail term without end (4,8)
12 Allotted quantity (5)
13 Soft leather shoe (8)
16 Single-handed (7)
18 Brown earth pigment (5)
19 Give nourishment to (4)
21 Foot extremity (3)

No. 166

Across

1 Betray (6-5)
9 Supplementary component (3-2)
10 Trouble in mind or body (3)
11 Measures duration (5)
12 Monster with nine heads (5)
13 Senseless (8)
16 Animal (8)
18 Competed in a speed contest (5)
21 Seeped (5)
22 Number of toes (3)
23 Musical instrument (5)
24 Devices popular before computers existed (11)

Down

2 Something left over (7)
3 Very unpleasant; unkind (7)
4 Small shrubs with pithy stems (6)
5 Cattle-breeding farm (5)
6 Prim and proper (5)
7 Immoderate (11)
8 Alert and thinking cogently (5-6)
14 Knife attached to a rifle (7)
15 Greedy drinker (7)
17 Park keeper (6)
19 Shrewd (5)
20 Male bee (5)

No. 167

Across

1 Offend; affront (6)
7 Cause frustration (8)
8 Sharp projection (3)
9 Periods of darkness (6)
10 School test (4)
11 Conditions (5)
13 Belgian language (7)
15 Excess of liabilities over assets (7)
17 Looking tired (5)
21 Coming immediately after (4)
22 Hit (6)
23 High ball in tennis (3)
24 Hopefulness about the future (8)
25 End a dispute (6)

Down

1 Force fluid into (6)
2 Reigns (anag.) (6)
3 Taut (5)
4 Quickly (7)
5 Pennant (8)
6 Wanders off; drifts (6)
12 Preserve (8)
14 Affinity (7)
16 Absolve (6)
18 Bangle worn at the top of the foot (6)
19 Take small bites out of (6)
20 Neatens (5)

No. 168

Across

1 Force lifting something up (8)
5 Pulls a vehicle (4)
9 State of the USA (5)
10 Useful (7)
11 Giggles (7)
12 Strange and mysterious (5)
13 Immature of its kind (of insects) (6)
14 Swimming costume (6)
17 Accustom (5)
19 Used for the storage of fat (of tissue) (7)
20 Keenly (7)
21 Currently in progress (5)
22 Check; exam (4)
23 Foliage (8)

Down

1 Not clever (13)
2 Kitchen appliance (7)
3 Large Brazilian city (3,2,7)
4 Division of a group (6)
6 Proposal of marriage; bid (5)
7 Obviously (4-9)
8 Unlawful (12)
15 Form of an element (7)
16 Woodcutter (6)
18 Strong desires (5)

No. 169

Across

1 Sermon (6)
4 Powerful (6)
9 Agrees or corresponds (7)
10 Contempt (7)
11 Took illegally (5)
12 Pierced by a bull's horn (5)
14 Impress a pattern on (5)
17 Correct (5)
19 Mark or wear thin (5)
21 Pancreatic hormone (7)
23 Quick musical tempo (7)
24 Metrical foot (6)
25 Shout down; harass (6)

Down

1 Sausage in a roll (3,3)
2 State of confusion (4)
3 Four-legged reptiles (7)
5 Solicits custom (5)
6 Sociable (8)
7 Device used to seal joints (6)
8 Charitable donation (11)
13 Form of government (8)
15 Portent (7)
16 e.g. Borneo (6)
18 Organ in the mouth of a mammal (6)
20 Misty (5)
22 Lie in ambush (4)

No. 170

Across

4 Wooden building material (6)
7 Sleep disorder (8)
8 Insane (3)
9 Cry of a goose (4)
10 Mix socially (6)
11 Leftovers (7)
12 Pointed weapon (5)
15 Renowned (5)
17 Wooed (7)
20 Wandering (6)
21 Pile (4)
22 Wetland (3)
23 Bridge above another road (8)
24 Over there (6)

Down

1 Repeat performance (6)
2 Piece of furniture (8)
3 Bewitch (7)
4 Domestic cat (5)
5 Treelike grass (6)
6 Girded (anag.) (6)
13 Pays homage to (8)
14 Harden (7)
15 Weakly (6)
16 Edge (6)
18 Pass by (6)
19 Lesser (5)

No. 171

Across

1 Left side of a ship (4)
3 Supported with money (8)
9 One's mental attitude (7)
10 Edits (anag.) (5)
11 Use of words that mimic sounds (12)
14 What you hear with (3)
16 Capital of Egypt (5)
17 Sound that a cow makes (3)
18 Bewitchingly (12)
21 Spin (5)
22 Musical wind instrument (7)
23 Wisdom (8)
24 Skin irritation (4)

Down

1 Put forward an idea (8)
2 Quantitative relation between two amounts (5)
4 Annoy (3)
5 Extremely large (12)
6 Silvery-white metal (7)
7 Stage of twilight (4)
8 Not intoxicating (of a drink) (12)
12 The Hunter (constellation) (5)
13 Person of varied learning (8)
15 Putting in order (7)
19 Remorse (5)
20 Is indebted to pay (4)
22 Widely cultivated cereal grass (3)

No. 172

Across

1 Forever (2,9)
9 Recede (3)
10 Alcoholic beverages (5)
11 Runs at a moderate pace (5)
12 Lively; cheerful (5)
13 Prison term (8)
16 Yearly (8)
18 Lump or bump (5)
20 Member of the weasel family (5)
21 Hang in the air (5)
22 Nevertheless (3)
23 Consisting of incomplete parts (11)

Down

2 Suspend; prevent (5)
3 Recently (5)
4 Inborn (6)
5 Install (7)
6 Not valid or true (7)
7 Re-evaluation (11)
8 Insults (11)
14 Reveal (7)
15 African wild pig (7)
17 Famous French museum (6)
18 Round cap (5)
19 Relay (anag.) (5)

No. 173

Across

1 Restored (8)
5 Look slyly (4)
8 Pays for (eg the bill) (5)
9 Very enthusiastic (7)
10 People who are in a club (7)
12 Tiredness (7)
14 Gave out (7)
16 Surpasses (7)
18 Tomb inscription (7)
19 First Pope (5)
20 Male children (4)
21 Migratory birds (8)

Down

1 Repeated jazz phrase (4)
2 Financial gain (6)
3 Bring about (9)
4 Biochemical catalyst (6)
6 Calls to mind (6)
7 Held out against (8)
11 Pertaining to a city (9)
12 Without identity (8)
13 Something done (6)
14 Shun (6)
15 Permanent skin marking (6)
17 Weapons (4)

No. 174

Across

1 Ruminant mammal (4)
3 A desert in south-western Africa (8)
9 Stammer (7)
10 Act of stealing (5)
11 Stadium (5)
12 Process of wearing away (7)
13 Small shoots (6)
15 Highly seasoned type of sausage (6)
17 Spacecraft that circles the planet (7)
18 Plant spike (5)
20 Set straight (5)
21 Considerate; diplomatic (7)
22 Making certain of (8)
23 Pottery material (4)

Down

1 Unemotional (13)
2 Give out; discharge (5)
4 Concurs (6)
5 Science of space travel (12)
6 United States (7)
7 Deliberately (13)
8 Starting here (anag.) (12)
14 Burrowing rodents (7)
16 Positively charged atomic particle (6)
19 Bits of meat of low value (5)

No. 175

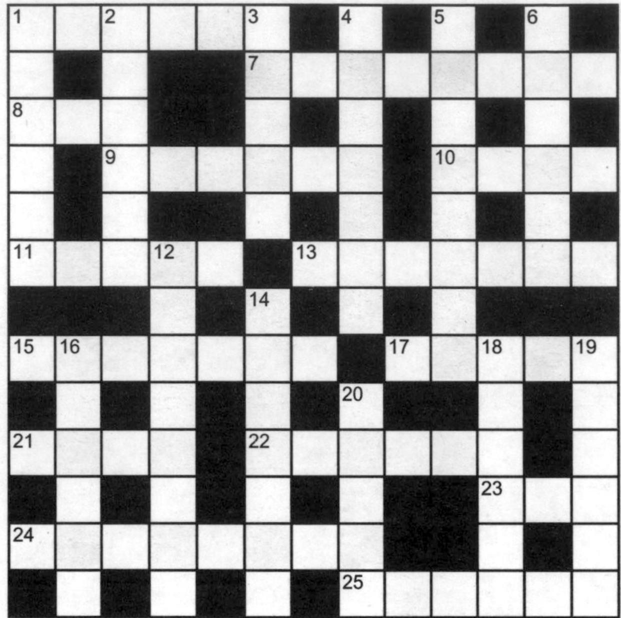

Across

1 Decorate with a raised design (6)
7 Without a fixed abode (8)
8 Mammal with a bushy tail (3)
9 Surpass (6)
10 Loose flowing garment (4)
11 Cleans (5)
13 Wishes for (7)
15 Immature fruit of a cucumber (7)
17 Parts (anag.) (5)
21 Floor covers (4)
22 Humorously sarcastic (6)
23 Young goat (3)
24 Investigate (8)
25 Comfort (6)

Down

1 Envelop (6)
2 Fist fighters (6)
3 Footwear (pl.) (5)
4 Smears (7)
5 Philanthropist (8)
6 Functional (6)
12 Beat easily (8)
14 Imitation (7)
16 Opposite of hell (6)
18 Loud disturbance (6)
19 Small body of rainwater (6)
20 Scottish lakes (5)

No. 176

Across

1 Grows more mature (8)
5 Ring a bell (4)
8 Pretend (5)
9 Turned down (7)
10 Musical performance (7)
12 Well-behaved (7)
14 Move slowly (7)
16 Walk with difficulty (7)
18 Clumsy (7)
19 Torn apart (5)
20 Playing cards between nines and jacks (4)
21 Complains (8)

Down

1 Foolish (4)
2 Expressed something in words (6)
3 Tarrying (9)
4 Dough used for pies (6)
6 Planetary paths around the sun (6)
7 Genteel and feminine in manner (8)
11 Riddle (9)
12 Get the better of through being clever (8)
13 Become angry (6)
14 Someone who buys and sells (6)
15 Worthless information (6)
17 Writing fluids (4)

No. 177

Across

1 Signs for public display (8)
5 Full of excitement (4)
9 Donald ___ : former US President (5)
10 Beat easily (7)
11 Bubbling (12)
13 Bent; not straight (6)
14 Forever (6)
17 Detective (12)
20 Mental collapse (7)
21 Effigies (5)
22 Seek (anag.) (4)
23 Understate (8)

Down

1 Places in position (4)
2 Water-bearing rock (7)
3 Foreboding (12)
4 Grammatical case (6)
6 Spirit in a bottle (5)
7 Best (8)
8 Act of discussing something; deliberation (12)
12 Scrawl (8)
15 Newtlike salamander (7)
16 Small restaurant (6)
18 Edge or border (5)
19 Get a glimpse of (4)

No. 178

Across

1 Dull and dreary (6)
7 e.g. uncle or sister (8)
8 Bath vessel (3)
9 Personal principles (6)
10 Accidental hole that lets liquid escape (4)
11 Untidy (5)
13 Insects with biting mouthparts (7)
15 A deified mortal (7)
17 Amounts of medicine (5)
21 Annoy (4)
22 South American cowboy (6)
23 Marry (3)
24 Breaks an agreement (8)
25 Showy and cheap (6)

Down

1 Opposite of top (6)
2 Precious red gems (6)
3 Make a sound expressing pain (5)
4 Make someone agitated (7)
5 Sharp heel (8)
6 Fly an aircraft (6)
12 Classic US comedy TV series (8)
14 Brave and persistent (7)
16 Evoke (6)
18 Displayed (6)
19 Day of rest (6)
20 Arduous search for something (5)

No. 179

Across

1 Work out logically (6)
4 Spread out awkwardly (6)
9 Exhilarated (7)
10 Wither (7)
11 Small loose stones (5)
12 Happen again (5)
14 e.g. screwdrivers and hammers (5)
17 Opposite of lows (5)
19 Dislikes intensely (5)
21 Personal belongings (7)
23 This starts on 1st January (3,4)
24 Relays (anag.) (6)
25 The boss at a newspaper (6)

Down

1 Water diviner (6)
2 Swinging barrier (4)
3 Change the form of something (7)
5 Written agreements (5)
6 Changing (8)
7 Soup spoons (6)
8 Aircraft (pl.) (11)
13 Shipwrecked person (8)
15 Moved (7)
16 French fashion designer (6)
18 Female sibling (6)
20 Lance (5)
22 US monetary unit (4)

No. 180

Across

1 Intrepid; courageous (8)
5 Greek god of war (4)
8 Blazes (5)
9 Having sharp features (7)
10 Changed gradually over time (7)
12 Division of the UK (7)
14 Pugilist (7)
16 Solidify (7)
18 Language spoken in Rome (7)
19 Good at (5)
20 Departs (4)
21 Canine that herds animals (8)

Down

1 High-pitched flute (4)
2 Exposing one's views (6)
3 Hopeless situation (4,5)
4 Exempted (6)
6 Experience again (6)
7 Device that chops up documents (8)
11 Arise; start (9)
12 Ejecting (8)
13 Infuriate (6)
14 Wince (6)
15 Spun-out filament of cotton (6)
17 Adult male deer (4)

No. 181

Across

1 Change in appearance (11)
9 Culinary herb (5)
10 Place where one sees animals (3)
11 Name applied to something (5)
12 Kind of wheat (5)
13 Exploits to excess (8)
16 Driven to action (8)
18 Established custom (5)
21 Establish as the truth (5)
22 Cry of a cat (3)
23 Starts off (5)
24 Basically (11)

Down

2 Walker without a fixed route (7)
3 Central cell part (7)
4 Edge (6)
5 Avarice (5)
6 Sharp blade (5)
7 General guideline (4,2,5)
8 Divine rule (11)
14 Part of the ocean (4,3)
15 Intoxicating element in wine (7)
17 Free from ostentation (6)
19 Round soup containers (5)
20 Ethos (anag.) (5)

No. 182

Across

1 Hawser (anag.) (6)
4 Positioned (6)
9 Keep out (7)
10 Subatomic particles such as electrons (7)
11 Take hold of (5)
12 Clean spiritually (5)
14 Deducts (5)
17 Moved slowly (5)
19 Well-mannered (5)
21 Profit from (7)
23 Disentangle (7)
24 Growing dimmer (6)
25 Takes up (6)

Down

1 Strike hard (6)
2 Liquid food (4)
3 Given; bequeathed (7)
5 Passes the tongue over (5)
6 Vessel for molten metal (8)
7 More profound (6)
8 Adequate in number (11)
13 Needed (8)
15 Perfumed (7)
16 The back of the neck (6)
18 Teachers (6)
20 Place of refuge (5)
22 Fail totally (4)

No. 183

Across

1 Metal fastener (4)
3 Profundity (8)
9 Arrogant person (7)
10 Insurgent or revolutionary (5)
11 Palpitate (5)
12 Absolutely incredible (7)
13 Shackle (6)
15 Loud cry (6)
17 River of South East Africa (7)
18 Assisted (5)
20 Deserves (5)
21 Bathing tub with bubbles (7)
22 Group of symptoms which occur together (8)
23 Obstacle (4)

Down

1 Copious abundance (13)
2 Focused light beam (5)
4 Background actors (6)
5 Persistence (12)
6 Involve in conflict (7)
7 25th anniversary of marriage (6,7)
8 Troublemaker (6-6)
14 Marmoset (7)
16 Deadlock (6)
19 Twelve (5)

No. 184

Across

1 Substance that arouses desire (11)
9 Tear (3)
10 Crevices (5)
11 Strong ringing sound (5)
12 Recipient of money (5)
13 Reproduce (8)
16 Medieval knightly system (8)
18 Blunder (5)
20 Ignite (5)
21 Positive electrode (5)
22 Large vessel (3)
23 Freedom from dirt (11)

Down

2 Young dog (5)
3 Extent or limit (5)
4 Scribble or draw aimlessly (6)
5 Female siblings (7)
6 Yearbook (7)
7 Obscurely (11)
8 Component parts (11)
14 Pertaining to the tongue (7)
15 Musical composition (7)
17 Pull back from (6)
18 Inexperienced (of a person) (5)
19 A ball game (5)

No. 185

Across

1 Every (4)
3 Take responsibility for (8)
9 Walks laboriously (7)
10 Water container; sink (5)
11 Study of human societies (12)
14 Legume (3)
16 Backbone (5)
17 Unhappy (3)
18 24th December (9,3)
21 Thin pancake (5)
22 Contaminate (7)
23 All people (8)
24 Chair (4)

Down

1 Measure of the heat content of a system (8)
2 Determine the number of (5)
4 Belonging to him (3)
5 Hard to fathom (12)
6 Quantities of medicine (7)
7 Monetary unit of South Africa (4)
8 In a hostile manner (12)
12 Impress on paper (5)
13 Person who supports a cause (8)
15 Accomplish (7)
19 Draw or bring out (5)
20 Highest point (4)
22 Joke (3)

No. 186

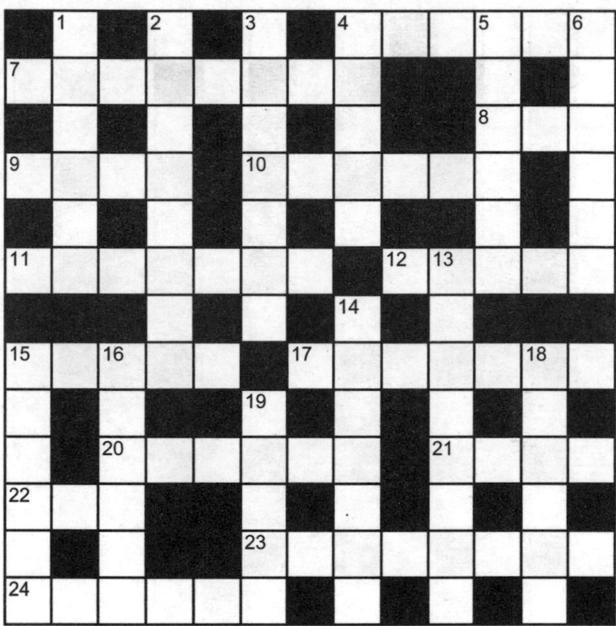

Across

4 Small drums (6)
7 Exclamation of joy (8)
8 Of a low standard (3)
9 An individual thing (4)
10 Calmness; composure (6)
11 Walks leisurely (7)
12 Obtain information from various sources (5)
15 Parasitic arachnids (5)
17 Pertaining to the skull (7)
20 Raise up (6)
21 Tiny amount (4)
22 What a hen lays (3)
23 Supreme being (8)
24 Provider of cheap accommodation (6)

Down

1 Celestial body (6)
2 Manual of instruction (8)
3 Liable to change (7)
4 Removes water from a boat (5)
5 Eat hurriedly (6)
6 Unexpected (6)
13 Desires; cravings (8)
14 Ancient galley (7)
15 Beat as if with a flail (6)
16 Expels air abruptly (6)
18 Sagacious (6)
19 Flower part; pales (anag.) (5)

No. 187

Across

1 To some degree (8)
5 Ride the waves (4)
9 Spring flower (5)
10 One of the archangels (7)
11 Molasses (7)
12 Invigorating medicine (5)
13 Person who fails to turn up (2-4)
14 Surrounded by (6)
17 Lubricated (5)
19 Mental process or idea (7)
20 Japanese fish dish (7)
21 Dispute or fight (3-2)
22 Three feet length (4)
23 Uses again (8)

Down

1 Impulsively (13)
2 Malady (7)
3 Abnormal anxiety about health (12)
4 Fell behind (6)
6 Marriage (5)
7 Congratulations (13)
8 In a sparing manner (12)
15 Not analogue (7)
16 Conflict (6)
18 Roles (anag.) (5)

No. 188

Across

1 True skin (6)
7 Third in order (8)
8 In what way (3)
9 Take into the body (of food) (6)
10 Type of starch (4)
11 Shield of Zeus (5)
13 Charged with a crime (7)
15 Celebrations (7)
17 Animal that walks on two legs (5)
21 Cat sound (4)
22 Unique (3-3)
23 Healthy (3)
24 Porcelain (8)
25 Wound together (6)

Down

1 Plant of the daisy family (6)
2 Arguing (6)
3 Warhorse (5)
4 Reviewers (7)
5 State of the USA (8)
6 Shoe (6)
12 Break in activity (8)
14 Type of respiration (7)
16 Good luck charm (6)
18 Seabird (6)
19 Marked with small spots (6)
20 Extravagant meal (5)

No. 189

1		2			3	4		5		6		7

Across

1 The actors in a show (4)
3 Ocean (8)
9 Flat-bottomed boat (7)
10 Suppress (5)
11 Now and then (12)
14 Rodent (3)
16 Female sovereign (5)
17 Unit of time (abbrev.) (3)
18 Inadequately manned (12)
21 Shade of purple (5)
22 Milk sugar (7)
23 Catastrophe (8)
24 True information (4)

Down

1 Piece of furniture (8)
2 Pertaining to sound (5)
4 Not (anag.) (3)
5 Person one knows (12)
6 Garden lattice (7)
7 Small room for a prisoner (4)
8 Effects or results (12)
12 Baking appliances (5)
13 Rigorous appraisal (4,4)
15 Prickles (7)
19 Plants of a region (5)
20 Lump of earth (4)
22 Sheltered side (3)

No. 190

Across

1 Predator (anag.) (8)
5 Melt (4)
9 Rugby formation (5)
10 Dirtier (7)
11 Constantly; always (12)
14 Ignited (3)
15 Small piece of land (5)
16 Violate a law of God (3)
17 The proprietor of an eating establishment (12)
20 Swift-flying songbird (7)
22 Not as young (5)
23 Transmit (4)
24 Unequal; biased (3-5)

Down

1 Throw a coin in the air (4)
2 Flight hub (7)
3 Nationally (12)
4 Unit of resistance (3)
6 Robbery (5)
7 Fretting (8)
8 Coming from outside (12)
12 Pertaining to the sun (5)
13 Flower sellers (8)
16 Sped along; skimmed (7)
18 European country (5)
19 Parched (4)
21 Came first in a race (3)

No. 191

Across

1 Quick reply (8)
5 Blunder (4)
9 Ape (5)
10 Computer peripheral (7)
11 Not with anybody (5)
12 Cereal grass (3)
13 Scoundrel (5)
15 Semiaquatic mammal (5)
17 Slip up (3)
19 Do extremely well at (5)
20 Pledged to marry (7)
21 Bring to the conscious mind (5)
22 Eyelid infection (4)
23 Trinkets (anag.) (8)

Down

1 Militant aggressiveness (13)
2 Large extinct elephant (7)
3 Study of microorganisms (12)
4 Managing (6)
6 External (5)
7 Absent-mindedness (13)
8 Give a false account of (12)
14 Bacterium (7)
16 Connective tissue (6)
18 Popular sport (5)

No. 192

Across

4 Configure in advance (6)
7 Brilliant performers (8)
8 Cut grass (3)
9 Greek cheese (4)
10 Howl (6)
11 Nestle up against (7)
12 Joins together (5)
15 Underground enlarged stem (5)
17 Bored into (7)
20 Short trip to perform a task (6)
21 Inspires fear (4)
22 Chatter (3)
23 Went beyond a quota (8)
24 Cared for (6)

Down

1 Common bird (6)
2 Spread out untidily (8)
3 Loudly (7)
4 Platforms leading out to sea (5)
5 Call for the presence of (6)
6 Absorbent cloths (6)
13 Destined to fail (3-5)
14 Make from raw materials (7)
15 Inhabitant of Troy (6)
16 One who makes beer (6)
18 Small hole (6)
19 Fader (anag.) (5)

No. 193

Across

1 Group of musicians (8)
5 Legendary creature (4)
9 Fourth month (5)
10 Force of civilians trained as soldiers (7)
11 Igneous rock (7)
12 Grasp tightly (5)
13 Habitual practice (6)
14 Small cave (6)
17 Sense experience (5)
19 A ripple (anag.) (7)
20 Small-scale model (7)
21 Smell (5)
22 Chinese monetary unit (4)
23 Person granted a permit (8)

Down

1 In an inflated manner (13)
2 Attendant (7)
3 Agreed upon by several parties (12)
4 Move slowly and awkwardly (6)
6 Additional; excess (5)
7 Not suitable (13)
8 Coat with a metal (12)
15 Camera stands (7)
16 Honolulu's state (6)
18 Minute pore (5)

No. 194

Across

1 Faint-hearted (8)
5 Shallow food container (4)
8 Grips with the teeth (5)
9 African country with capital Windhoek (7)
10 Provider of financial cover (7)
12 Tranquil (7)
14 Tense (7)
16 Violent troublemakers (7)
18 Enduring (7)
19 Completely; really (5)
20 Access illegally (4)
21 Marriage ceremony (8)

Down

1 Taxis (4)
2 Rawest (anag.) (6)
3 Become evident again (9)
4 Edible pulse (6)
6 Innate (6)
7 Support at the top of a seat (8)
11 Current state of affairs (6,3)
12 Rebuke (8)
13 Group of 12 constellations (6)
14 Customary practices (6)
15 Metamorphic rock (6)
17 Remove the skin from (4)

No. 195

Across

1 Conceals with a cloth (6)
7 Feeler (8)
8 24-hour period (3)
9 Not written in any key (of music) (6)
10 Pointer on a clock (4)
11 Lines (anag.) (5)
13 Absorb all the attention of (7)
15 Sculptured figures (7)
17 Church songs (5)
21 Protest march (abbrev.) (4)
22 Values highly (6)
23 Legal ruling (3)
24 Set free (8)
25 Moved back and forth (6)

Down

1 Club (6)
2 Journey by sea (6)
3 Wounded by a wasp (5)
4 Fishing (7)
5 Paternal (8)
6 Mixes together (6)
12 Atmospheric gas (8)
14 Scorn (7)
16 Recurrent topics (6)
18 Misplace (6)
19 Packed carefully and neatly (6)
20 e.g. crows and magpies (5)

No. 196

Across

1 Quick look (6)
4 Strong gusts of wind (6)
9 Type of bill (7)
10 Attentive (7)
11 Flour and water mixture (5)
12 Sequence (5)
14 Ravine (5)
17 Undergarments (5)
19 Solid geometric figure (5)
21 Insect body segment (7)
23 Restoration to life (7)
24 Walk with long steps (6)
25 Less fresh (of bread) (6)

Down

1 Style of architecture (6)
2 Skin condition on the face (4)
3 Making sore by rubbing (7)
5 Resided (5)
6 Impetus (8)
7 Bubble violently (6)
8 Orca (6,5)
13 Successful person (8)
15 Plain and clear (7)
16 Refrains from injuring (6)
18 Device that detects a physical property (6)
20 Relocated (5)
22 Letters and parcels generally (4)

No. 197

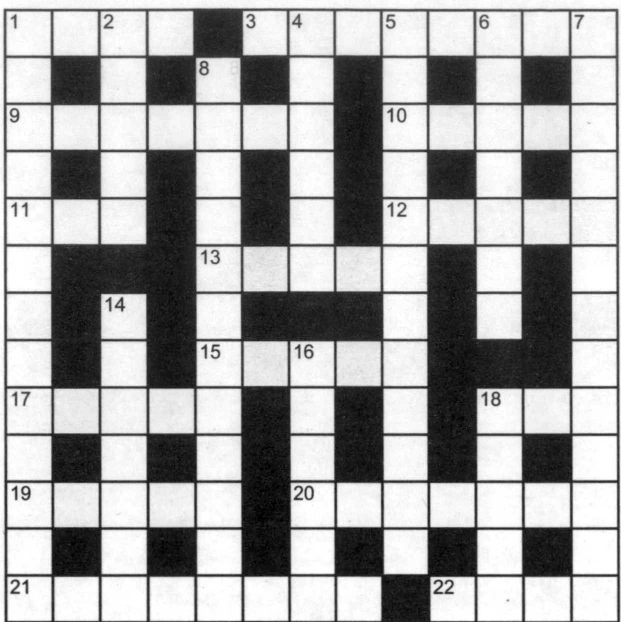

Across

1 Applaud (4)
3 Circuitous (8)
9 Matured (7)
10 Tennis score (5)
11 Pot (3)
12 Does not succeed (5)
13 Natural elevation (5)
15 Gives as a reference (5)
17 Arrive at (5)
18 Nevertheless (3)
19 Loop with a running knot (5)
20 Famous astronomer (7)
21 Establish firmly (8)
22 Unit of heredity (4)

Down

1 Line that bounds a circle (13)
2 Trembling poplar (5)
4 Inclined one's head to show approval (6)
5 Not capable of justification (12)
6 Escaping (7)
7 Hidden store of valuables (8,5)
8 Perform below expectation (12)
14 As fast as possible (4,3)
16 Calamitous (6)
18 Attractive young lady (5)

No. 198

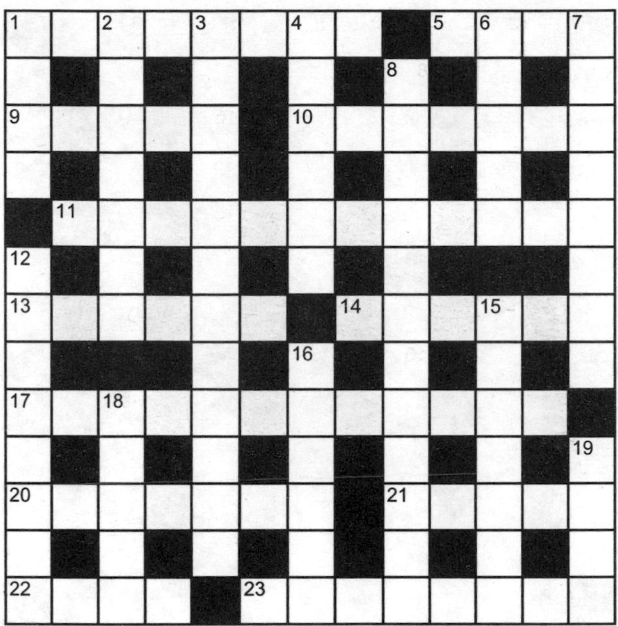

Across

1 Amazes (8)
5 Country in South America (4)
9 Dish of mixed vegetables (5)
10 Ballroom dance (7)
11 Excessive stress (12)
13 Turn aside (6)
14 Exist permanently in (6)
17 Most perfect example of a quality (12)
20 Opposed to (7)
21 Plant flower (5)
22 Greek god of love (4)
23 Acutely (8)

Down

1 In addition to (4)
2 Large Israeli city (3,4)
3 Insuring (12)
4 Slander (6)
6 Peers (5)
7 Unproven (8)
8 Capable of being traded (12)
12 Sufficient (8)
15 Shut in (7)
16 Tropical fly (6)
18 Mature insect (5)
19 Prestigious TV award (4)

No. 199

Across

1 Do better than expected (11)
9 Fix the result in advance (3)
10 Breathing organs (5)
11 Instruct; teach (5)
12 Musical compositions (5)
13 Long-tailed parrot (8)
16 Talk with (8)
18 Adult human female (5)
20 Entertain (5)
21 Spear (5)
22 Vessel; jolt (3)
23 Introductory (11)

Down

2 One who avoids animal products (5)
3 Regulations (5)
4 Where one finds Quebec (6)
5 In the place of (7)
6 Journeys by sea (7)
7 Highest class in society (11)
8 Official (11)
14 Ring-shaped (7)
15 Grow more mature (7)
17 Wrongdoer (6)
18 Take away by force (5)
19 Important and significant (5)

No. 200

Across

1 Fault-finding programs (11)
9 Secret agents (5)
10 Nip (anag.) (3)
11 Prevent (5)
12 Tool used for digging (5)
13 Pain or anguish (8)
16 Woodwind instrument (8)
18 Municipalities (5)
21 Opposite of best (5)
22 Finish (3)
23 Sets of six balls in cricket (5)
24 Diaphanous (11)

Down

2 Ardent (7)
3 Movement conveying an expression (7)
4 Willow twigs (6)
5 Exams (5)
6 Dried kernel of the coconut (5)
7 A parent's Dad (11)
8 Restrained (11)
14 Program for viewing web pages (7)
15 Firmly establish (7)
17 Batting order (4-2)
19 Long-legged bird (5)
20 Item of cutlery (5)

No. 201

Across

1 To the point (6)
7 Distinctive feature (8)
8 Animal doctor (3)
9 Removes from one's property (6)
10 Affirm with confidence (4)
11 Breathing organs of fish (5)
13 Paid a debt (7)
15 Obtain (7)
17 Area of sand (5)
21 African antelope (4)
22 Mexican cloak (6)
23 Father (3)
24 Monster that changes form during a full moon (8)
25 Extravagant meals (6)

Down

1 Jumping into water (6)
2 Narrate a story once again (6)
3 Opposite of thin (5)
4 Categories (7)
5 Fortify against attack (8)
6 Zephyr (6)
12 University teacher (8)
14 Inert gaseous element (7)
16 Paths (6)
18 Homes (6)
19 Throngs (6)
20 Breathe in audibly (5)

No. 202

1		2		■	3	4		5		6		7
	■		■	8	■		■		■		■	
9							■	10				
	■		■		■		■		■		■	
11			■		■		■	12				
	■	■	■	13					■		■	
	■	14	■		■	■	■		■		■	
	■		■	15		16			■	■	■	
17					■		■		■	18		
	■		■		■		■		■		■	
19					■	20						
	■		■		■		■		■		■	
21								■	22			

Across

1 Unspecified in number (4)
3 Unselfish concern for others (8)
9 Brazilian dance (7)
10 A central point (5)
11 Seventh Greek letter (3)
12 Grew fainter (5)
13 Small marine fish (5)
15 Variety of chalcedony (5)
17 Staple (5)
18 Snow runner (3)
19 In a slow tempo (of music) (5)
20 Illness (7)
21 Commonplace (8)
22 Listen to (4)

Down

1 25th anniversary celebration (6,7)
2 Venomous African snake (5)
4 Ruler (6)
5 Not special (3-2-3-4)
6 Entered in a hostile manner (7)
7 Manage badly (13)
8 Adequate (12)
14 Rise again (7)
16 Domesticated llama (6)
18 Strain (5)

No. 203

Across

1 e.g. rooks and knights (8)
5 Bone of the forearm (4)
9 Rope used to catch cattle (5)
10 Coiffure (7)
11 Pilot (7)
12 Motet (anag.) (5)
13 Church instruments (6)
14 Take into custody (6)
17 Accumulate over a period of time (5)
19 Flexible (7)
20 Intrusions (7)
21 Absolute (5)
22 Topical information (4)
23 Scantily (8)

Down

1 Cooperation (13)
2 Following immediately (7)
3 Small meteor (8,4)
4 Urge (6)
6 Lawful (5)
7 In a reflex manner (13)
8 Sound of quick light steps (6-6)
15 Ennoble (7)
16 Botch (4-2)
18 Pointed projectile (5)

No. 204

Across

1 Legal ambiguity (8)
5 Pack down tightly (4)
9 Extreme displeasure (5)
10 State of the USA (7)
11 Ineptness (12)
14 Monstrous humanoid creature (3)
15 Group of shots (5)
16 Flightless bird (3)
17 Scientific research rooms (12)
20 Remedy for everything (7)
22 Period of time in history (5)
23 West's opposite (4)
24 Loss of hearing (8)

Down

1 Deceiver (4)
2 Derived from living matter (7)
3 Terrified or extremely shocked (6-6)
4 Fall behind (3)
6 Inert gas that is present in air (5)
7 Egg-laying mammal (8)
8 DIY stands for this (2-2-8)
12 Person who flies an aircraft (5)
13 Cave in (8)
16 Ugly building (7)
18 Curves (5)
19 Therefore (4)
21 Consumed food (3)

No. 205

Across

4 Chamber of the heart (6)
7 Legendary island (8)
8 Removed from sight (3)
9 Arduous journey (4)
10 Plan of action (6)
11 Crash together (7)
12 Gives a meal to (5)
15 Uneven (of a road) (5)
17 Decide firmly (7)
20 Be aggrieved by (6)
21 Not spicy (4)
22 Damp (3)
23 Refined (8)
24 Spoof (6)

Down

1 Sound system (6)
2 Reverse somersault (8)
3 Drives aground (a boat) (7)
4 Awry; lopsided (5)
5 Breathe in (6)
6 Particular designs or versions (6)
13 Huge (8)
14 Rallying speech (3,4)
15 Fill a balloon with air (4,2)
16 Mixture used to bond bricks (6)
18 Held in great esteem (6)
19 Compassion (5)

No. 206

Across

1 Small children (4)
3 Relating to education and scholarship (8)
9 Not tidy (7)
10 Large bags (5)
11 Cameraman (12)
14 Part of a pen (3)
16 A score of two under par on a hole (golf) (5)
17 Leap on one foot (3)
18 Total confusion (12)
21 Breadth (5)
22 Ingest (7)
23 A reduction in price (8)
24 Individual article or unit (4)

Down

1 Hitting hard (8)
2 Capital of Japan (5)
4 Snip (3)
5 Vanishing (12)
6 Shakespeare play about a Scottish nobleman (7)
7 Portfolio (4)
8 Made poor (12)
12 Stiff (5)
13 Against the current (8)
15 Electric appliance (7)
19 Show triumphant joy (5)
20 Moved through water (4)
22 Domestic bovine animal (3)

No. 207

Across

1 Creative (11)
9 Beam of light (3)
10 Uses a keyboard (5)
11 Sully or blemish (5)
12 Requiring much mastication (5)
13 Wide-ranging (8)
16 Concluding section (8)
18 Gaped (anag.) (5)
20 Rock group (5)
21 Rotate (5)
22 Enjoyable (3)
23 Quality of being timeless (11)

Down

2 Perhaps (5)
3 Full of nerve (5)
4 Son of one's brother or sister (6)
5 Scuffles (7)
6 Organic nutrient (7)
7 Past performances (5,6)
8 Air sport (4-7)
14 Sibilant (7)
15 Close to the shore (7)
17 Undoes (6)
18 Large mast (5)
19 Presents (5)

No. 208

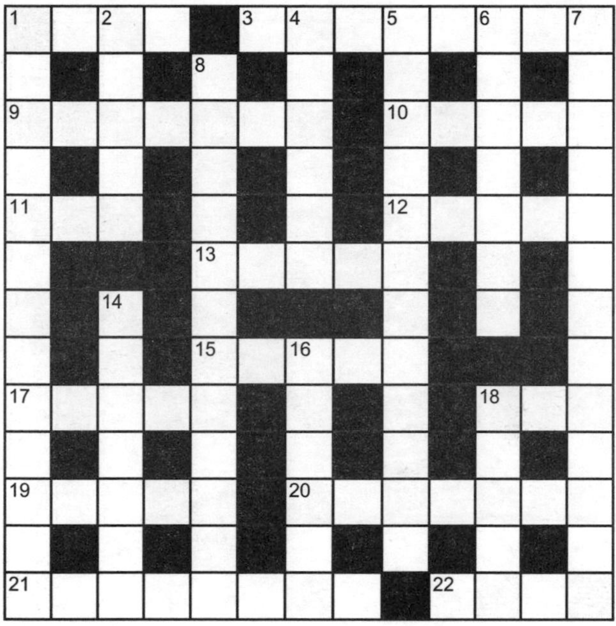

Across

1 Depressions (4)
3 Greeted warmly (8)
9 Serving no purpose (7)
10 We breathe through these (5)
11 False statement (3)
12 Crawl (5)
13 Pertaining to the moon (5)
15 Dispose of (5)
17 Golf clubs (5)
18 Interdict (3)
19 Garbage or drivel (5)
20 Important dietary component (7)
21 Laughably small (8)
22 Fencing sword (4)

Down

1 Having unusually flexible joints (6-7)
2 Annoy (5)
4 Banner or flag (6)
5 Compulsory military service (12)
6 Baffling puzzle (7)
7 Act of vanishing (13)
8 Altruism (12)
14 More spacious (7)
16 Machine that harvests a crop (6)
18 Short high-pitched tone (5)

No. 209

Across

1 Put right (6)
7 Researched in detail (8)
8 Method; road (3)
9 Dealer in cloth (6)
10 First son of Adam and Eve (4)
11 Small canoe (5)
13 Bouncer (7)
15 Unit of heat energy (7)
17 Company emblems (5)
21 Send through the mail (4)
22 Cause sudden excitement (6)
23 Chain attached to a watch (3)
24 Ragged (8)
25 Fortified wine (6)

Down

1 Amend; change (6)
2 Distress signal (6)
3 High-pitched cries (5)
4 Garden bird (7)
5 Piece for a soloist and orchestra (8)
6 Part of the eye (6)
12 Religious deserter (8)
14 Triumph (7)
16 Without ethics (6)
18 e.g. Rory McIlroy (6)
19 Run-down and in poor condition (6)
20 Networks of lines (5)

No. 210

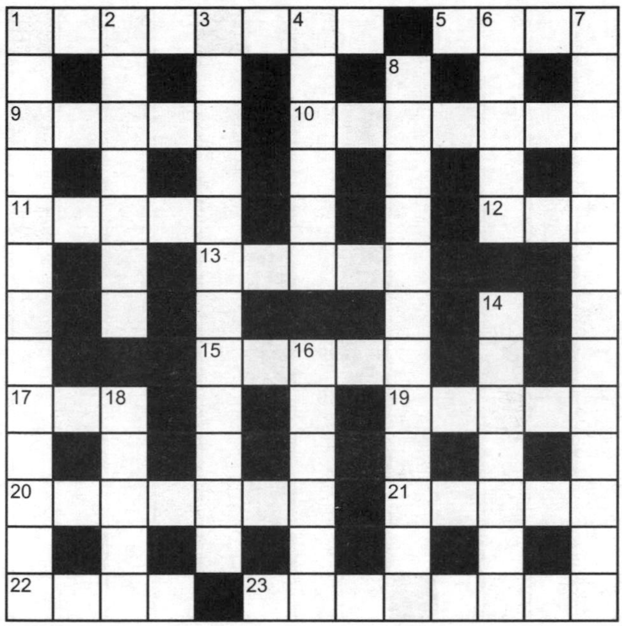

Across

1 Dawn (8)
5 Read quickly (4)
9 Admirable (5)
10 Canopies (7)
11 Turn inside out (5)
12 Mock (3)
13 Individual things (5)
15 Escape from (5)
17 Affirmative vote (3)
19 Broadcast again (5)
20 Exerts control over (7)
21 Small tuned drum (5)
22 Invalid (4)
23 Whole numbers (8)

Down

1 Close mental application (13)
2 Spiders spin these (7)
3 Inventiveness (12)
4 Not allowing light to pass through (6)
6 Country in East Africa (5)
7 Of mixed character (13)
8 Not capable of reply (12)
14 Place in order (7)
16 Agreement or concord (6)
18 Remove from school (5)

No. 211

Across

1 Thrashing (8)
5 Metallic element (4)
9 Vertical part of a step (5)
10 Idealistic (7)
11 Chatter (7)
12 Type of confection (5)
13 The science of light (6)
14 Layered cake (6)
17 Consumed (5)
19 River in Africa (7)
20 Template (7)
21 Slow down (5)
22 Ridge of rock (4)
23 Hand-woven pictorial design (8)

Down

1 Computer program for writing documents (4,9)
2 A precise point in time (7)
3 Firework display (12)
4 Not masculine or feminine (6)
6 Epic poem ascribed to Homer (5)
7 Successively (13)
8 Not catching fire easily (12)
15 Graceful in form (7)
16 Type of rhododendron (6)
18 Subject of a talk (5)

No. 212

Across

1 Fingers (6)
4 Small in degree (6)
9 Decaying (7)
10 Copy (7)
11 Direct (5)
12 Adolescence (5)
14 Three-note chord (5)
17 Angered; irritated (5)
19 Assesses performance (5)
21 Pain in the lower back (7)
23 Type of pheasant (7)
24 Hay-cutting tool (6)
25 Firm and dry (of food) (6)

Down

1 Very much (6)
2 Swallow eagerly (4)
3 This evening (7)
5 Stringed instruments (5)
6 Wily (8)
7 Large felines (6)
8 Virtually (11)
13 Unstable (8)
15 Percussion musician (7)
16 Vine fruits (6)
18 Hanging down limply (6)
20 Apathy (5)
22 Ends; goals (4)

No. 213

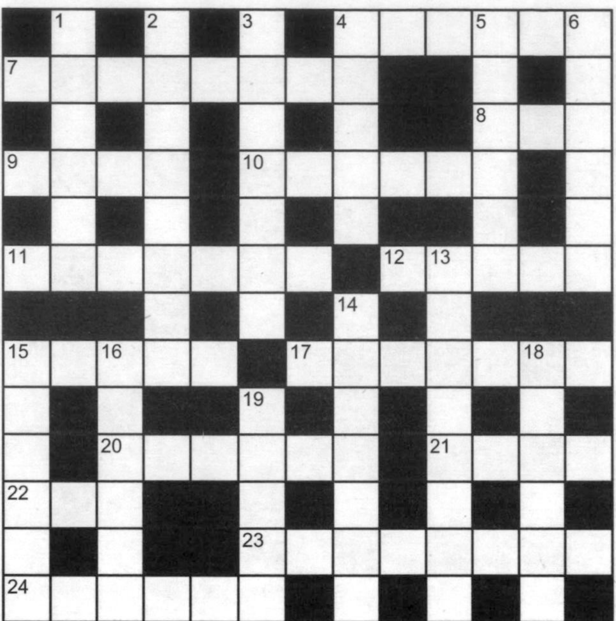

Across

4 Next after third (6)
7 Complete (8)
8 Bird of the crow family (3)
9 A person's individuality (4)
10 Ferocious (6)
11 Reaches a specified level (7)
12 Oily; greasy (5)
15 Wished (5)
17 Powdered spice (7)
20 Eccentricity (6)
21 Sell (4)
22 Give a nickname to (3)
23 Slender coiling leaves (8)
24 Cooks in the oven (6)

Down

1 Not present (6)
2 Combine into one (8)
3 Polishing (7)
4 Less (5)
5 Turn down (6)
6 Period of prosperity (6)
13 Large burrowing African mammal (8)
14 Fluctuating (7)
15 Hamper (6)
16 Irrational fear (6)
18 Regal (6)
19 Thin fogs (5)

No. 214

Across

1 Frames used by artists (6)
7 Approximate (8)
8 Fellow (3)
9 Saturated (6)
10 Useful implement (4)
11 Take part in combat (5)
13 Stinted (anag.) (7)
15 Large areas of land (7)
17 You usually do this whilst asleep (5)
21 Curve in a road (4)
22 Edible plant tuber (6)
23 Excavate (3)
24 Frenzied (8)
25 Start a fire (6)

Down

1 Surround (6)
2 Maxim (6)
3 Capital of South Korea (5)
4 Examines in detail (7)
5 Copycat (8)
6 Backless seats (6)
12 Board used to display adverts (8)
14 Notwithstanding (7)
16 Guides a vehicle (6)
18 Wore away gradually (6)
19 Ruin; crush (6)
20 Block of wood (5)

No. 215

Across

1 Restlessly (11)
9 Smack (3)
10 Crucial person or point (5)
11 Bird sound; chirp (5)
12 Stiff with age (5)
13 Physically strong and active (8)
16 Critical explanation (8)
18 Type of bread roll (5)
20 Walk (5)
21 Repasts (5)
22 School of Mahayana Buddhism (3)
23 Type of artist (11)

Down

2 Small dust particles (5)
3 Sufficiently (5)
4 Turn upside down (6)
5 Stylishly (7)
6 Freedom (7)
7 Curative (11)
8 Type of weather system (11)
14 Keepsake; reminder (7)
15 Permit entry again (7)
17 Leaping antelope (6)
18 Attack on all sides (5)
19 Stares (5)

No. 216

Across

1 Composer or singer (8)
5 Killer whale (4)
9 Protective garment worn in the kitchen (5)
10 Come out on top (7)
11 In a greedy manner (12)
14 Particle that is electrically charged (3)
15 Haggard (5)
16 Horse shade (3)
17 Body of voters in a specified region (12)
20 Self-important (7)
22 Sea duck (5)
23 Otherwise (4)
24 Exaggerated emotion (8)

Down

1 Ditch filled with water (4)
2 Inverts (anag.) (7)
3 Gathering of people (12)
4 Unit of current (3)
6 Studies a subject at university (5)
7 Lessening (8)
8 Disregarding the rules (5,3,4)
12 Outer layer of bread (5)
13 Follower (8)
16 Deciphering machine (7)
18 Titles (5)
19 Extent of a surface (4)
21 Timid (3)

No. 217

Across

1 Nitrous oxide (8,3)
9 Skirmish (5)
10 Total (3)
11 Condescend (5)
12 District council head (5)
13 Area of the zodiac (4,4)
16 Highly educated (4-4)
18 Prize (5)
21 Moderate and well-balanced (5)
22 Piece of wood (3)
23 Dole out (5)
24 Philosophical doctrine (11)

Down

2 Skilled worker (7)
3 Flexible athlete (7)
4 Doing nothing (6)
5 Twinkle (5)
6 Test or examine (5)
7 Not wanted (11)
8 Needleworker (11)
14 Sparkle (7)
15 Insects found where you sleep (7)
17 Symbol or representation (6)
19 Standpoint (5)
20 Hang with cloth (5)

No. 218

Across

1 Resisting (8)
5 Remnant (4)
9 Woodland spirit (5)
10 Large ships (7)
11 Action of breaking a law (12)
14 Purchase (3)
15 Grin (5)
16 Organ of sight (3)
17 Destruction of bacteria (12)
20 Makes possible (7)
22 Seawater (5)
23 Clean up (4)
24 Abandoned (8)

Down

1 Expel; drive out (4)
2 Power; strength (7)
3 Shockingly (12)
4 e.g. almond or pecan (3)
6 Sheet (anag.) (5)
7 Infatuated (8)
8 Not discernible (12)
12 Foolishly credulous (5)
13 Complying with orders (8)
16 Boastful person (7)
18 Piece of broken pottery (5)
19 Long-running dispute (4)
21 Issue legal proceedings (3)

No. 219

Across

1 Imperial unit (4)
3 Tepid (8)
9 People who insist on sticking to formal rules (7)
10 Domesticates (5)
11 Fault; mistake (5)
12 From beginning to end (7)
13 Lying on the back (6)
15 Fine cloth; type of paper (6)
17 Cloudiness (7)
18 Tortilla topped with cheese (5)
20 Lacking meaning (5)
21 Stinging plants (7)
22 Think deeply for a period of time (8)
23 Optimistic (4)

Down

1 Style of painting (13)
2 Type of tree (5)
4 Saddens (6)
5 Exorbitant (12)
6 Fulmars (anag.) (7)
7 Naughtily (13)
8 Inflexible (12)
14 Poster (7)
16 Young swan (6)
19 Stringed instrument (5)

No. 220

Across

1 Longevity of an individual (8)
5 Unit of land area (4)
8 Flowering plant (5)
9 Cost (7)
10 Ancient jar (7)
12 Small boxes (7)
14 Fell over (7)
16 Easily broken (7)
18 Orbs (7)
19 Unspecified object (5)
20 Drains of energy (4)
21 Person with a degree (8)

Down

1 Tax (4)
2 Shows displeasure facially (6)
3 Form of pasta (9)
4 Stadiums (6)
6 Large artillery gun (6)
7 Raised (8)
11 Allowed (9)
12 Befuddles (8)
13 Do the dishes (4-2)
14 Type of muscle (6)
15 Thin layer of sedimentary rock (6)
17 Fit of shivering (4)

No. 221

Across

1 Pleasingly pretty (4)
3 Explicit and clearly stated (8)
9 Stuck on the bottom (of a ship) (7)
10 Woody-stemmed plant (5)
11 Mountain range in South America (5)
12 Disentangle (7)
13 Streak (anag.) (6)
15 Shining (6)
17 Notes down (7)
18 Very pale (5)
20 Thermosetting resin (5)
21 Unfasten (7)
22 Experienced pain (8)
23 Move wings; flutter (4)

Down

1 Dull and uninteresting (13)
2 Weary (5)
4 Lectern (6)
5 Science of deciphering codes (12)
6 Imaginary (7)
7 Artisanship (13)
8 Short story or poem for children (7,5)
14 Start (4,3)
16 Guarantee (6)
19 Place providing accommodation (5)

No. 222

Across

1 Commotion (8)
5 Run quickly (4)
9 Abatement (5)
10 Spanish beverage (7)
11 Ruinously (12)
13 Presented the case for (6)
14 Machine that creates motion (6)
17 Demands or needs (12)
20 Issue forth (7)
21 Made a mistake (5)
22 Hardens (4)
23 In a direct and frank way (3,2,3)

Down

1 Unattractive (4)
2 Smacking (7)
3 Pertaining to letters (12)
4 Plus points (6)
6 Large amounts of land (5)
7 Stocky (8)
8 Formal notice (12)
12 People who shape horseshoes (8)
15 Time between events (7)
16 Swiss city (6)
18 Liquid measure (5)
19 Biblical garden (4)

No. 223

Across

1 Sweat (8)
5 Loud cry (4)
9 Japanese dish (5)
10 Proportionately (3,4)
11 Failure to act with prudence (12)
14 Material from which metal is extracted (3)
15 Area of open land (5)
16 Snare or trap (3)
17 Dictatorial (12)
20 Country in northwestern Africa (7)
22 Form of identification (5)
23 Perceives (4)
24 Listen to again (4,4)

Down

1 Opposite of pull (4)
2 Ear test (anag.) (7)
3 Most prominent position (5,2,5)
4 Knock vigorously (3)
6 Avoid (5)
7 Secret relationships (8)
8 Significantly (12)
12 Make a physical or mental effort (5)
13 Outfits (8)
16 Father of a parent (7)
18 Number in a trilogy (5)
19 Bill (4)
21 Lubricate (3)

No. 224

1		2		3		4		■	5	6		7
	■		■		■		■	8	■		■	
9					■	10						
	■		■		■		■		■		■	
■	11											
12	■		■		■		■		■	■	■	
13						■	14			15		
	■	■	■		■	16	■		■		■	
17		18										■
	■		■		■		■		■		■	19
20							■	21				
	■		■		■		■		■		■	
22				■	23							

Across

1 Bookish (8)
5 Con; swindle (4)
9 Leader or ruler (5)
10 Pertaining to marriage (7)
11 Dreamy; odd and unfamiliar (12)
13 Hearts (anag.) (6)
14 Spiny tree (6)
17 Heartbroken (12)
20 Imaginary mischievous sprite (7)
21 Coldly (5)
22 Hearing organs (4)
23 Male relation (8)

Down

1 Scottish lake (4)
2 Cheep (7)
3 Invigoratingly (12)
4 Celebrity (6)
6 Young boy or girl (5)
7 Our galaxy (5,3)
8 Gratitude (12)
12 Item of sweet food (8)
15 Temperature scale (7)
16 Point where two edges meet (6)
18 Make less miserable (5)
19 Church song (4)

No. 225

Across

1 Large metal pot (8)
5 Rode (anag.) (4)
9 Network points where lines intersect (5)
10 Layer or band of rock (7)
11 People who make money (7)
12 Teacher (5)
13 Musical ensembles (6)
14 Smear or blur (6)
17 Sound of any kind (5)
19 Salad vegetable (7)
20 Foolishly (7)
21 Soothes (5)
22 Require (4)
23 Great adulation (8)

Down

1 Attitude of superiority or arrogance (13)
2 Be subjected to (7)
3 Dispirited (12)
4 Be preoccupied with a topic (6)
6 Group of eight (5)
7 Pitilessly (13)
8 Relating to numeric calculations (12)
15 Short close-fitting jacket (7)
16 Took part in a game (6)
18 Annoyed (5)

No. 226

Across

1 Ruler who has absolute power (8)
5 Norway's capital (4)
9 Slight error; oversight (5)
10 Very eager to get something (7)
11 Significant (12)
13 River in Europe (6)
14 Controlling (6)
17 Mentally acute (5-7)
20 Rags (7)
21 Embarrass (5)
22 Utters (4)
23 Secondary personality (5,3)

Down

1 Associate (4)
2 Tropical cyclone (7)
3 Fast food item (12)
4 e.g. trophies and medals (6)
6 Cleanse by rubbing (5)
7 Be heavier than (8)
8 Street (12)
12 Teaches (8)
15 Perform repeatedly (7)
16 Prayer book (6)
18 Act of going in (5)
19 State of the USA (4)

No. 227

Across

1 Rose fruits (4)
3 Agreeable (8)
9 Teemed (7)
10 Protective containers (5)
11 Perceptions (12)
14 Frozen water (3)
16 Stanza of a poem (5)
17 Snappy dog (3)
18 Planned in advance (12)
21 Wading bird (5)
22 State of the USA (7)
23 Starved (8)
24 Agitate (4)

Down

1 Belonging to the past (8)
2 Joins in a game (5)
4 Was in first place (3)
5 Practice of designing buildings (12)
6 Chemical element with atomic number 33 (7)
7 Long pointed tooth (4)
8 Enhancements (12)
12 Bitterly pungent (5)
13 Animal that hunts (8)
15 Tympanic membrane (7)
19 Type of fish (5)
20 Cook (4)
22 Compete (3)

No. 228

Across

1 Precision (8)
5 Block a decision (4)
8 Deep fissure (5)
9 Sour in taste (7)
10 States as a fact (7)
12 Social reject (7)
14 Cowboy hat (7)
16 Receiver (7)
18 Dense masses of vegetation (7)
19 Derisive smile (5)
20 A lyric poet (4)
21 Gathering (8)

Down

1 Curved shape (4)
2 Red wine (6)
3 Contemplative people (9)
4 Item of neckwear (6)
6 Remains of a fire (6)
7 Particular event (8)
11 Sample; preview (9)
12 At work (2-3-3)
13 Way of doing something (6)
14 Stagnation or inactivity (6)
15 Majestic (6)
17 Wear away (4)

No. 229

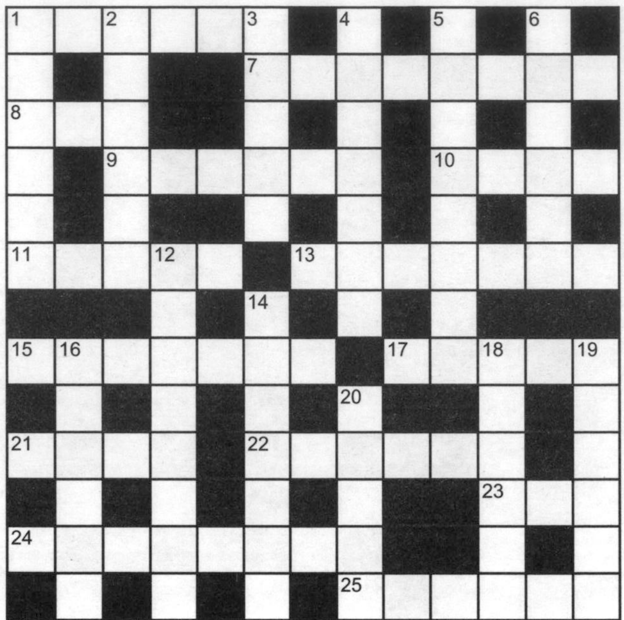

Across

1 Mischievous (6)
7 Roman leaders (8)
8 Stream of liquid (3)
9 Blocks of metal (6)
10 Sail (anag.) (4)
11 Dough raiser (5)
13 Pseudoscience (7)
15 In an unspecified manner (7)
17 Wide (5)
21 Unit of power (4)
22 Turned over and over (6)
23 Opposite of high (3)
24 One who steers a boat (8)
25 Slick and shiny (6)

Down

1 Physical wound (6)
2 Surface film; coating (6)
3 Biblical king (5)
4 Disciple (7)
5 Person who gives a sermon (8)
6 Event which precedes another (6)
12 Most saccharine (8)
14 Opening to a room (7)
16 Public speaker (6)
18 Large quantity (6)
19 Lethargic; sleepy (6)
20 Hurled (5)

No. 230

Across

1 Dubs (anag.) (4)
3 An engraved design (8)
9 Aperture or hole (7)
10 Tight; taut (5)
11 Cairo is in this country (5)
12 Small holes in cloth or leather (7)
13 Concealed from view (6)
15 Basic metrical unit in a poem (6)
17 Make less intense (7)
18 Laborious task (5)
20 Fortune-telling card (5)
21 Friendly understanding (7)
22 Spread out (8)
23 Modify (4)

Down

1 Overwhelmed with sorrow (6-7)
2 Common garden flower (5)
4 Required (6)
5 Quality of being genuine (12)
6 Portable lamp (7)
7 Exaggeration (13)
8 Chatter (6-6)
14 Arid areas (7)
16 Precious stones (6)
19 Possessed (5)

No. 231

Across

1 Concern; worry (4)
3 Deny (8)
9 In a friendly manner (7)
10 Narrow pieces of land (5)
11 Creator of film scripts (12)
14 Soft animal hair (3)
16 Store of hoarded wealth (5)
17 19th Greek letter (3)
18 Able to use both hands well (12)
21 Plummeted (5)
22 Snarled (anag.) (7)
23 Firmness (8)
24 Cut (4)

Down

1 Arrange by category (8)
2 Send someone to a medical specialist (5)
4 Climbing vine (3)
5 Private (12)
6 Very old (7)
7 Opposite of least (4)
8 Lost in thought (6-6)
12 Complete (5)
13 Surpass (8)
15 Act of getting rid of something (7)
19 Antiquated (5)
20 Not evens (4)
22 Division of a tennis match (3)

No. 232

Across

4 Prevents access to (6)
7 Negative aspect (8)
8 Extend out (3)
9 Mischievous god in Norse mythology (4)
10 Japanese dress (6)
11 Keeps hold of (7)
12 In what place (5)
15 Animal enclosures (5)
17 Rod used in weightlifting (7)
20 Attract powerfully (6)
21 Snatched (4)
22 Young dog (3)
23 Someone who talks in a foolish way (8)
24 Sweltering (6)

Down

1 Sullen and gloomy (6)
2 Signal (8)
3 Becoming submerged (7)
4 Smiles radiantly (5)
5 Coax into doing something (6)
6 Seat for two or more persons (6)
13 Natural homes of animals (8)
14 Entrance (7)
15 Body of written texts (6)
16 Thing that is totally true (6)
18 Viewed; saw (6)
19 Short and stout (5)

No. 233

Across

1 Wood preserver (8)
5 Musical staff sign (4)
9 Cowboy exhibition (5)
10 Ship worker (7)
11 Scornful (12)
14 Consume food (3)
15 Periods of 60 minutes (5)
16 Type of statistical chart (3)
17 Clearly evident (12)
20 Artistic movement (3,4)
22 Electronic message (5)
23 Flesh of a pig (4)
24 Trestles (anag.) (8)

Down

1 Bend or coil (4)
2 Last in a series (7)
3 Cheated someone financially (5-7)
4 Twitch (3)
6 West Indian dance (5)
7 Completes a race (8)
8 Second part of the Bible (3,9)
12 Climb onto (5)
13 Car light (8)
16 Plunder (7)
18 Move as fast as possible (5)
19 Woes; problems (4)
21 Lyric poem (3)

No. 234

Across

1 Terminate (6)
4 Stress mark (6)
9 Not ethically right (7)
10 These follow Sundays (7)
11 Strike firmly (5)
12 Absorbent cloth (5)
14 Piece of bread (5)
17 Tiny arachnids (5)
19 Religious acts (5)
21 Cyclone (7)
23 Playful composition (7)
24 Dull (6)
25 Perceived (6)

Down

1 Way something is set out (6)
2 Noble gas (4)
3 Spreads out (7)
5 Arrives (5)
6 Soonest (8)
7 Inclined at an angle (6)
8 Agent who supplies goods to stores (11)
13 Glowing with heat (5-3)
15 Clasp (7)
16 Wall painting or mural (6)
18 Unemotional (6)
20 Puts in order (5)
22 Diving seabirds (4)

No. 235

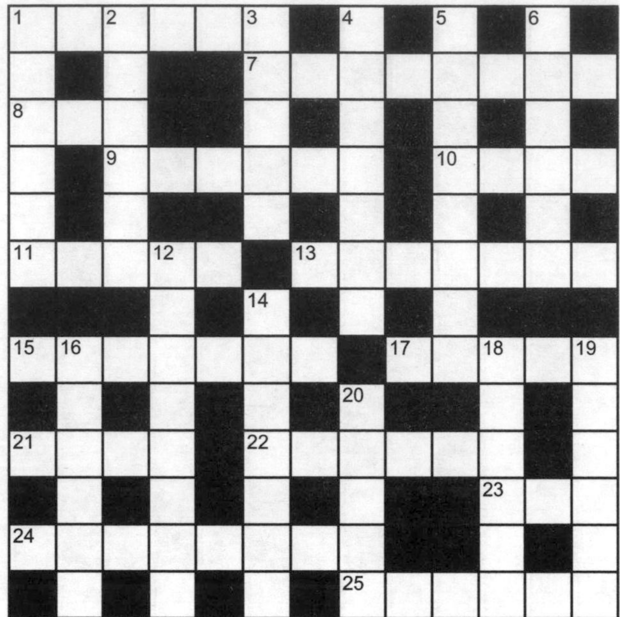

Across

1 Unstable (6)
7 Makes bigger (8)
8 Hit high into the air (3)
9 By mouth (6)
10 Seep; exude (4)
11 Scale representation (5)
13 Relies upon (7)
15 Release from captivity (3,4)
17 Assert that something is the case (5)
21 Digestive juice (4)
22 Spanish festival (6)
23 Taxi (3)
24 Absolute (8)
25 Notable inconvenience (6)

Down

1 Sagacity (6)
2 Further-reaching than (6)
3 Screams (5)
4 Portable enclosure for infants (7)
5 Relating to trees (8)
6 Grabbed (6)
12 Make weak (8)
14 Without flaws (7)
16 Complex problem (6)
18 Calculating machine (6)
19 Form of limestone (6)
20 Mooring for a ship (5)

No. 236

Across

4 Domed roof (6)
7 Text of an opera (8)
8 Note down (3)
9 Literary composition (4)
10 Type of nursery (6)
11 Dignified conduct (7)
12 Suitably (5)
15 Blended (5)
17 Moved round an axis (7)
20 Destroy (6)
21 Nous (anag.) (4)
22 One more than five (3)
23 Swindler (8)
24 Opposite of winners (6)

Down

1 Type of basic aerial (6)
2 Garden flower (8)
3 Overly conceited and arrogant (5-2)
4 Managed to deal with (5)
5 Physical item (6)
6 Far from the target (6)
13 Free from sensual desire (8)
14 Persuasive relevance (7)
15 Small piece of food (6)
16 Ancient Persian king (6)
18 Displayed freely (6)
19 Groups of musicians (5)

No. 237

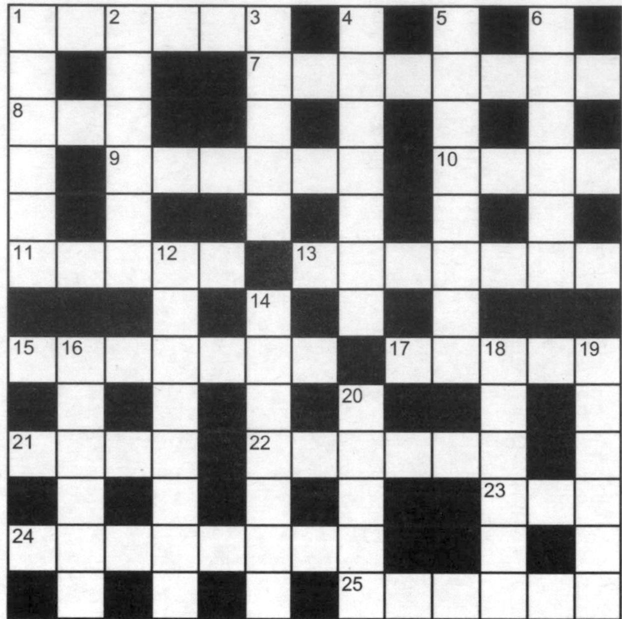

Across

1 Immature insects (6)
7 Citizen (8)
8 Partly digested animal food (3)
9 Apprehend someone (6)
10 Male sheep (pl.) (4)
11 Extent (5)
13 Financial award (7)
15 Arranging a piece of music (7)
17 Garden tool for cutting grass (5)
21 Large US feline (4)
22 Sound reflections (6)
23 Fruit of a rose (3)
24 Radioactive element (8)
25 Elapsed (of time) (6)

Down

1 Cut slightly (6)
2 Amusingly eccentric (6)
3 Injure with very hot liquid (5)
4 Conquer by force (7)
5 In the open air (8)
6 Agriculturalist (6)
12 Small turtle (8)
14 Acquire as an heir (7)
16 Clasp (6)
18 Cleans with water (6)
19 Torn (of clothes) (6)
20 Ape (abbrev.) (5)

No. 238

Across

4 Signal (anag.) (6)
7 Seemly (8)
8 Allow (3)
9 Spiritual teacher (4)
10 Cooked slowly in liquid (6)
11 Rubbish (7)
12 Device used to connect to the internet (5)
15 Precious gem (5)
17 Undo (7)
20 Person who fishes (6)
21 Place where a wild animal lives (4)
22 Remuneration (3)
23 Surrounded on all sides (8)
24 Wading birds (6)

Down

1 Source of caviar (6)
2 State capital of South Carolina (8)
3 Flower arrangement (7)
4 Put a question to (5)
5 Privileged and well off (6)
6 Humorous television drama (6)
13 Fail to notice (8)
14 Furtiveness (7)
15 Small hairpiece (6)
16 Participant in a game (6)
18 Moves smoothly (6)
19 Works one's trade steadily (5)

No. 239

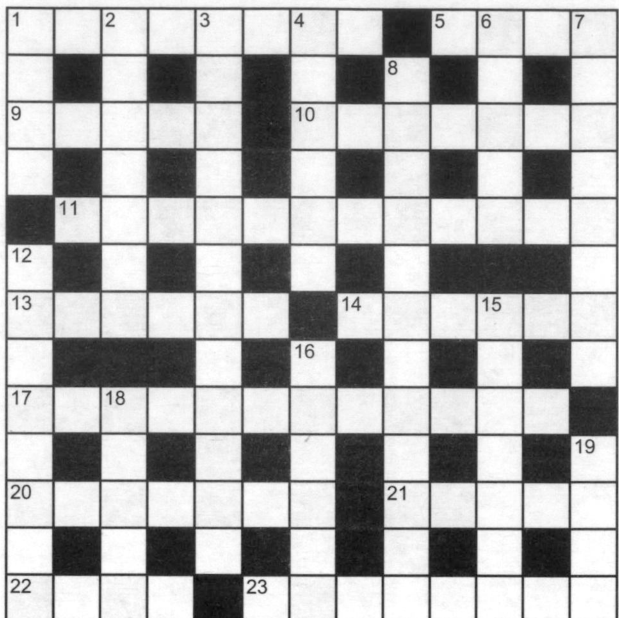

Across

1 Most foolish (8)
5 Test (anag.) (4)
9 Unabridged (5)
10 Wine merchant (7)
11 Intuitively designed (of a system) (4-8)
13 Garner; collect (6)
14 Heed (6)
17 Conjectural (12)
20 Quivering singing effect (7)
21 Neutral shade (5)
22 US actress and singer (4)
23 Physical power (8)

Down

1 Fail to speak clearly (4)
2 Migratory grasshoppers (7)
3 Act of seizing something en route (12)
4 Cuts off (6)
6 In pitch (5)
7 Delaying (8)
8 Not capable of being checked (12)
12 Definite and clear (8)
15 Ripping (7)
16 Pious (6)
18 Portion (5)
19 Wire lattice (4)

No. 240

Across

1 Knocks lightly (4)
3 Curved surface of a liquid in a tube (8)
9 Long-lasting and recurrent (7)
10 Type of snake (5)
11 Ate too much (12)
13 Whole (6)
15 Hot spring (6)
17 Feeling depressed (5-7)
20 Express; complete (5)
21 Waterproof fabric (7)
22 Finely chopped (8)
23 Soft cheese (4)

Down

1 Relating to construction (8)
2 Money container (5)
4 Encrypt (6)
5 Immune (12)
6 Evergreen conifer (7)
7 Tender to the touch (4)
8 Not found (12)
12 Circumspection (8)
14 Small loudspeaker (7)
16 Select (6)
18 Buyer (5)
19 Pulls at (4)

No. 241

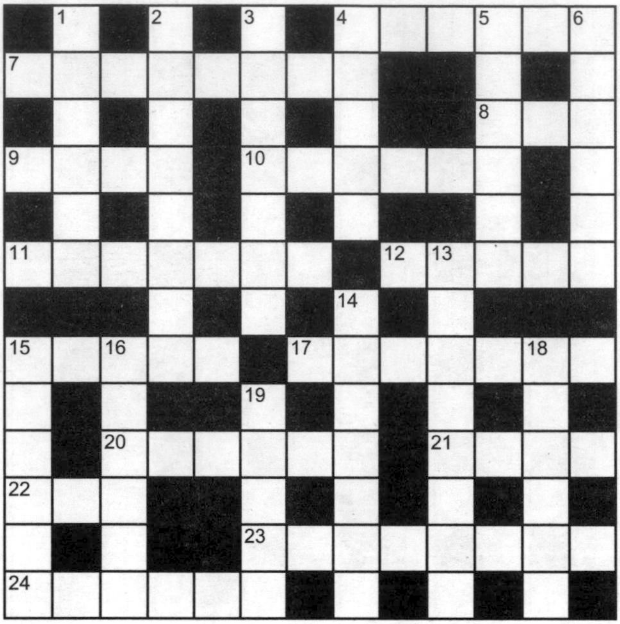

Across

4 On a ship or train (6)
7 Large cask (8)
8 Pitcher (3)
9 Desert in northern China (4)
10 Fierce woman (6)
11 Summary of events (5-2)
12 Person who eats in a restaurant (5)
15 Reddish (5)
17 Visually appealing (7)
20 Arrangement of flowers (6)
21 Beast of burden (4)
22 Flower that is not yet open (3)
23 Bowl-shaped strainer (8)
24 Get-up-and-go (6)

Down

1 Pygmy chimpanzee (6)
2 Allocated (8)
3 Apprehensive (7)
4 Decorate (5)
5 Border (6)
6 Miner (6)
13 Cruel (8)
14 Gently (7)
15 Mob (6)
16 Move slowly (6)
18 Soothed (6)
19 Whim or caprice; find attractive (5)

No. 242

Across

1 Good fortune (11)
9 Spy (5)
10 Strong drink (3)
11 Visual perception (5)
12 Out of fashion (5)
13 Pliable sheet of material (8)
16 Symmetrical open plane curve (8)
18 Metallic compound (5)
21 Residence (5)
22 Toothed wheel (3)
23 Hit hard (5)
24 Irritable (3-8)

Down

2 Final stage of an extended process (7)
3 Opposite of western (7)
4 Visit informally (4,2)
5 Arise unexpectedly (3,2)
6 Gets weary (5)
7 Likeness (11)
8 Instantly (11)
14 Plant-eating aquatic mammal (7)
15 Large German city (7)
17 In flower (6)
19 Allowed by official rules (5)
20 Sailing vessel (5)

No. 243

Across

1 Messengers of God (6)
7 Women noted for great courage (8)
8 Triangular sail (3)
9 Knocked into (6)
10 Release; give out (4)
11 Melodies (5)
13 Books of maps (7)
15 Newspaper audience (7)
17 Long tubes (5)
21 Indication (4)
22 Ten raised to the power 100 (6)
23 Cover with steam (of a glass surface) (3)
24 Make; produce (8)
25 Magnitude (6)

Down

1 Alter or move slightly (6)
2 Small arboreal ape (6)
3 Retail stores (5)
4 Dryness (7)
5 Intelligentsia (8)
6 Gadget (6)
12 Put at risk (8)
14 Country in South America (7)
16 Banished (6)
18 Steal (6)
19 Solitary (6)
20 Fed up (5)

No. 244

Across

4 Washed lightly (6)
7 Capital of Finland (8)
8 Vitality (3)
9 Endure (4)
10 Sandstone constituent (6)
11 Decorative altar cloth (7)
12 e.g. copper or calcium (5)
15 Seals (anag.) (5)
17 Marched (7)
20 Actually (6)
21 Heavy hammer (4)
22 Month of the year (3)
23 The decade from 1990 - 1999 (8)
24 Difficult (6)

Down

1 Coating (6)
2 Alienate (8)
3 Uncommon (7)
4 Small streams (5)
5 Learned person (6)
6 Maiden (6)
13 Immensity (8)
14 Making a petition to God (7)
15 Peak (6)
16 Voice box (6)
18 Slips through the net (6)
19 Held on to something tightly (5)

No. 245

Across

1 Absolution (11)
9 Drinking tube (5)
10 Obtained (3)
11 Metal worker (5)
12 Show indifference with the shoulders (5)
13 Airport checking devices (8)
16 Supervisor (8)
18 Bunches (5)
21 Type of bandage (5)
22 Very small child (3)
23 Operatic songs (5)
24 Watching over one's flock (11)

Down

2 Relating to sight (7)
3 Flowing profusely (7)
4 Church official (6)
5 Amphibians (5)
6 Sweet substance (5)
7 Revive (11)
8 Fear in front of an audience (5,6)
14 Dessert (anag.) (7)
15 Large web-footed bird (7)
17 City in North East Italy (6)
19 Retrieve (5)
20 Skin on top of the head (5)

No. 246

Across

1 Letters of a language (8)
5 Couple (4)
9 Cut a joint of meat (5)
10 Protectors (7)
11 Indifferent (12)
14 Quick sleep (3)
15 Length of interlaced hair (5)
16 Sprint (3)
17 Fence closure (anag.) (12)
20 Round building (7)
22 Equip (5)
23 Disposed of for money (4)
24 Continues obstinately (8)

Down

1 Curved shapes (4)
2 Root vegetable (7)
3 Astonishing; amazing (3-9)
4 Large deer (3)
6 Wide-awake (5)
7 Permanent inhabitant (8)
8 Notwithstanding (12)
12 Tests (5)
13 Work outfits (8)
16 Retreats (7)
18 Up to the time when (5)
19 Possesses (4)
21 Mature (3)

No. 247

Across

1 Causing a blockage (11)
9 Short cylindrical piece of wood (3)
10 Capital of France (5)
11 Trick or feat of daring (5)
12 Doctrine (5)
13 Cut across (8)
16 Least old (8)
18 Intimidated and weakened (5)
20 Unexpected plot element (5)
21 Fruit of the oak (5)
22 Our star (3)
23 Of noble birth (4-7)

Down

2 Brass instrument (5)
3 Lukewarm (5)
4 Turmoil (6)
5 Throwing a coin in the air (7)
6 Infective agents (7)
7 Prophetic of the end of the world (11)
8 Amazingly good (11)
14 Obedient (7)
15 Disturb (7)
17 Walk casually (6)
18 Showing a willingness to achieve results (3-2)
19 Use inefficiently (5)

No. 248

Across

1 Potential (11)
9 Spread by scattering (5)
10 Court (3)
11 Speed in nautical miles per hour (5)
12 Ancient object (5)
13 Observer (8)
16 Venerated (8)
18 Representative; messenger (5)
21 Carrying chair (5)
22 Pop music performance (3)
23 Lives (anag.) (5)
24 One in charge of a school (4,7)

Down

2 Pulls back from (7)
3 Meeting of an official body (7)
4 Continent (6)
5 Tall narrow building (5)
6 Speech sound (5)
7 Admit to be true (11)
8 Agreement (11)
14 Traditional example (7)
15 Wrap in garments (7)
17 Complex silicate mineral (6)
19 The prevailing fashion (5)
20 Give up (5)

No. 249

Across

1 Ruler who is unconstrained by law (8)
5 Liquid precipitation (4)
9 Type of jazz (5)
10 e.g. hate or joy (7)
11 Sporadic (12)
14 Appropriate (3)
15 Keen (5)
16 Farewell remark (3)
17 Having existed for a considerable time (4-8)
20 Reaches a destination (7)
22 Use to one's advantage (5)
23 Items that unlock doors (4)
24 Orations (8)

Down

1 Touches gently (4)
2 Piece of furniture (7)
3 Uneasy (12)
4 Single in number (3)
6 Burning (5)
7 Final teenage year (8)
8 Person studying after a first degree (12)
12 Hot rock (5)
13 Summon to return (4,4)
16 Below (7)
18 Anxious (5)
19 Sell (anag.) (4)
21 Drink a little (3)

No. 250

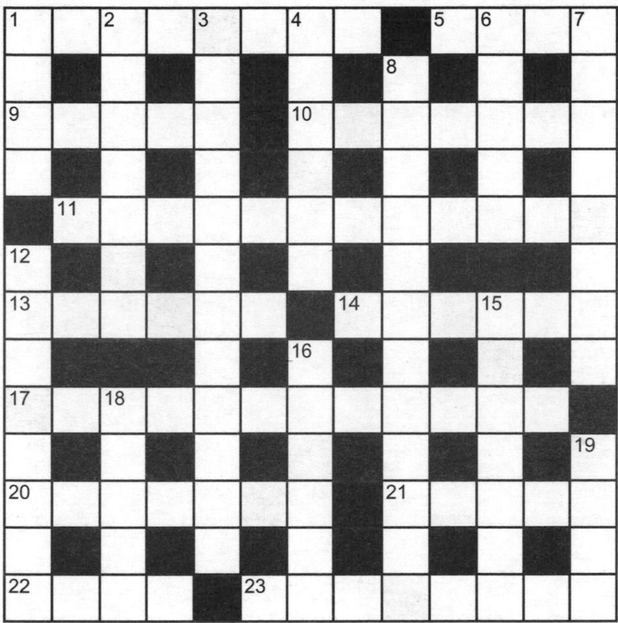

Across

1 Escape from prison (8)
5 From a distance (4)
9 Round steering device (5)
10 Novice driver (7)
11 Contentment (12)
13 More likely than not (4-2)
14 Takes the place of (6)
17 Unnecessarily careful (12)
20 Fragment (7)
21 Fabric with parallel ribs (5)
22 Loop of cloth worn around the waist (4)
23 Frozen dessert (3,5)

Down

1 Buckles (4)
2 Green gemstone (7)
3 Children's toy (12)
4 Raise (6)
6 What a mycologist studies (5)
7 Scarceness (8)
8 Vain (12)
12 Gigantic statue (8)
15 Procedure; standard (7)
16 Rural (6)
18 Leaves (5)
19 Edible fruit (4)

No. 251

Across

1 Difficult choices (8)
5 Examine quickly (4)
9 In the middle of (5)
10 Archer's weapon (7)
11 Designed to distract (12)
14 Unit of energy (3)
15 Solid blow (5)
16 Enemy (3)
17 Medicine taken when blocked-up (12)
20 Seize and take legal custody of (7)
22 Of the nose (5)
23 Freedom from difficulty (4)
24 Inactivity (8)

Down

1 Moist (4)
2 Living in another's home (7)
3 First language (6,6)
4 Every (3)
6 Venomous snake (5)
7 Recently married (5-3)
8 Ineptness (12)
12 Food relish (5)
13 Time by which a task must be completed (8)
16 Skill (7)
18 Sleeveless cloaks (5)
19 Large deer (pl.) (4)
21 Thing that fails to work properly (3)

No. 252

Across

1 Long-haired breed of dog (6)
7 Capable of being used (8)
8 Sticky yellowish substance (3)
9 Amended (6)
10 Jar lids (4)
11 Small garden statue (5)
13 Flower shop (7)
15 Formal speech (7)
17 Confronts; deals with (5)
21 Just and unbiased (4)
22 Help or support (6)
23 Female chicken (3)
24 Achieved (8)
25 Place of origination (6)

Down

1 Stitching (6)
2 Dinner jacket (6)
3 Tree anchors (5)
4 Willingly (7)
5 Microorganisms (8)
6 Slants (6)
12 Cloth or fabric (8)
14 Crying heavily (7)
16 Responds to (6)
18 Code (6)
19 Spiritual meeting (6)
20 Sour substances (5)

No. 253

Across

1 Brood (4)
3 Send off to a destination (8)
9 Quibble (7)
10 Antelope (5)
11 Framework for washed garments (7,5)
14 Word expressing negation (3)
16 Trimmed (5)
17 Floor covering (3)
18 Cooling device in the kitchen (12)
21 Lift up (5)
22 Variety of rummy (7)
23 Lack of flexibility (8)
24 Computer memory unit (4)

Down

1 Threatening (8)
2 Paved area (5)
4 Pen fluid (3)
5 Surpassing in influence (12)
6 Wooden bar across a window (7)
7 Conceal (4)
8 Joyously unrestrained (4-8)
12 Small branch (5)
13 Study the night sky (8)
15 Abounding (7)
19 Petulant (5)
20 Norse god of thunder (4)
22 Feline (3)

No. 254

Across

1 Thing serving as an appropriate model (8)
5 Engrave with acid (4)
9 Dance hall (5)
10 Rowdy (7)
11 Awkward (12)
13 Constructs a building (6)
14 Visible warning device (6)
17 Mapmaker (12)
20 Reserved and shy (7)
21 Urge into action (5)
22 Current of air (4)
23 Huge sums of money (8)

Down

1 Finishes (4)
2 Vital content (7)
3 Commensurate (12)
4 Reach a destination (6)
6 Ironic metaphor (5)
7 Suffering from indecision (8)
8 Compensate for (12)
12 Educating (8)
15 Reduce the price of (7)
16 Quickly (6)
18 Travels by bicycle (5)
19 Bonus; positive (4)

No. 255

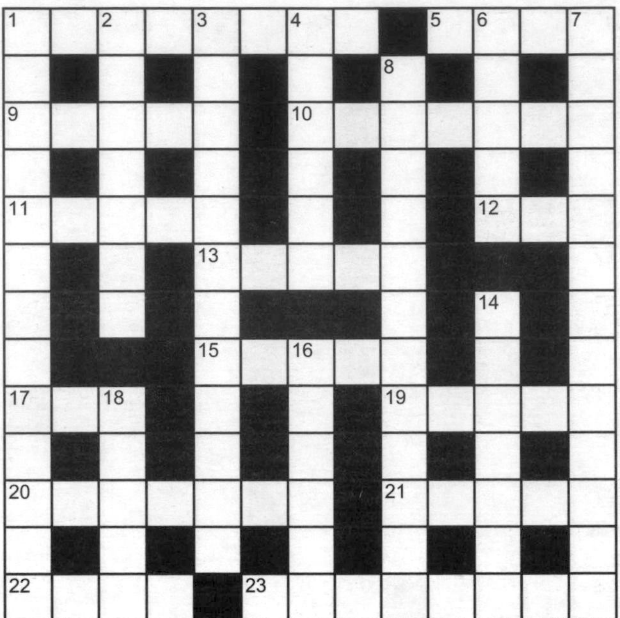

Across

1 Unstrap (8)
5 Percussion instrument (4)
9 Self-evident truth (5)
10 Game played on a lawn (7)
11 Reduce the temperature of (5)
12 Deciduous tree (3)
13 Not concealed (5)
15 European country (5)
17 Rocky hill (3)
19 Measure heaviness (5)
20 Bunch of flowers (7)
21 Conveys an action without words (5)
22 Days before major events (4)
23 Plant with decorative leaves (8)

Down

1 Inexplicable (13)
2 Sheriff's officer (7)
3 Dark towering cloud (12)
4 Track down (6)
6 Recycle (5)
7 Process of transformation (of an insect) (13)
8 Female fellow national (12)
14 Victory (7)
16 Very cold (of weather) (6)
18 Path or road (5)

No. 256

Across

1 Devices that illuminate (6)
4 Geneva (anag.) (6)
9 Former (3-4)
10 Element needed by the body (7)
11 Holy person (5)
12 Symbol (5)
14 Entrance barriers (5)
17 Apportions a punishment (5)
19 Heroic tales (5)
21 Lack of (7)
23 Wear out completely (7)
24 Mottled marking (6)
25 Organic compounds (6)

Down

1 Surgical knife (6)
2 Respiratory organ of fish (4)
3 Moving along the ground (of aircraft) (7)
5 Opinions (5)
6 Least quiet (8)
7 Kicks out (6)
8 Tame (11)
13 Position of a male monarch (8)
15 Breaks into pieces (7)
16 Climb (6)
18 Soaks in liquid (6)
20 Bony structure in the head (5)
22 Three squared (4)

No. 257

Across

1 Trifling sum of money (5,6)
9 Opposite of old (5)
10 Hit gently (3)
11 Judged (5)
12 Become ready to eat (of fruit) (5)
13 Permitting (8)
16 Overindulged (8)
18 Nearby (5)
21 A number between an eighth and a tenth (5)
22 Gallivant (3)
23 Stove (anag.) (5)
24 Taped in advance (3-8)

Down

2 Human beings (7)
3 Give up or surrender something (3,4)
4 Child of your aunt or uncle (6)
5 Tool for boring holes (5)
6 Rise to one's feet (3,2)
7 Branch of medicine dealing with skin disorders (11)
8 Straightforward (4-3-4)
14 Financial supporter (7)
15 Small explosive bomb (7)
17 Pertaining to vinegar (6)
19 Alcoholic beverage (5)
20 Intimate companion (5)

No. 258

Across

1 Praise (11)
9 Bite sharply (3)
10 Male relation (5)
11 Fits of violent anger (5)
12 Deciduous coniferous tree (5)
13 Resolute; obstinate (8)
16 e.g. when lunch or dinner is eaten (8)
18 Top degree mark (5)
20 Moved by air (5)
21 Motionless (5)
22 Fish appendage (3)
23 Insensitivity (11)

Down

2 A written document (5)
3 Rocky; harsh (5)
4 Container with a handle (6)
5 Thus; as a result (7)
6 Get too big for something (7)
7 Combustible (11)
8 Suggesting indirectly (11)
14 Balearic Island (7)
15 Object used in the kitchen (7)
17 One's environment (6)
18 Criminal (5)
19 Floating timber platforms (5)

No. 259

Across

1 Dedicate (6)
4 Support (6)
9 Child's room (7)
10 Wanderer (7)
11 Hank of wool (5)
12 Quick (5)
14 Very small amount (5)
17 Harsh and grating in sound (5)
19 Chopped finely (5)
21 Human-like robot (7)
23 Shining (7)
24 Discontinuance; neglect (6)
25 Groups of lions (6)

Down

1 Sculptor (6)
2 Dynasty in China (4)
3 e.g. Borneo and Java (7)
5 Cat sounds (5)
6 Component parts (8)
7 Working steadily with a tool (6)
8 Put questions to (11)
13 Goes before (8)
15 Vessel that cleans rivers (7)
16 Loved deeply (6)
18 Songlike cries (6)
20 Reads (anag.) (5)
22 Still to be paid (4)

No. 260

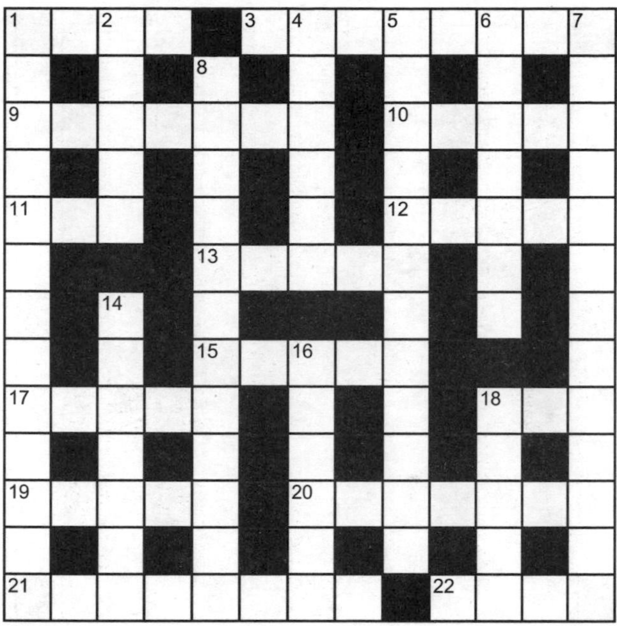

Across

1 Social insects (4)
3 Where one finds Glasgow (8)
9 Small stones (7)
10 Intense sorrow (5)
11 Title of a married woman (3)
12 Follow the position of (5)
13 e.g. molar or incisor (5)
15 Take place; happen (5)
17 Pertaining to the ear (5)
18 Acquire; obtain (3)
19 Creative thoughts (5)
20 European country (7)
21 Mobster (8)
22 Allot a punishment (4)

Down

1 Easy to deal with (13)
2 Pipes (5)
4 Gambling house (6)
5 Fellowship (12)
6 Creatures (7)
7 Distinguish between (13)
8 Decomposition by a current (12)
14 Flourish (7)
16 Glass container (6)
18 Spiny yellow plant (5)

No. 261

Across

1 Sudden cry expressing surprise (11)
9 Adult males (3)
10 Christmas song (5)
11 Looks slyly (5)
12 Gives temporarily (5)
13 Assume control of (4,4)
16 Harmful in effect (8)
18 Inferior to (5)
20 Very foolish (5)
21 Peak (5)
22 Stomach (3)
23 Inevitably (11)

Down

2 Heavy noble gas (5)
3 Fastens shut with a key (5)
4 Dock for small yachts (6)
5 Totals up (7)
6 See (7)
7 Petty (5-6)
8 Tools; utensils (11)
14 Quarrel (7)
15 Two-wheeled vehicle (7)
17 Changes (6)
18 Liquid essential for life (5)
19 Royal (5)

No. 262

Across

1 Awkward (8)
5 Break suddenly (4)
9 Not moving (5)
10 More jolly (7)
11 Number of years in a century (7)
12 Manner of speaking (5)
13 Tools for drilling holes (6)
14 Recompense for hardship (6)
17 Have faith in (5)
19 Extremely disordered (7)
20 Torment or harass (7)
21 Perfect (5)
22 Pitcher (4)
23 Evaluator (8)

Down

1 Unsuitable for living in (13)
2 Better for the environment (7)
3 Explanatory (12)
4 11th Greek letter (6)
6 Very loud (5)
7 Upright; vertical (13)
8 Question in great detail (5-7)
15 Ingenuous (7)
16 Climbs (6)
18 Unwarranted (5)

No. 263

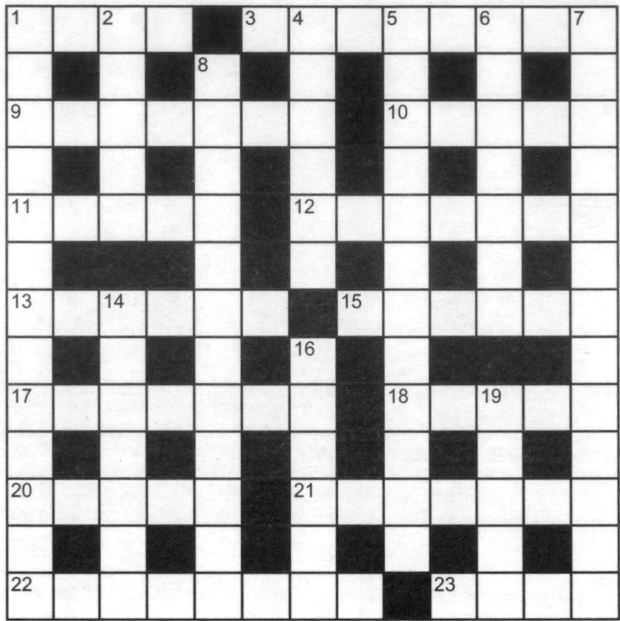

Across

1 Manure (4)
3 Without warning (8)
9 Commendation (7)
10 Shaping machine (5)
11 Completely correct (5)
12 Downwind (7)
13 Supplies with food (6)
15 Country in central Africa (6)
17 Liberate; release (7)
18 Brick-shaped lump of metal (5)
20 Commerce (5)
21 Improve (7)
22 Longing (8)
23 Poses a question (4)

Down

1 Where you were born (6,7)
2 Porcelain (5)
4 Sewing instrument (6)
5 Boxing class division (12)
6 Learn new skills (7)
7 Loyalty in the face of trouble (13)
8 Underground (12)
14 Musical composition (7)
16 Confine as a prisoner (6)
19 Groups of criminals (5)

No. 264

Across

1 Type of bag (8)
5 Familiar name for a potato (4)
9 Knotty protuberance on a tree (5)
10 Highest vantage point of a building (7)
11 Changes to a situation (12)
14 Blade for rowing a boat (3)
15 Tailored fold (5)
16 Adult male (3)
17 Unplugged (12)
20 A curse; wicked look (4,3)
22 Gate fastener (5)
23 Marine flatfish (4)
24 Recreational area for children (8)

Down

1 Beer containers; casks (4)
2 Non-professional (7)
3 Working for oneself (4-8)
4 Four-wheeled road vehicle (3)
6 Feign (3,2)
7 Removing from office (8)
8 Insistently (12)
12 Large body of water (5)
13 Liking for something (8)
16 A very skilled performer (7)
18 Ability (5)
19 Fancy (4)
21 Measure of length (3)

No. 265

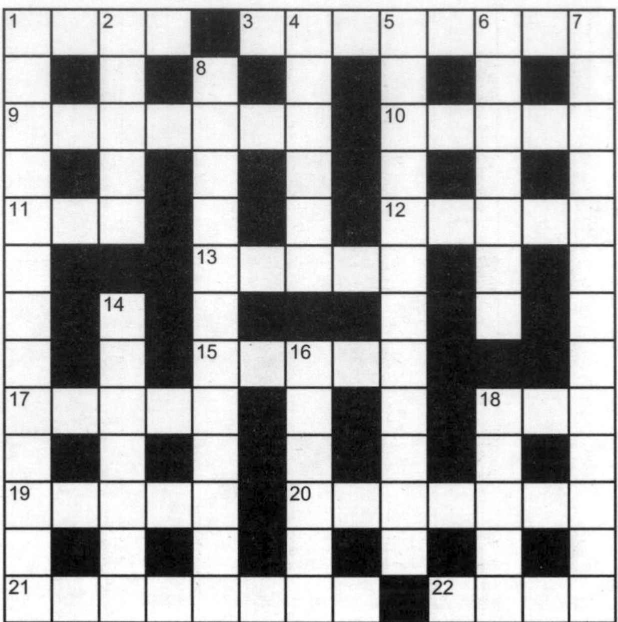

Across

1 Hens lay these (4)
3 Sign of approval (6-2)
9 Bedroom (7)
10 More pleasant (5)
11 Protective cover (3)
12 Fall heavily (5)
13 Latin American dance (5)
15 Wander aimlessly (5)
17 Vast multitude (5)
18 University teacher (3)
19 Dismiss from office (5)
20 Look something over (7)
21 Entirety (8)
22 Gull-like bird (4)

Down

1 Ornamentation (13)
2 Stuck together (5)
4 Toughen (6)
5 Maker (12)
6 Isolate (7)
7 Miscellaneous equipment (13)
8 Occurring at the same time (12)
14 Item of clothing (7)
16 Purpose (6)
18 Imbibed (5)

No. 266

Across

1 Rocked (8)
5 Photographic material (4)
9 Supply with; furnish (5)
10 Wooded areas (7)
11 Gives an account of (7)
12 Harsh and serious in manner (5)
13 Cleaned up (6)
14 Contort (6)
17 Ancient measure of length (5)
19 Characteristics; features (7)
20 Simple song for a baby (7)
21 Ice dwelling (5)
22 Open the mouth wide when tired (4)
23 Not necessary (8)

Down

1 Conceptually (13)
2 Punched (7)
3 Derived from past events (12)
4 Exude (6)
6 Important topic (5)
7 Misinterpreted (13)
8 Dictatorial (12)
15 Excited agreeably (7)
16 Subatomic particle such as a nucleon (6)
18 Under (5)

No. 267

Across

1 Document confirming an achievement (11)
9 Sharp end (5)
10 Before the present (of time) (3)
11 Competes in a speed contest (5)
12 Prodded (5)
13 Gave a summary of (8)
16 Hairstyle (8)
18 Heavy iron block (5)
21 Make indistinct (5)
22 Magic spell (3)
23 Awaken (5)
24 Pretentious display (11)

Down

2 Teach (7)
3 Surface layer of earth (7)
4 Eccentricity (6)
5 Chop into pieces (3,2)
6 Express gratitude (5)
7 Practice of drawing maps (11)
8 Bird of prey (6,5)
14 Unconventional (7)
15 Bison (7)
17 Supernatural (6)
19 Annoys (5)
20 Huge (5)

No. 268

Across

1 Suffered the consequences (4)
3 Chinese language (8)
9 Art of paper-folding (7)
10 Reception room (5)
11 Should (5)
12 Rip hats (anag.) (7)
13 Units of heat (6)
15 Point in an orbit furthest from earth (6)
17 Last longer than (7)
18 Ticked over (of an engine) (5)
20 Getting rid of (5)
21 Central bolt (7)
22 Throwing out (8)
23 Delight (4)

Down

1 Corresponding (13)
2 Decorating a cake (5)
4 Get off (6)
5 Detailed reports (12)
6 Turning over and over (7)
7 Failure to be present at (13)
8 Boxing class (12)
14 Wind together (7)
16 Mythical sea monster (6)
19 Folded back part of a coat (5)

No. 269

Across

1 Confuse (8)
5 Hold as an opinion (4)
8 Ponders (5)
9 Flamboyant confidence of style (7)
10 Omission of a sound when speaking (7)
12 Excess (7)
14 Edible parts of nuts (7)
16 Melodious (7)
18 Confound (7)
19 Drain away from soil (of a chemical) (5)
20 Scottish singer-songwriter (4)
21 Impudent (8)

Down

1 Collide with (4)
2 Quicker (6)
3 Incredulity (9)
4 Temporary failures of concentration (6)
6 Greek mathematician (6)
7 Humility and gentleness (8)
11 Very confused situation (9)
12 Lazy (8)
13 Unfold (6)
14 Horn (6)
15 Hire for work (6)
17 Stimulate the appetite (4)

No. 270

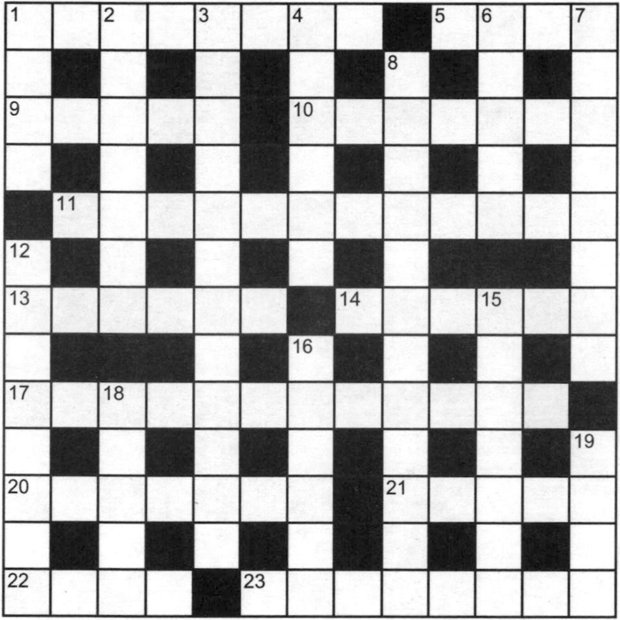

Across

1 Very confusing (8)
5 First man (4)
9 Exploiting (5)
10 Make damp (7)
11 Directions (12)
13 Title used for a French woman (6)
14 Make beloved (6)
17 Destruction (12)
20 Multiplied by two (7)
21 Expel from a country (5)
22 Christmas (4)
23 Vision (8)

Down

1 Boxing match (4)
2 Pretended (7)
3 Lawfully (12)
4 Large dark cloud (6)
6 Mark of repetition (5)
7 The priesthood (8)
8 Clarity (12)
12 Give someone the courage to do something (8)
15 Conjuring up feelings (7)
16 Day after Thursday (6)
18 Ousel (anag.) (5)
19 Home for a bird (4)

No. 271

Across

4 Helix (6)
7 Create an account deficit (8)
8 Not many (3)
9 Inspired by reverence (4)
10 Martial art (4,2)
11 Thin coating of metal (7)
12 Break the rules (5)
15 Pointed; acute (5)
17 Question after a mission (7)
20 Fame (6)
21 Tardy (4)
22 Trivial lie (3)
23 Taped (8)
24 Flipped a coin (6)

Down

1 Open declaration of affirmation (6)
2 Person owed money (8)
3 Slowing down (7)
4 Long-necked birds (5)
5 Prove to be false (6)
6 Towels (anag.) (6)
13 Pageantry (8)
14 Propriety and modesty (7)
15 Underside of an arch (6)
16 Commercial aircraft (6)
18 One or the other of two (6)
19 Watch over (5)

No. 272

Across

1 Unwrap or untie (4)
3 Heated exchange of views (8)
9 Extremely cruel (7)
10 Capital of Ghana (5)
11 Wireless (5)
12 Curved sword (7)
13 A score (6)
15 Tool used to hit things (6)
17 Provide with food (7)
18 Lock of hair (5)
20 Asian country (5)
21 Pasta pockets (7)
22 Collected or stored (8)
23 Restrain (4)

Down

1 Comprehension (13)
2 Vaulted (5)
4 Excessively ornate (of literature) (6)
5 Ugly (12)
6 Cry out (7)
7 Violation of a law (13)
8 Teach to accept a belief uncritically (12)
14 Republic in South America (7)
16 Accuse; run at (6)
19 Decay (5)

No. 273

Across

1 Tonic (4-2-2)
5 Ingredient in vegetarian cooking (4)
9 Seven (anag.) (5)
10 Pay homage to (7)
11 Egg-shaped solid (5)
12 Regret with sadness (3)
13 Swerves off course (5)
15 Approaches (5)
17 For each (3)
19 Piece of furniture (5)
20 Pays no attention to (7)
21 Strong gust of wind (5)
22 Religious sisters (4)
23 Space rock (8)

Down

1 Presupposition (13)
2 Cigar (7)
3 Mishap (12)
4 Foolish (6)
6 Opposite one of two (5)
7 Unparalleled (13)
8 Overwhelmingly compelling (12)
14 Wavering vocal quality (7)
16 Entertains (6)
18 Angry dispute (3-2)

No. 274

Across

1 Mean (5-6)
9 Not wet (3)
10 Irritate (5)
11 Injures (5)
12 Prison compartments (5)
13 Inventive; creative (8)
16 Contained as part of a whole (8)
18 Pierces with a horn (5)
20 Attractively stylish (5)
21 Intense (5)
22 Small truck (3)
23 Official agreements (11)

Down

2 Faithful (5)
3 Remains (5)
4 Swordsman (6)
5 Very great (3-4)
6 Competitor (7)
7 Serving to enlighten; instructive (11)
8 Annoying (11)
14 Confused struggle (7)
15 Floating (7)
17 Reason for not doing something (6)
18 Diving waterbird (5)
19 Short bolt or pin (5)

No. 275

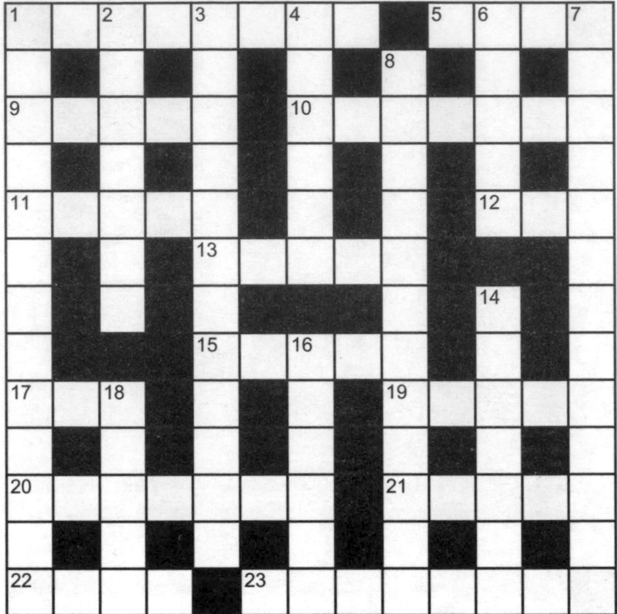

Across

1 Defeated (8)
5 Primates (4)
9 African country whose capital is Niamey (5)
10 Not sudden (7)
11 Trunk of the body (5)
12 Public transport vehicle (3)
13 Vault under a church (5)
15 Acer tree (5)
17 Not new (3)
19 Assumed name (5)
20 Have as a part (7)
21 Musical times (5)
22 Playthings (4)
23 Yielded (8)

Down

1 Zoologist who studies birds (13)
2 Swell with fluid (7)
3 Type of cloud (12)
4 Strong (6)
6 In a vertical line (5)
7 Complacent and happy with oneself (4-9)
8 Lacking courage (5-7)
14 Of enormous effect (7)
16 Show-off (6)
18 Decomposition (5)

No. 276

Across

1 Assumed propositions (6)
7 Not guilty (8)
8 For what reason (3)
9 Dragged (6)
10 Fall slowly (of water) (4)
11 Republic in the Middle East (5)
13 Foes (7)
15 Moving to music (7)
17 Stared into space (5)
21 Business (4)
22 Using all one's resources (3,3)
23 Witch (3)
24 Elks idea (anag.) (8)
25 Deprive of food (6)

Down

1 Restrained and subtle (3-3)
2 Chaos (6)
3 Daft (5)
4 Painkilling drug or medicine (7)
5 The scholastic world (8)
6 Lure (6)
12 Hamper (8)
14 Live in (7)
16 Beast (6)
18 Folk instrument (6)
19 Hang loosely (6)
20 Sticks together (5)

No. 277

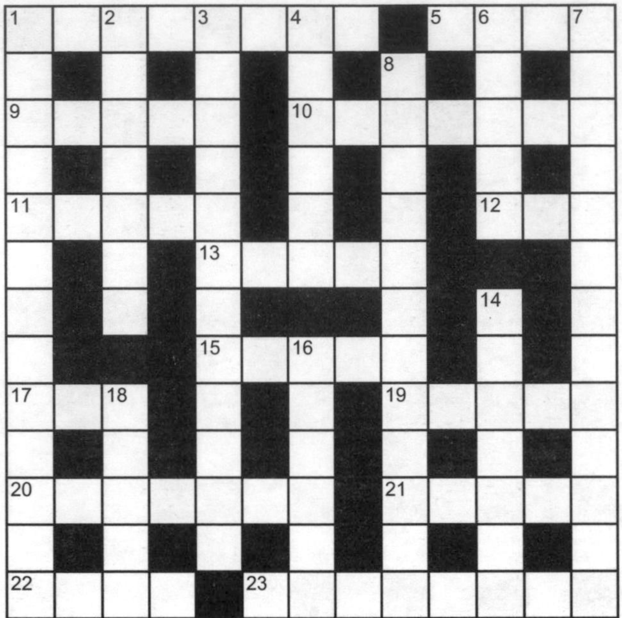

Across

1 Extremely accomplished (8)
5 Total spread of a bridge (4)
9 Allocate money (5)
10 Snack food (7)
11 Composition for a solo instrument (5)
12 Empty space between two objects (3)
13 Mammal that eats bamboo (5)
15 Fill with high spirits (5)
17 Convent dweller (3)
19 Stare (anag.) (5)
20 Hermit (7)
21 Cloth woven from flax (5)
22 Gardening tools used for weeding (4)
23 Individually crafted by a person (8)

Down

1 Direction to which a compass points (8,5)
2 Degree of eminence (7)
3 Someone who sets up their own business (12)
4 Subatomic particle such as an electron (6)
6 Pointed part of a fork (5)
7 Failure to be present (13)
8 Stretched out completely (12)
14 Aerial (7)
16 Greek goddess (6)
18 Shallow recess (5)

No. 278

Across

1 Spiny cactus fruit (7,4)
9 Amp (anag.) (3)
10 Animal life of a region (5)
11 Group of singers (5)
12 Enumerates (5)
13 Green vegetable (8)
16 Grandiosity of language (8)
18 Frustrated and annoyed (3,2)
20 Come to a point (5)
21 Discourage (5)
22 Place (3)
23 Extend by inference (11)

Down

2 Strong cords (5)
3 Small restaurants (5)
4 Less quiet (6)
5 Impressive bird (7)
6 Container releasing a fine spray (7)
7 Makes better (11)
8 Take part in (11)
14 Bewilder (7)
15 Person who accumulates things (7)
17 Arch of the foot (6)
18 Wild and untamed (5)
19 Repository (5)

No. 279

Across

4 Capital of Lebanon (6)
7 Monument (8)
8 Cutting tool (3)
9 Bate (anag.) (4)
10 Leg bone (6)
11 Pours off liquid (7)
12 Glasses (abbrev.) (5)
15 Overly self-confident (5)
17 Unrecoverable money owed (3,4)
20 Breathing passage (6)
21 Secluded narrow valley (4)
22 Hairpiece (3)
23 Small bunches of flowers (8)
24 e.g. using a towel (6)

Down

1 Moon goddess in Greek mythology (6)
2 Light axe (8)
3 Outsiders (7)
4 Amorphous shapes (5)
5 Act of selling on goods (6)
6 Tall castle structures (6)
13 Method and practice of teaching (8)
14 Infantile (7)
15 Masticated (6)
16 Rough and uneven (of a cliff) (6)
18 Farewell remark (3-3)
19 Move back and forth (5)

No. 280

Across

1 Bringing into use (11)
9 Facsimile (abbrev.) (3)
10 Body of rules (5)
11 Having three dimensions (5)
12 TV presenters (5)
13 Musical pieces for solo instruments (8)
16 Remote; cut off (8)
18 Petite (5)
20 Mexican tortilla wraps (5)
21 Shaped up (5)
22 Domesticated pig (3)
23 Rural scenery (11)

Down

2 Focal point (5)
3 Loose scrums (rugby) (5)
4 Electric generator (6)
5 Make by mixing ingredients (7)
6 Very young infant (7)
7 Where one finds Kabul (11)
8 Group of islands (11)
14 e.g. Mount Etna (7)
15 Motor-driven revolving cylinder (7)
17 Nearer (anag.) (6)
18 Teams (5)
19 Plant pest (5)

No. 281

Across

1 Safe place (6)
4 Exhausts (6)
9 Repeat performances (7)
10 Plant with bright flowers (7)
11 Foam or froth (5)
12 Direct competitor (5)
14 Caused persistent dull pain (5)
17 Walks through water (5)
19 Not together (5)
21 Degree of compactness (7)
23 Personal (7)
24 Recapture (6)
25 Inclined at an angle (6)

Down

1 Thief (6)
2 Canine tooth (4)
3 Kind of breakfast cereal (7)
5 Eats like a bird (5)
6 Brought up; cared for (8)
7 Long strips of cloth (6)
8 Unnecessarily forceful (5-6)
13 Singer (8)
15 Diminish (7)
16 Stylishly dressed (6)
18 Fashioned (6)
20 Trail (5)
22 Tehran is the capital here (4)

No. 282

Across

1 Images recorded on film (11)
9 Select; choose (5)
10 Evergreen coniferous tree (3)
11 Stinky (5)
12 Synthetic fabric (5)
13 Relating to the heart (8)
16 Baseless distrust of others (8)
18 Roman country house (5)
21 Overly sentimental (5)
22 Limb used for walking (3)
23 Aqualung (5)
24 Car pedal (11)

Down

2 Warming devices (7)
3 Buying and selling (7)
4 Scowl (6)
5 Opposite of before (5)
6 Weighty (5)
7 For all practical purposes (11)
8 Gorge in Arizona (5,6)
14 Plant with starchy tuberous roots (7)
15 Submarine weapon (7)
17 Refer to indirectly (6)
19 Good sense (5)
20 Passage between rows of seats (5)

No. 283

Across

4 What a spider makes (6)
7 Captive (8)
8 Knot with a double loop (3)
9 Give a particular title to (4)
10 Confused noise (6)
11 Embryonic root (7)
12 A sense (5)
15 Horse carts (5)
17 Promising young actress (7)
20 Safety device in a car (6)
21 Recording medium (4)
22 Flexible container (3)
23 Fanaticism (8)
24 Not real or genuine (6)

Down

1 Fleet of ships (6)
2 Harshness of manner (8)
3 Mound made by insects (7)
4 Babies' beds (5)
5 Waver (6)
6 Lament (6)
13 Long foot race (8)
14 Symbols of disgrace (7)
15 Make a hole (6)
16 Sayings (6)
18 Person with detailed knowledge (6)
19 Humming (5)

No. 284

Across

1 e.g. Shakespeare and Bernard Shaw (11)
9 Precious stone (3)
10 Financial resources (5)
11 e.g. covered with bricks (5)
12 Hazardous; dangerous (5)
13 Deluge (8)
16 Hindquarters (8)
18 Remove errors from software (5)
20 Sheep sound (5)
21 Legal process (5)
22 State of armed conflict (3)
23 Money spent (11)

Down

2 Unshapely masses; swellings (5)
3 Delicious (5)
4 Explanation (6)
5 Panting (7)
6 Unimportant (7)
7 Fear of open spaces (11)
8 Parakeets (11)
14 Music player (7)
15 Coal bucket (7)
17 Desired for oneself (6)
18 Glazed earthenware (5)
19 Shady spot under trees (5)

No. 285

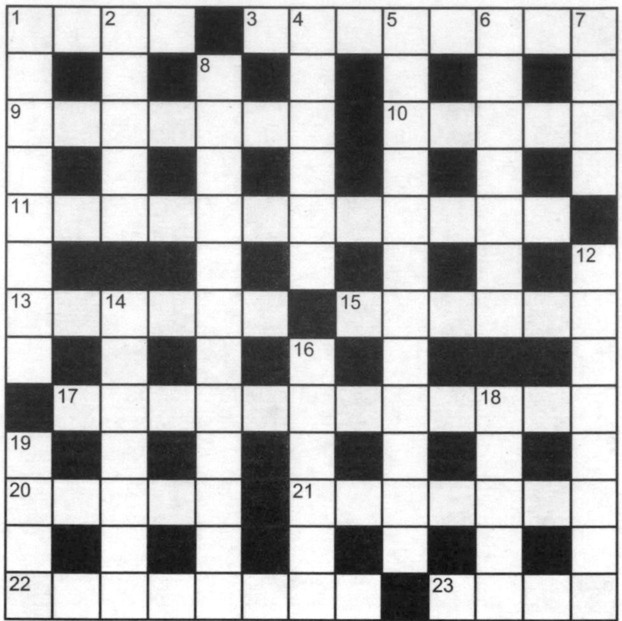

Across

1 Fastened with stitches (4)
3 Support (8)
9 Material made from animal skin (7)
10 U-shaped curve in a river (5)
11 Contagiously (12)
13 Oppose (6)
15 Christmas decoration (6)
17 Insincere (12)
20 Spoken for (5)
21 Firm providing flights (7)
22 Circle of constant longitude (8)
23 Gets older (4)

Down

1 Military people (8)
2 Fixed platform by water (5)
4 Scandinavian (6)
5 Developmental (12)
6 Small stones (7)
7 Small amphibian (4)
8 Insensitive to criticism (5-7)
12 Close groups (8)
14 One who neglects a duty (7)
16 Crested lizard (6)
18 Outstanding (of a debt) (5)
19 Plant stalk (4)

No. 286

Across

1 Becoming agitated (8)
5 Female sheep (pl.) (4)
9 Visual representation (5)
10 Foot support (7)
11 Painting medium (7)
12 Breed of dog (5)
13 Makes spick and span (6)
14 Admit to a post (6)
17 Stares at in a lecherous way (5)
19 Mundane (7)
20 Japanese warrior (7)
21 Expect (5)
22 Thread (4)
23 Note (4,4)

Down

1 Teasingly (13)
2 Shocked (7)
3 Ancestors (12)
4 Capital of the Bahamas (6)
6 Electrician (5)
7 Worldly-wise (13)
8 Very sad (12)
15 Ignorant of something (7)
16 Top aim (anag.) (6)
18 Small primate (5)

No. 287

Across

1 Sports grounds (8)
5 Point-winning serves (tennis) (4)
9 Agreeable sound or tune (5)
10 Bishop's jurisdiction (7)
11 Dairy product (5)
12 Droop (3)
13 Immature insects (5)
15 Steer (anag.) (5)
17 Bashful (3)
19 Remote in manner (5)
20 Character in Hamlet (7)
21 Seventh sign of the zodiac (5)
22 Retail store (4)
23 Calculated and careful (8)

Down

1 Partially awake (13)
2 Responses (7)
3 Contradictory (12)
4 Fictional (4,2)
6 Salad plant (5)
7 Legerdemain (7,2,4)
8 Majestic birds of prey (6,6)
14 Iron lever (7)
16 Recount (6)
18 Loutish person (5)

No. 288

Across

1 Ragtimes (anag.) (8)
5 Tiny parasite (4)
8 Ring-shaped object (5)
9 Challenges the truth of (7)
10 Impinges upon (7)
12 Inventor (7)
14 Made a bubbling sound (7)
16 Respectable; refined (7)
18 Called on (7)
19 Fruit of the vine (5)
20 Precious metal (4)
21 Explosive shells (8)

Down

1 Microscopic arachnid (4)
2 Motor vehicle storage building (6)
3 Forceful (9)
4 Cure-all (6)
6 Amount of money left in a will (6)
7 Aided (8)
11 Grouselike game bird (9)
12 Expelling air abruptly (8)
13 Cry and sniffle (6)
14 Engineless aircraft (6)
15 Reptile (6)
17 Charges (4)

No. 289

Across

4 Have sufficient money to pay for (6)
7 Moored (8)
8 Surpass (3)
9 Slip (anag.) (4)
10 States an opinion (6)
11 Sincere (7)
12 Humorous (5)
15 Closes and opens an eye (5)
17 Leave quickly and in secret (7)
20 Son of Daedalus in Greek mythology (6)
21 Small symbol or graphic (4)
22 Soft fruit with seeds (3)
23 Highly regarded (8)
24 Follows (6)

Down

1 Whole (6)
2 Burrowing ground squirrel (8)
3 Strong desire for a thing (7)
4 Mingle with something else (5)
5 Beginning (6)
6 Person who acts for another (6)
13 Leans (8)
14 Corpulence (7)
15 Talk nonsense (6)
16 Equine sounds (6)
18 Loops with running knots (6)
19 Liberates (5)

No. 290

Across

1 Scam (anag.) (4)
3 Making a duck sound (8)
9 Solid inorganic substance (7)
10 ___ acid: protein part (5)
11 Acquire knowledge of (5)
12 Indefinitely many (7)
13 Threaten (6)
15 Form-fitting garment (6)
17 In name only (7)
18 Elevated step (5)
20 Concur (5)
21 Spun around (7)
22 Christmas season (8)
23 Not at home (4)

Down

1 Given free of charge (13)
2 Faint southern constellation (5)
4 Diacritical mark of two dots (6)
5 Type of contest (12)
6 Chilly attitude (7)
7 Amiably (4-9)
8 Exceptional (12)
14 Digit (7)
16 Shone (6)
19 Let (5)

No. 291

Across

1 Type of treatment using needles (11)
9 Book leaves (5)
10 Bleat of a sheep (3)
11 Cloudy; not clear (5)
12 Satisfied a desire (5)
13 Long scolding speeches (8)
16 Ability to act as one wishes (4,4)
18 Governed (5)
21 Informal language (5)
22 Chemical element (3)
23 Solemn promises (5)
24 Dejection (11)

Down

2 Cup (7)
3 Ancient parchment (7)
4 Invalidate (6)
5 Things to be done (5)
6 Refute by evidence (5)
7 State of being well known (11)
8 Weak form of illumination (11)
14 Print anew (7)
15 Colossal (7)
17 Putrid (6)
19 Sudden movement (5)
20 Sink; sag (5)

No. 292

Across

1 Soak; drench (8)
5 Heat up (4)
9 Bore into (5)
10 Quantities (7)
11 Breastbone (7)
12 Mediterranean island (5)
13 Small (6)
14 Spoken form of communication (6)
17 Shallow carrying containers (5)
19 Small valleys (7)
20 Delightful (7)
21 Impair (5)
22 Long deep cut (4)
23 Giant ocean waves (8)

Down

1 Very funny (4-9)
2 Three-pronged weapon (7)
3 Incessantly (12)
4 Emotional shock (6)
6 Declare invalid (5)
7 State of the USA (13)
8 Worldly (12)
15 Selfishness (7)
16 Verifies (6)
18 Bottomless pit (5)

No. 293

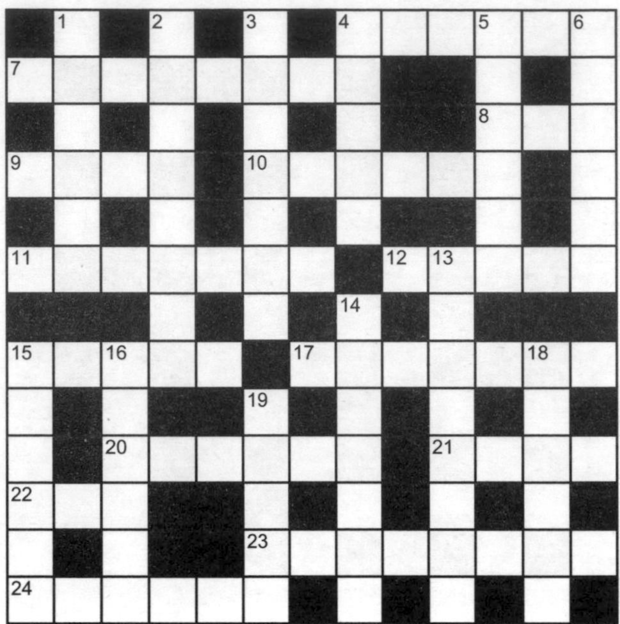

Across

4 Roman military unit (6)
7 Fictitious (8)
8 Small winged insect (3)
9 Lane (anag.) (4)
10 Avoids (6)
11 Particular version of a text (7)
12 Type of water lily (5)
15 Makeshift shelter (5)
17 Crazy about someone (7)
20 A husband or wife (6)
21 Bitter-tasting substance (4)
22 Throat of a voracious animal (3)
23 Person who hears (8)
24 Where one finds Oslo (6)

Down

1 Rode a bike (6)
2 Relating to speech sounds (8)
3 Formation of troops (7)
4 Fastening device (5)
5 Compensate for (6)
6 Lymphoid organ (6)
13 No longer in fashion (8)
14 Steep in; engross (7)
15 Sailor (6)
16 Reply (6)
18 Those expelled from a country (6)
19 Tarnish (5)

No. 294

Across

1 International waters (4,4)
5 Look at amorously (4)
8 Reject with disdain (5)
9 Number of attendees (7)
10 Rower (7)
12 Accounts inspector (7)
14 Set in motion; agitated (7)
16 Capital of Georgia in the US (7)
18 Started a fire (7)
19 Jostle and push (5)
20 Rough or harsh sound (4)
21 Very annoying (8)

Down

1 Silence (4)
2 Estimated (6)
3 Feeling (9)
4 Writer (6)
6 Tidies one's appearance (6)
7 Stretched out (8)
11 Recall past experiences (9)
12 Aggressor (8)
13 Catapults (6)
14 Make unhappy (6)
15 Revived or regenerated (6)
17 In a good way (4)

No. 295

Across

1 Escorted (11)
9 Mark of insertion (5)
10 Steal (3)
11 Hit with the fist (5)
12 Respected person in a field (5)
13 Block (8)
16 Native of the United States (8)
18 Spiritual nourishment (5)
21 Make fun of in a playful manner (5)
22 Haul (3)
23 Suit (5)
24 Tendency to disintegrate (11)

Down

2 Nationality of a citizen of Beijing (7)
3 Land with fruit trees (7)
4 Astronomical distance (6)
5 Well-known (5)
6 Ahead of time (5)
7 Not exact (11)
8 Withdrawal of support (11)
14 Set down on paper (7)
15 Writes untidily (7)
17 Resolute or brave (6)
19 More recent (5)
20 Collection of songs (5)

No. 296

Across

1 Moved at an easy pace (6)
7 Surrounds on all sides (8)
8 Layer of a folded material (3)
9 Within a space (6)
10 Speak angrily (4)
11 Smooth transition (5)
13 Ponderously (7)
15 Sports arena (7)
17 Fills a suitcase (5)
21 Rip up (4)
22 Rigid; very cold (6)
23 Wild ox (3)
24 Courteous and pleasant (8)
25 Substance found in wine (6)

Down

1 Fruits with pips (6)
2 Barking loudly (6)
3 Lived (anag.) (5)
4 Plans (7)
5 Liberia's capital (8)
6 Shelter for a dog (6)
12 Play a role with great restraint (8)
14 Clown (7)
16 Speculative view (6)
18 Deep gorge (6)
19 Uttered (6)
20 Amplify a signal (5)

No. 297

Across

4 Scarcity (6)
7 Cocktail (8)
8 Exclamation of amazement (3)
9 Statistics and facts (4)
10 Bird; crazy (6)
11 Provoked or teased (7)
12 Summed together (5)
15 Jewel from an oyster shell (5)
17 Tried a new product (7)
20 Strong public protest (6)
21 Roman poet (4)
22 Evergreen tree (3)
23 Tells a story (8)
24 Long narrow hilltops (6)

Down

1 Make empty (6)
2 Spend wastefully (8)
3 Went around and around (7)
4 Trench (5)
5 Rephrase (6)
6 Offered goods for sale (6)
13 International negotiator (8)
14 Wood cutters (7)
15 Request made to God (6)
16 Declared (6)
18 US rapper (6)
19 Examines quickly (5)

No. 298

Across

1 Disturb the status quo (4,3,4)
9 Quavering sound (5)
10 Cut of pork (3)
11 Conjuring trick (5)
12 Smarter (5)
13 An indirect and sometimes snide implication (8)
16 Bothers (8)
18 Decal (anag.) (5)
21 Very large (5)
22 At the present time (3)
23 Nimble (5)
24 A parent's Mum (11)

Down

2 Beginnings (7)
3 Room used for preparing food (7)
4 Applauded (6)
5 Local authority rule (2-3)
6 Remains of a fire (5)
7 Mixing together (11)
8 Impersonations (11)
14 Topic (7)
15 Quick look (7)
17 Element discovered by the Curies (6)
19 Crouch down in fear (5)
20 Draw off liquid from (5)

No. 299

Across

1 Go around (6)
7 Working dough (8)
8 Hit forcibly (3)
9 Ordered arrangements (6)
10 Greases (4)
11 Fully prepared (5)
13 Mends (7)
15 Removed from office forcefully (7)
17 Moneys owed (5)
21 Performs in a play (4)
22 Small fasteners (6)
23 Cooking appliance (3)
24 Formerly Ceylon (3,5)
25 Adornment of hanging threads (6)

Down

1 Device pressed by game show contestants (6)
2 Tropical fruit (6)
3 Seabirds (5)
4 Restrained (7)
5 Publicly recommend (8)
6 Deer horn (6)
12 Sleepily (8)
14 Mocking (7)
16 Bodyguard (6)
18 Hits hard (6)
19 Token (6)
20 Big (5)

No. 300

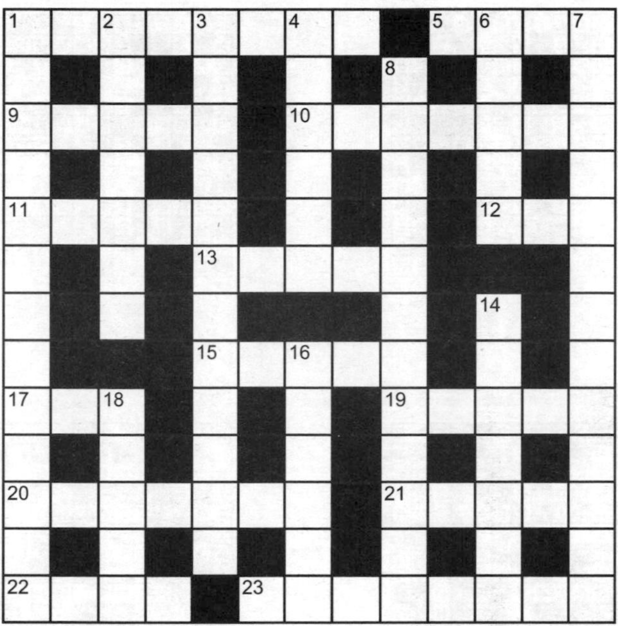

Across

1 Sudden release of emotion (8)
5 Became older (4)
9 Lively Bohemian dance (5)
10 Render utterly perplexed (7)
11 Precipitates (5)
12 Asp (anag.) (3)
13 Change (5)
15 Supple (5)
17 Family or variety (3)
19 Feign (5)
20 Frozen water spears (7)
21 A satellite of Uranus (5)
22 Observed (4)
23 Reassign (8)

Down

1 Chances to do things (13)
2 Speaking (7)
3 Impregnable (12)
4 Poem of fourteen lines (6)
6 Very strong winds (5)
7 Repugnantly (13)
8 Lacking a backbone (12)
14 Pertaining to a river (7)
16 Scuffle (6)
18 Cutting instrument (5)

No. 1

R	O	U	L	E	T	T	E		O	M	I	T
E		N		L		R		A		E		A
C	A	C	H	E		I	N	C	I	T	E	S
E		L		C		A		K		E		T
P	L	A	N	T	E	D		N	E	R	V	E
T		S		R		S		O				L
I	M	P	A	I	R		T	W	E	L	V	E
V				F		L		L		E		S
E	V	E	R	Y		E	L	E	G	I	E	S
N		G		I		S		D		S		N
E	R	R	A	N	D	S		G	A	U	G	E
S		E		G		E		E		R		S
S	I	T	E		N	E	E	D	L	E	S	S

No. 2

O	R	A	T	E	S		I		A		D	
N		S			C	O	M	M	U	N	A	L
W	R	Y			O		P		T		R	
A		L	E	G	U	M	E		O	A	K	S
R		U			T		R		M		E	
D	U	M	P	S		R	I	V	A	L	R	Y
			R		C		L		T			
B	R	I	O	C	H	E		C	A	V	E	S
	E		T		O		F			E		T
O	G	R	E		P	I	L	L	A	R		A
	G		C		P		I			B	O	Y
P	A	N	T	H	E	O	N			A		E
	E		S		R		T	I	T	L	E	D

No. 3

B	O	R	R	O	W	E	D		H	E	A	D
U		H		B		F				X		I
Z	A	I	R	E		F	O	R	B	I	D	S
Z		N		D		O				S		O
		A		I		R	E	A	C	T	O	R
S	A	L	I	E	N	T		S		S		D
O				N				S				E
M		U		C		C	H	E	A	T	E	R
B	U	G	B	E	A	R		M		O		
R		L				I		B		U		W
E	P	I	G	R	A	M		L	U	R	C	H
R		E				E		E		E		E
O	A	R	S		C	A	N	D	I	D	L	Y

No. 4

C	A	V	E		T	W	O	F	A	C	E	D
U		A		E		A		O		R		U
R	E	L	A	X	E	D		R	O	U	G	E
T		E		T				T		S		S
A	F	T	E	R	T	H	O	U	G	H	T	
I				A		O		I		E		T
N	E	T		V	I	S	I	T		D	E	W
S		R		A		T		O				E
	C	O	N	G	R	A	T	U	L	A	T	E
T		U		A				S		M		Z
R	O	B	I	N		E	L	L	I	P	S	E
I		L		Z		K		Y		L		R
O	P	E	R	A	T	E	S		H	E	R	S

No. 5

S	A	R	D	O	N	I	C		I	M	P	S
O		A		L		N		B		O		H
U	R	G	E	D		S	I	R	O	C	C	O
L		T		T		E		E		H		R
S	P	I	T	E		R		A		A	N	T
E		M		S	I	T	E	S				T
A		E		T				T		H		E
R				A	V	E	R	S		O		M
C	O	L		M		R		T	R	A	M	P
H		A		E		A		R		R		E
I	N	T	E	N	T	S		O	R	D	E	R
N		E		T		E		K		E		E
G	A	R	B		A	S	C	E	N	D	E	D

No. 6

C	U	F	F		D	E	V	I	L	I	S	H
O		A		D		U		N		N		Y
U	N	C	L	E	A	R		S	W	A	M	P
N		E		L		E		U		N		E
T	U	T		I		K		F	R	I	A	R
E				C	H	A	F	F		T		C
R		A		A				E		Y		R
A		S		T	I	G	E	R				I
T	R	I	T	E		R		A		S	I	T
T		N		S		A		B		A		I
A	D	I	O	S		P	O	L	E	M	I	C
C		N		E		H		E		B		A
K	E	E	N	N	E	S	S		F	A	L	L

No. 7

	A	G	O	R	A	P	H	O	B	I	C	
C		A		O		R		V		N		E
H	U	M		A	R	O	S	E		G		N
A		E		D		V		R	U	R	A	L
R	U	S	T	S		E		A		A		A
I					E	D	U	C	A	T	O	R
S		A		B				T		E		G
M	A	V	E	R	I	C	K					E
A		O		I		A		B	E	D	I	M
T	U	C	K	S		V		E		O		E
I		A		K	R	I	L	L		D	E	N
C		D		E		A		I		O		T
	P	O	L	T	E	R	G	E	I	S	T	

No. 8

	D	I	S	T	R	E	S	S	I	N	G	
C		N		R		X		T		O		G
H		H		A	W	O	K	E		M	A	R
O	M	I	T	S		T		E		A		E
R		B		H		I		L	A	D	L	E
E	V	I	D	E	N	C	E					N
O		T		D				F		A		H
G					E	S	P	R	E	S	S	O
R	O	W	D	Y		P		A		P		U
A		I		A		R		N	A	I	L	S
P	I	P		R	E	A	C	T		R		E
H		E		D		I		I		I		S
	P	R	O	S	A	N	D	C	O	N	S	

No. 9

D	O	V	E	C	O	T	E		I	D	O	L
O		E		A		E		D		R		E
S	T	R	U	T		A	R	I	Z	O	N	A
E		B		A				S		S		P
	B	O	I	S	T	E	R	O	U	S	L	Y
M		S		T		D		B				E
N	E	E		R	A	I	S	E		R	I	A
E				O		F		D		E		R
M	E	T	A	P	H	Y	S	I	C	A	L	
O		O		H				E		L		C
N	A	G	G	I	N	G		N	E	I	G	H
I		A		C		N		C		S		I
C	A	S	H		S	U	P	E	R	M	A	N

No. 10

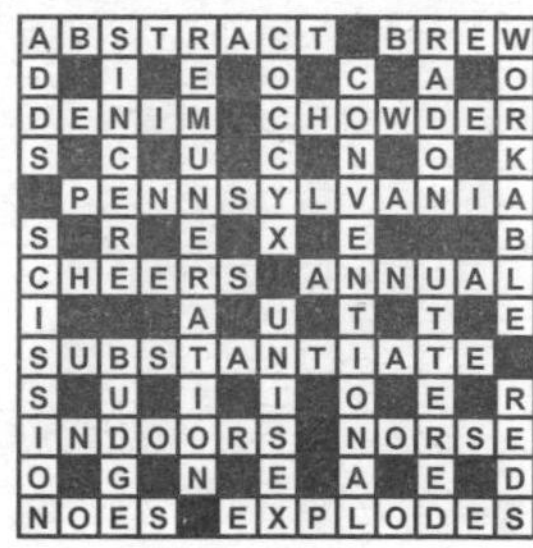

A	B	S	T	R	A	C	T		B	R	E	W
D		I		E		O		C		A		O
D	E	N	I	M		C	H	O	W	D	E	R
S		C		U		C		N		O		K
	P	E	N	N	S	Y	L	V	A	N	I	A
S		R		E		X		E				B
C	H	E	E	R	S		A	N	N	U	A	L
I				A		U		T		T		E
S	U	B	S	T	A	N	T	I	A	T	E	
S		U		I		I		O		E		R
I	N	D	O	O	R	S		N	O	R	S	E
O		G		N		E		A		E		D
N	O	E	S		E	X	P	L	O	D	E	S

No. 11

U	T	A	H		A	R	T	I	S	T	I	C
N		L		S		E		N		R		O
D	R	A	S	T	I	C		T	R	A	I	L
E		R		R		E		R		M		L
R	U	M	B	A		S	C	O	R	P	I	O
E				I		S		D		L		Q
S	T	O	D	G	E		B	U	R	E	A	U
T		V		H		S		C				I
I	N	E	R	T	I	A		T	I	B	I	A
M		R		A		L		O		U		L
A	G	L	O	W		M	A	R	T	I	N	I
T		A		A		O		Y		L		S
E	M	P	T	Y	I	N	G		E	D	A	M

No. 12

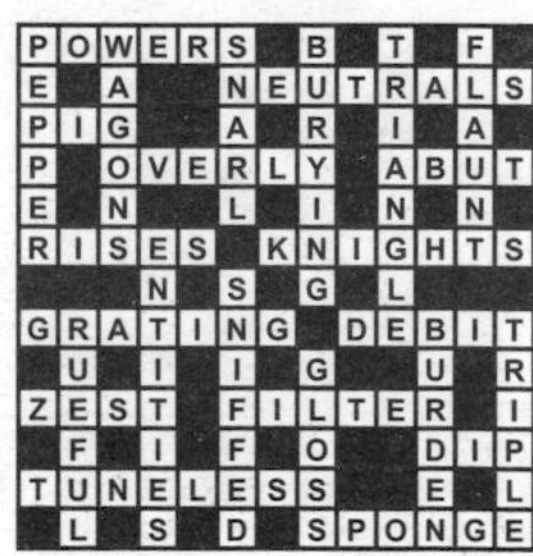

P	O	W	E	R	S		B		T		F	
E		A			N	E	U	T	R	A	L	S
P	I	G			A		R		I		A	
P		O	V	E	R	L	Y		A	B	U	T
E		N			L		I		N		N	
R	I	S	E	S		K	N	I	G	H	T	S
			N		S		G		L			
G	R	A	T	I	N	G		D	E	B	I	T
	U		I		I		G			U		R
Z	E	S	T		F	I	L	T	E	R		I
	F		I		F		O			D	I	P
T	U	N	E	L	E	S	S			E		L
	L		S		D		S	P	O	N	G	E

No. 13

P	E	D	A	N	T		I	C	O	N	I	C
O		O		E		D		I		E		H
C		W		S		O	B	V	I	A	T	E
K	I	N	E	T	I	C		I		R		E
E				E		U		L	A	N	E	S
T	Y	I	N	G		M				E		E
		N		G	U	E	S	S		S		
S		C				N		P	E	S	T	S
C	R	I	M	P		T		I				E
H		S		I		A	L	L	O	V	E	R
E	M	I	T	T	E	R		L		E		I
M		O		H		Y		E		E		E
A	N	N	O	Y	S		A	D	O	R	E	S

No. 14

I	N	E	X	P	E	R	T		A	X	L	E
R		A		U		O		C		Y		S
R	A	R	E	R		L	E	A	F	L	E	T
E		N		P		L		N		E		A
C	R	E	D	O		E		T		M	O	B
O		S		S	Y	R	I	A				L
V		T		E				N		P		I
E				F	L	O	C	K		I		S
R	I	D		U		V		E	A	R	T	H
A		I		L		E		R		A		M
B	U	R	G	L	A	R		O	U	N	C	E
L		G		Y		D		U		H		N
E	V	E	N		C	O	N	S	T	A	N	T

No. 15

	I	M	A	G	I	N	A	T	I	O	N	
F		A		R		I		U		R		C
U		G		O	R	C	A	S		B	O	O
R	E	N	E	W		E		K		I		M
T		U		I		S		S	I	T	U	P
H	U	M	A	N	I	T	Y					L
E		S		G				W		O		I
R					E	U	P	H	O	R	I	C
M	E	A	T	S		R		A		G		A
O		R		P		S		T	R	A	I	T
R	A	G		R	E	I	G	N		N		E
E		U		E		N		O		Z		D
	R	E	V	E	R	E	N	T	I	A	L	

No. 16

A	P	P	L	A	U	S	E		H	A	L	L
P		L		R		U		C		L		I
P	H	O	T	O		L	E	A	P	I	N	G
R		V		M		L		R		E		H
O	P	E	R	A		E		B		N	I	T
X		R		T	A	N	G	O				F
I		S		H				H		S		I
M				E	S	S	A	Y		T		N
A	R	K		R		P		D	O	I	N	G
T		N		A		H		R		N		E
E	X	A	M	P	L	E		A	U	G	U	R
L		C		Y		R		T		E		E
Y	O	K	E		R	E	F	E	R	R	E	D

No. 17

M	A	D	M	A	N		W	H	I	T	E	N
Y		O		F		C		U		O		U
S		U		F		A	D	M	I	R	E	R
T	U	R	M	O	I	L		P		T		S
I				R		C		S	N	I	P	E
C	U	P	I	D		U				L		S
		E		S	U	L	K	S		L		
I		N				A		H	E	A	T	H
M	O	U	N	D		T		U				U
P		M		A		I	N	F	O	R	M	S
E	M	B	A	R	G	O		F		A		T
L		R		E		N		L		F		L
S	H	A	R	D	S		P	E	S	T	L	E

No. 18

I	F	F	Y		M	E	C	H	A	N	I	C
M		U		N		X		O		U		O
P	A	T	R	I	O	T		P	R	A	W	N
R		O		G		E		E		N		F
A	W	N		H		N		L	U	C	R	E
C				T	I	T	H	E		E		C
T		H		C				S		S		T
I		E		L	I	M	B	S				I
C	A	R	G	O		A		N		E	G	O
A		E		T		T		E		L		N
B	A	T	C	H		R	E	S	I	D	U	E
L		I		E		O		S		E		R
E	X	C	U	S	I	N	G		A	R	M	Y

No. 19

L	I	V	E	L	Y		S		A		F	
A		O			E	N	T	A	N	G	L	E
V	O	W			A		A		A		E	
I		E	S	P	R	I	T		C	U	E	S
S		L			S		U		O		C	
H	U	S	K	Y		S	T	U	N	N	E	D
			E		G		E		D			
A	L	G	E	R	I	A		C	A	B	A	L
	E		P		N		L			U		O
B	E	E	S		G	R	A	I	N	S		N
	W		A		H		N			H	U	G
B	A	C	K	P	A	C	K			E		E
	Y		E		M		Y	E	L	L	E	D

No. 20

No. 21

No. 22

No. 23

No. 24

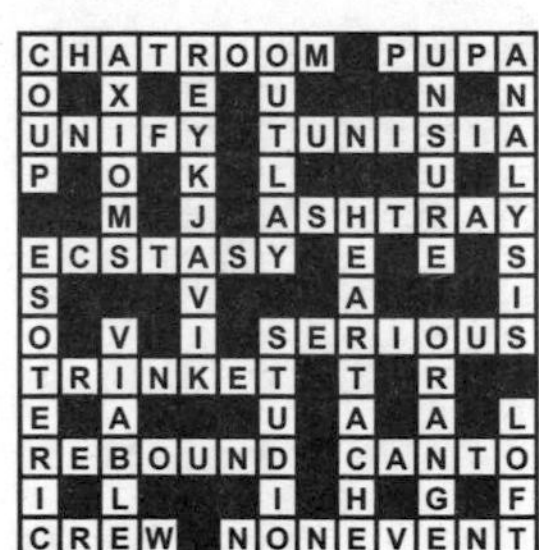

No. 25

M	O	D	I	F	I	E	D		B	E	A	U
A		E		L		N		C		T		N
T	O	A	D	Y		M	A	R	C	H	E	D
E		D		O		E		O		I		I
R	E	S	E	N	T	S		S	E	C	T	S
I		E		T		H		S				C
A	P	A	T	H	Y		S	C	A	M	P	I
L				E		S		O		A		P
I	N	L	A	W		C	O	U	N	S	E	L
S		E		A		A		N		O		I
T	O	D	D	L	E	R		T	E	N	O	N
I		G		L		C		R		R		E
C	H	E	W		D	E	W	Y	E	Y	E	D

No. 26

No. 27

E	A	T	S		H	A	R	D	S	H	I	P
X		E		C		B		I		O		E
P	A	N	T	H	E	R		A	L	T	A	R
R		E		I		U		G		T		C
E	N	T	E	R		P	A	R	V	E	N	U
S				O		T		A		S		S
S	I	T	U	P	S		S	M	I	T	E	S
I		R		R		C		M				I
O	V	E	R	A	L	L		A	U	D	I	O
N		A		C		I		T		U		N
I	N	S	E	T		N	A	I	R	O	B	I
S		O		O		C		C		M		S
M	O	N	A	R	C	H	Y		C	O	S	T

No. 28

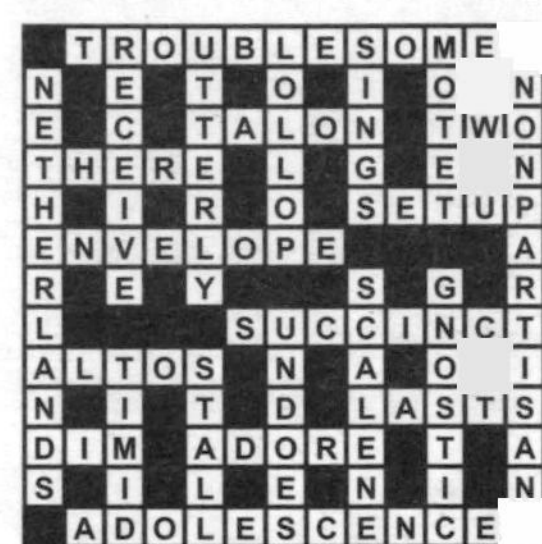

No. 29

No. 30

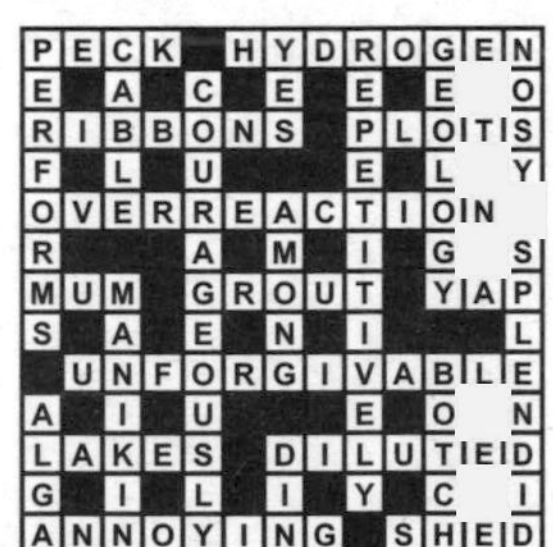

No. 31

	A	N	N	I	V	E	R	S	A	R	Y	
M		O		M		N		H		E		I
A		T		P	L	A	C	E		P	E	N
S	H	E	L	L		B		L		L		C
S		P		O		L		F	O	Y	E	R
P	R	A	I	R	I	E	S					E
R		D		E				J		M		M
O					A	C	C	O	L	A	D	E
D	O	M	E	S		O		U		L		N
U		A		P		S		R	O	A	S	T
C	O	T		L	U	M	E	N		R		A
E		C		A		I		A		I		L
	W	H	I	T	E	C	O	L	L	A	R	

No. 32

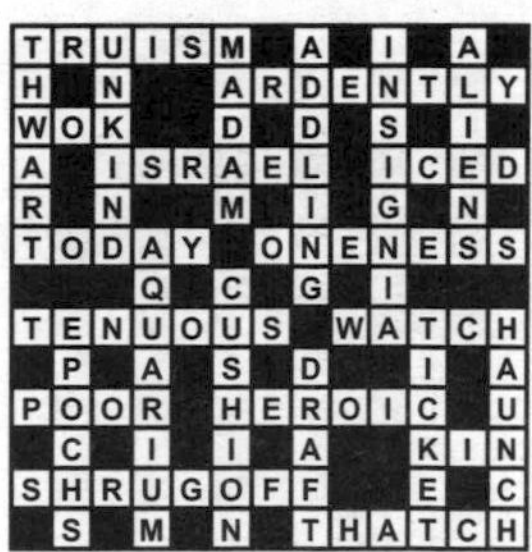

No. 33

No. 34

No. 35

No. 36

No. 37

S	H	A	M	P	O	O	S	■	H	U	R	T
I	■	V	■	E	■	C	■	■	■	N	■	O
C	L	A	M	P	■	C	H	A	N	C	E	L
K	■	T	■	P	■	U	■	■	■	L	■	E
■	■	A	■	E	■	P	I	O	N	E	E	R
P	O	R	T	R	A	Y	■	U	■	S	■	A
E	■	■	■	O	■	■	■	T	■	■	■	T
R	■	I	■	N	■	F	I	S	S	U	R	E
J	A	M	A	I	C	A	■	P	■	N	■	■
U	■	P	■	■	■	L	■	O	■	S	■	S
R	E	A	L	I	S	T	■	K	N	E	L	T
E	■	C	■	■	■	E	■	E	■	E	■	E
D	O	T	S	■	B	R	A	N	D	N	E	W

No. 38

M	A	N	A	M	A	■	O	P	I	N	E	D
I	■	I	■	E	■	C	■	A	■	E	■	U
S	■	L	■	T	■	O	U	T	L	A	S	T
F	R	E	S	H	E	N	■	C	■	T	■	I
I	■	■	■	O	■	T	■	H	E	N	C	E
T	A	M	E	D	■	I	■	■	■	E	■	S
■	■	A	■	S	I	N	U	S	■	S	■	■
O	■	P	■	■	■	U	■	H	U	S	K	S
B	U	M	P	S	■	A	■	A	■	■	■	I
L	■	A	■	T	■	L	Y	R	I	C	A	L
I	N	K	W	E	L	L	■	P	■	A	■	E
G	■	E	■	P	■	Y	■	E	■	K	■	N
E	G	R	E	S	S	■	I	N	S	E	C	T

No. 39

O	C	C	I	D	E	N	T	■	I	C	E	S
I	■	A	■	I	■	O	■	■	■	A	■	P
L	U	R	K	S	■	V	E	R	A	N	D	A
Y	■	M	■	C	■	E	■	■	■	V	■	C
■	■	E	■	R	■	L	E	A	K	A	G	E
M	O	N	K	E	Y	S	■	N	■	S	■	M
E	■	■	■	D	■	■	■	N	■	■	■	A
T	■	H	■	I	■	H	O	A	R	S	E	N
R	E	E	N	T	R	Y	■	P	■	U	■	■
I	■	L	■	■	■	B	■	U	■	P	■	T
C	L	I	M	B	E	R	■	R	U	P	E	E
A	■	U	■	■	■	I	■	N	■	L	■	N
L	I	M	A	■	A	D	J	A	C	E	N	T

No. 40

No. 41

No. 42

No. 43

	C		T		M		C	L	I	C	H	E
B	A	S	E	B	A	L	L			O		I
	V		T		N		O			W	A	G
P	O	S	H		A	B	S	O	R	B		H
	R		E		C		E			O		T
S	T	A	R	T	L	E		G	L	Y	P	H
			E		E		C		I			
H	E	R	D	S		R	O	S	T	R	U	M
A		I			A		U		E		N	
N		B	E	R	L	I	N		R	O	W	S
G	A	B			O		T		A		E	
U		O			F	O	R	E	T	E	L	L
P	U	N	D	I	T		Y		E		L	

No. 44

D	E	C	A	M	P		O	B	T	A	I	N
I		O		A		C		O		P		U
S		M		R		O	N	G	O	I	N	G
C	H	E	R	V	I	L		U		A		G
O				E		D		S	E	R	V	E
S	T	O	O	L		B				I		T
		V		S	P	L	I	T		S		
S		E				O		R	A	T	T	Y
L	Y	R	E	S		O		A				E
O		C		I		D	I	P	L	O	M	A
W	R	A	N	G	L	E		E		A		R
E		S		N		D		Z		T		L
D	E	T	E	S	T		J	E	R	S	E	Y

No. 45

	E	S	T	A	B	L	I	S	H	E	D	
A		A		G		O		T		X		A
B	I	D		A	M	I	D	E		H		S
B		L		P		T		R	A	I	L	S
R	H	Y	M	E		E		I		B		I
E					D	R	I	L	L	I	N	G
V		D		G				E		T		N
I	N	E	Q	U	I	T	Y					M
A		B		E		U		B	I	B	L	E
T	E	A	M	S		N		O		U		N
E		U		S	O	N	A	R		F	A	T
D		C		E		E		O		F		S
	G	H	O	S	T	L	I	N	E	S	S	

No. 46

No. 47

No. 48

No. 49

S	A	F	E		P	A	S	T	R	A	M	I
E		J		V		N		R		N		N
L	O	O	K	O	U	T		A	N	G	S	T
F		R		C		H		N		E		R
C	O	D		I		E		S	A	L	S	A
O				F	O	R	U	M		U		N
N		C		E				I		S		S
S		E		R	O	C	K	S				I
C	O	N	G	O		H		S		N	A	G
I		T		U		O		I		Y		E
O	P	A	L	S		S	H	O	W	M	A	N
U		U		L		E		N		P		C
S	P	R	A	Y	I	N	G		S	H	O	E

No. 50

No. 51

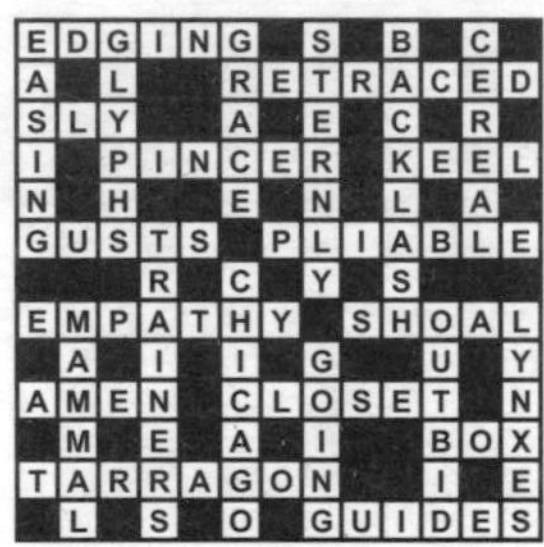

No. 52

No. 53

No. 54

No. 55

U	P	O	N		M	U	R	M	U	R	E	D
N		S		O		N		U		E		I
I	N	C	I	S	O	R		L	O	C	U	S
M		A		T		I		T		I		A
P	U	R	E	E		P	A	I	N	T	E	D
E				N		E		L		E		V
A	D	A	P	T	S		S	I	E	S	T	A
C		L		A		S		N				N
H	A	B	I	T	A	T		G	R	A	F	T
A		A		I		O		U		D		A
B	I	N	G	O		L	E	A	V	I	N	G
L		I		U		E		L		E		E
E	L	A	P	S	I	N	G		R	U	E	D

No. 56

A	R	T	I	F	I	C	E		I	D	E	A
L		R		I		O		T		O		B
T	R	I	B	E		P	E	R	T	U	R	B
E		G		L		I		A		S		R
R	A	G	E	D		E		N		E	W	E
N		E		G	I	R	L	S				V
A		R		L				F		G		I
T				A	L	I	V	E		R		A
I	N	N		S		N		R	O	O	S	T
V		A		S		F		A		W		I
E	X	T	R	E	M	E		B	A	N	J	O
L		A		S		C		L		U		N
Y	A	L	E		A	T	T	E	M	P	T	S

No. 57

	S	U	P	E	R	L	A	T	I	V	E	
C		N		N		A		E		I		P
O		A		G	L	U	O	N		T	O	Y
M	O	R	A	L		R		C		A		R
M		M		I		E		H	E	L	L	O
U	T	E	N	S	I	L	S					T
N		D		H				D		A		E
I					P	E	R	I	O	D	I	C
C	L	A	N	G		S		S		J		H
A		L		A		C		C	R	O	W	N
T	U	G		B	R	A	V	O		U		I
E		A		L		P		R		R		C
	N	E	V	E	R	E	N	D	I	N	G	

No. 58

N	A	V	E		D	O	G	F	I	G	H	T
A		E		M		U		R		R		E
M	O	R	D	A	N	T		O	Z	O	N	E
E		B		L				N		U		M
D	I	S	I	N	F	E	C	T	A	N	T	
R				O		D		I		D		L
O	R	B		U	N	I	T	S		S	E	A
P		O		R		T		P				R
	P	L	A	I	N	S	A	I	L	I	N	G
S		S		S				E		N		E
K	E	T	C	H		P	I	C	K	L	E	S
I		E		E		U		E		A		S
P	A	R	A	D	I	G	M		L	Y	R	E

No. 59

D	O	L	T		C	A	S	H	M	E	R	E
O		A		D		N		O		X		F
U	N	T	Y	I	N	G		M	O	T	I	F
B		E		S		O		E		E		E
L	U	X		A		R		L	I	N	E	R
E				G	L	A	R	E		D		V
C		D		R				S		S		E
H		R		E	D	G	E	S				S
E	L	I	D	E		A		N		A	R	C
C		B		A		M		E		R		E
K	E	B	A	B		B	A	S	T	I	O	N
E		L		L		L		S		S		C
D	E	E	P	E	N	E	D		W	E	R	E

No. 60

H	A	P	P	I	E	S	T		A	U	R	A
A		A		N		U				R		B
V	A	U	N	T		P	I	E	R	C	E	S
E		S		E		P				H		T
		E		G		L	U	C	K	I	E	R
E	L	D	E	R	L	Y		O		N		U
S				I				N				S
C		C		T		A	B	S	O	L	V	E
A	L	L	O	Y	E	D		T		E		
P		A				O		A		V		D
I	N	S	U	L	A	R		B	R	I	B	E
N		S				E		L		E		F
G	U	Y	S		F	R	I	E	N	D	L	Y

No. 61

B	L	U	E	B	I	R	D		O	V	E	R
L		N		U		E		E		I		E
U	N	D	E	R		M	A	N	A	G	U	A
R		Y		G		A		T		I		S
	K	I	L	L	E	R	W	H	A	L	E	S
H		N		A		K		U				E
A	U	G	U	R	Y		A	S	I	D	E	S
N				A		A		I		R		S
D	O	U	B	L	E	D	E	A	L	E	R	
L		N		A		S		S		S		D
I	N	F	E	R	N	O		T	A	S	T	Y
N		I		M		R		I		E		E
G	E	T	S		O	B	S	C	U	R	E	D

No. 62

No. 63

No. 64

No. 65

No. 66

No. 67

B	O	U	N	C	E	R	S		M	Y	T	H
U		P		A		U		S		O		O
S	P	E	L	L		B	R	O	A	D	E	N
H		N		L		R		M		E		E
	A	D	D	I	T	I	O	N	A	L	L	Y
C		E		G		C		A				B
O	R	D	E	R	S		I	M	P	E	D	E
M				A		S		B		L		E
M	A	S	S	P	R	O	D	U	C	E	D	
O		H		H		F		L		M		S
N	E	A	R	E	S	T		I	N	E	P	T
L		R		R		E		S		N		A
Y	A	K	S		A	N	I	M	A	T	O	R

No. 68

C	A	P	T	A	I	N	S		H	A	I	R
O		R		S		O				V		O
R	I	O	T	S		Z	O	O	L	O	G	Y
D		M		U		Z				U		A
		P		R		L	O	G	I	C	A	L
S	I	T	U	A	T	E		E		H		I
P				N				N				S
E		A		C		R	E	E	N	A	C	T
C	O	L	L	E	G	E		R		C		
I		S				P		A		C		S
A	L	A	N	I	N	E		T	O	U	C	H
L		C				N		O		S		I
S	P	E	D		S	T	U	R	G	E	O	N

No. 69

H	O	S	T	E	L	R	Y		M	A	L	I
Y		T		C		E		C		F		R
P	I	A	N	O		P	R	O	F	F	E	R
O		R		N		E		M		I		E
C	O	R	P	O	R	A		M	I	X	U	P
H		E		M		L		E				R
O	R	D	A	I	N		I	N	C	I	T	E
N				C		A		S		N		S
D	O	G	M	A		B	L	U	S	H	E	S
R		A		L		J		R		A		I
I	M	P	U	L	S	E		A	D	L	I	B
A		E		Y		C		T		E		L
C	A	S	K		A	T	T	E	N	D	E	E

No. 70

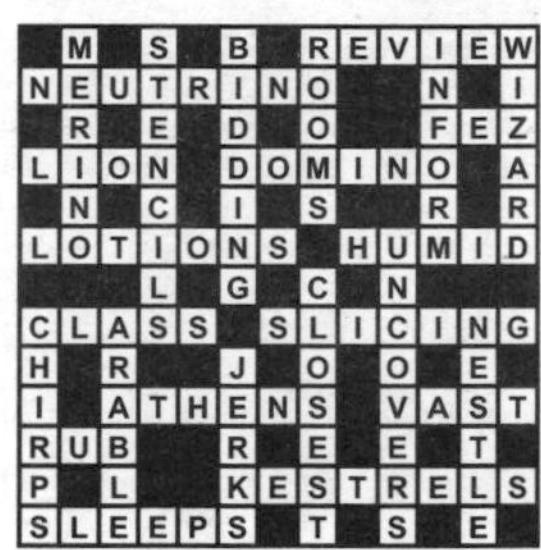

	M		S		B		R	E	V	I	E	W
N	E	U	T	R	I	N	O			N		I
	R		E		D		O			F	E	Z
L	I	O	N		D	O	M	I	N	O		A
	N		C		I		S			R		R
L	O	T	I	O	N	S		H	U	M	I	D
			L		G		C		N			
C	L	A	S	S		S	L	I	C	I	N	G
H		R			J		O		O		E	
I		A	T	H	E	N	S		V	A	S	T
R	U	B			R		E		E		T	
P		L			K	E	S	T	R	E	L	S
S	L	E	E	P	S		T		S		E	

No. 71

C	U	B	I	S	T		F	U	S	S	E	D
A		E		H		D		N		U		E
S		E		U		E	N	D	I	N	G	S
H	E	P	A	T	I	C		I		B		I
E				O		E		D	A	L	E	S
W	H	I	F	F		I				O		T
		N		F	E	V	E	R		C		
S		T				I		H	I	K	E	R
T	H	I	E	F		N		O				A
I		M		A		G	A	M	B	L	E	D
C	H	A	T	T	E	L		B		O		I
K		T		E		Y		U		A		A
Y	I	E	L	D	S		U	S	E	F	U	L

No. 72

C	A	T	A	P	U	L	T		R	O	O	F
O		O		R		O		D		W		A
N	U	R	S	E		C	H	I	G	N	O	N
T		O		F		U		S		E		T
R	U	N	N	E	R	S		A	O	R	T	A
A		T		R		T		P				S
V	I	O	L	E	T		U	P	R	O	O	T
E				N		L		O		U		I
N	I	G	H	T		I	D	I	O	T	I	C
T		R		I		N		N		P		A
I	S	O	L	A	T	E		T	R	A	W	L
O		U		L		A		E		C		L
N	A	P	S		D	R	U	D	G	E	R	Y

No. 73

D	E	B	I	L	I	T	Y		L	A	M	B
U		O		U		A				L		R
N	A	V	A	L		T	E	Q	U	I	L	A
E		I		L		T				B		G
		N		A		L	O	O	T	I	N	G
T	R	E	M	B	L	E		V		S		A
O				I				E				R
R		E		E		A	I	R	L	I	F	T
R	E	V	I	S	E	D		D		N		
E		A				A		R		F		T
N	U	D	G	I	N	G		A	B	I	D	E
T		E				I		F		R		X
S	U	D	S		C	O	N	T	E	M	P	T

No. 74

No. 75

S	O	F	T		S	T	I	F	L	I	N	G
Y		O		C		H		R		C		I
N	U	R	T	U	R	E		A	R	E	A	S
O		T		R				U		B		T
P	O	S	T	M	E	R	I	D	I	E	M	
S				U		E		U		R		B
I	M	P		D	R	A	W	L		G	E	L
S		I		G		L		E				U
	I	N	T	E	R	M	I	N	A	B	L	E
M		B		O				T		R		B
A	G	A	I	N		V	U	L	T	U	R	E
M		L		L		I		Y		T		L
A	L	L	E	Y	W	A	Y		W	E	A	L

No. 76

No. 77

No. 78

No. 79

ASTRONOMERS
R K I A E I P
O E DOTED FOR
CITED I I T E
K C L V CASED
ATHLETES E
N Y S C P C
D TOILSOME
REVEL C E R S
O A O U MYTHS
LUG FALSE I O
L U T A N C R
DEHYDRATION

No. 80

No. 81

No. 82

No. 83

No. 84

No. 85

P	U	M	I	C	E		S	H	A	P	E	D
R		E		U		C		I		A		A
O		M		D		O	U	T	I	N	G	S
T	R	O	D	D	E	N		C		O		H
E				L		T		H	O	R	S	E
M	O	U	S	E		R				A		S
		N		D	R	A	W	S		M		
P		F				S		W	E	A	V	E
L	E	A	D	S		T		I				N
U		S		C		I	N	F	A	N	T	S
S	I	T	D	O	W	N		T		A		U
E		E		P		G		E		P		R
S	E	N	D	E	R		F	R	E	E	Z	E

No. 86

No. 87

No. 88

No. 89

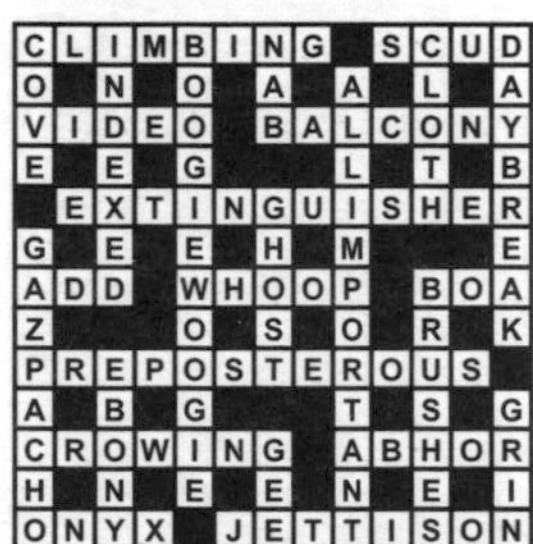

No. 90

No. 91

	A	G	G	R	A	V	A	T	I	N	G	
E		A		E		I		O		I		C
L	A	P		S	A	V	E	R		G		H
A		E		T		A		S	H	E	E	R
B	I	D	E	S		C		I		R		O
O					D	E	M	O	T	I	O	N
R		C		C				N		A		O
A	V	O	C	A	D	O	S					G
T		M		L		W		V	O	T	E	R
E	M	P	T	Y		N		I		O		A
L		E		P	E	E	L	S		A	S	P
Y		R		S		R		O		S		H
	R	E	M	O	N	S	T	R	A	T	E	

No. 92

No. 93

R	E	A	P	P	E	A	R		L	A	V	A
I		R		R		R		A		S		S
G	A	M	M	A		O	P	P	O	S	E	S
H		R		I		U		P		E		E
T	R	E	S	S	E	S		R	O	T	O	R
E		S		E		E		O				T
O	T	T	A	W	A		S	A	F	A	R	I
U				O		L		C		C		V
S	P	O	O	R		A	T	H	L	E	T	E
N		G		T		W		A		T		N
E	A	R	T	H	L	Y		B	R	O	K	E
S		E		Y		E		L		N		S
S	O	S	O		F	R	E	E	Z	E	R	S

No. 94

No. 95

No. 96

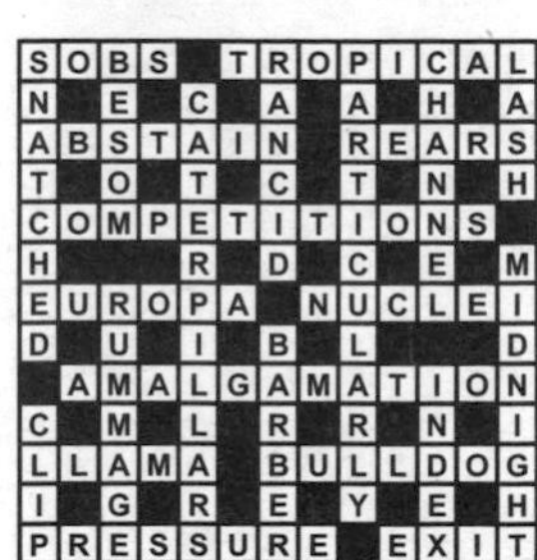

No. 97

C	U	B	E		E	T	C	H	I	N	G	S
O		U		S		A		E		E		T
N	U	R	S	I	N	G		A	M	A	Z	E
S		M		G				R		T		P
P	L	A	I	N	C	L	O	T	H	E	S	
I				I		A		R		N		O
R	A	M		F	A	R	C	E		S	A	P
E		O		I		V		N				E
	S	P	I	C	K	A	N	D	S	P	A	N
B		P		A				I		E		E
A	V	I	A	N		B	O	N	E	D	R	Y
R		N		C		E		G		A		E
B	A	G	U	E	T	T	E		C	L	A	D

No. 98

S	P	L	A	S	H	E	S		B	A	N	G
E		A		I		R				L		L
E	B	B	E	D		R	E	G	A	L	I	A
P		E		E		I				E		S
		L		L		N	O	O	D	L	E	S
G	O	S	L	I	N	G		V		E		F
L				N				E				U
A		O		E		C	A	R	A	M	E	L
C	R	U	I	S	E	R		J		O		
I		T				A		O		S		I
E	E	R	I	E	S	T		Y	E	A	R	N
R		U				E		E		I		N
S	I	N	G		P	R	E	D	I	C	T	S

No. 99

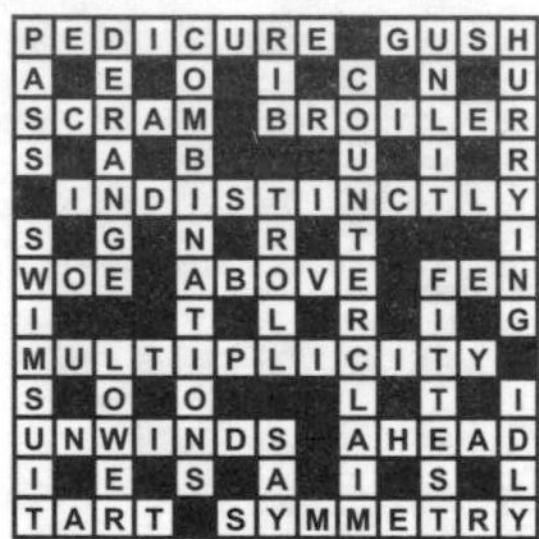

P	E	D	I	C	U	R	E		G	U	S	H
A		E		O		I		C		N		U
S	C	R	A	M		B	R	O	I	L	E	R
S		A		B				U		I		R
	I	N	D	I	S	T	I	N	C	T	L	Y
S		G		N		R		T				I
W	O	E		A	B	O	V	E		F	E	N
I				T		L		R		I		G
M	U	L	T	I	P	L	I	C	I	T	Y	
S		O		O				L		T		I
U	N	W	I	N	D	S		A	H	E	A	D
I		E		S		A		I		S		L
T	A	R	T		S	Y	M	M	E	T	R	Y

No. 100

	F		P		S		J	E	T	S	A	M
J	A	P	A	N	E	S	E			U		I
	C		T		T		W			B	E	D
C	I	T	E		T	H	E	I	S	M		D
	L		N		E		L			I		A
V	E	N	T	U	R	E		D	I	T	T	Y
			E		S		S		N			
C	U	B	E	S		P	U	T	D	O	W	N
H		A			T		P		O		A	
O		L	A	T	H	E	R		L	O	N	E
P	O	T			U		E		E		T	
P		I			D	O	M	I	N	I	O	N
Y	A	C	H	T	S		E		T		N	

No. 101

U	R	D	U		S	A	U	S	A	G	E	S
N		E		C		C		A		L		E
A	F	F	R	O	N	T		C	R	A	W	L
N		E		M		I		R		C		F
T	H	R	U	M		V	O	I	C	I	N	G
I				E		E		L		E		O
C	R	O	W	N	S		H	E	N	R	Y	V
I		U		C		S		G				E
P	O	T	T	E	R	Y		I	N	C	U	R
A		F		M		S		O		H		N
T	I	L	D	E		T	S	U	N	A	M	I
E		O		N		E		S		I		N
D	O	W	N	T	I	M	E		F	R	O	G

No. 102

M	A	S	T	H	E	A	D		T	O	N	E
A		U		A		V		W		R		N
R	E	C	A	P		E	C	H	O	I	N	G
S		R		P		N		O		B		A
	B	O	D	Y	B	U	I	L	D	I	N	G
A		S		G		E		E				I
T	R	E	M	O	R		S	H	O	O	I	N
Y				L		M		E		C		G
P	R	O	T	U	B	E	R	A	N	C	E	
I		P		C		N		R		L		K
C	R	I	C	K	E	T		T	R	U	C	E
A		N		Y		A		E		D		E
L	E	E	K		B	L	U	D	G	E	O	N

No. 103

	U	N	N	E	C	E	S	S	A	R	Y	
E		A		M		N		C		E		A
X		T		P	A	S	T	A		P	I	T
C	R	U	E	T		U		R		E		M
E		R		I		E		F	O	L	I	O
P	R	E	T	E	N	D	S					S
T		S		D				F		L		P
I					C	E	N	O	T	A	P	H
O	B	E	Y	S		N		R		C		E
N		N		E		J		F	L	O	O	R
A	W	E		D	I	O	D	E		N		I
L		M		G		I		I		I		C
	C	Y	B	E	R	N	E	T	I	C	S	

No. 104

F	I	L	T	H	Y		A	F	R	A	I	D
L		O		E		I		U		B		E
O		G		R		N	O	S	T	R	I	L
C	R	O	S	S	E	D		E		O		A
K				E		I		S	O	G	G	Y
S	W	E	L	L		F				A		S
		X		F	I	F	T	Y		T		
A		P				E		T	W	E	A	K
B	L	E	N	D		R		T				I
O		D		R		E	N	R	A	G	E	D
U	N	I	C	O	R	N		I		I		N
N		T		V		T		U		R		E
D	E	E	M	E	D		E	M	P	L	O	Y

No. 105

E	X	E	M	P	T	E	D		H	A	L	T
R		V		O		X				C		A
G	U	E	S	T		C	A	S	H	I	E	R
O		N		P		E				D		T
		T		O		S	T	A	T	I	O	N
D	I	S	C	U	S	S		L		C		E
I				R				L				S
S		M		R		G	R	E	A	S	E	S
C	H	O	R	I	Z	O		V		T		
O		U				V		I		R		T
U	P	S	U	R	G	E		A	M	I	T	Y
N		S				R		T		C		P
T	O	E	S		U	N	S	E	T	T	L	E

No. 106

No. 107

No. 108

No. 109

R	A	I	N	C	O	A	T		S	M	U	G
O		N		O		I		S		A		I
P	I	T	O	N		M	E	L	A	N	I	N
E		O		C				E		T		G
	I	N	T	E	R	M	E	D	I	A	T	E
U		E		N		O		G				R
N	O	D		T	I	T	L	E		I	L	L
I				R		T		H		V		Y
C	O	L	L	A	B	O	R	A	T	O	R	
Y		Y		T				M		R		E
C	H	I	M	E	R	A		M	O	I	S	T
L		N		D		S		E		E		N
E	D	G	Y		C	H	A	R	I	S	M	A

No. 110

No. 111

T	R	E	N	C	H	E	S		R	H	E	A
A		X		O		R		U		A		D
S	A	T	I	N		A	N	N	E	L	I	D
K		I		T				P		V		I
	U	N	D	E	R	G	A	R	M	E	N	T
C		C		M		R		O				I
H	U	T		P	R	O	O	F		W	H	O
I				T		O		I		R		N
C	O	N	F	I	R	M	A	T	I	O	N	
K		O		B				A		U		O
P	A	T	E	L	L	A		B	E	G	I	N
E		C		E		I		L		H		L
A	C	H	Y		U	R	G	E	N	T	L	Y

No. 112

No. 113

No. 114

No. 115

M	A	S	S	E	U	R	S		O	U	R	S
O		E		N		A				N		I
B	I	N	G	E		B	E	H	A	V	E	D
S		O		R		B				E		E
		R		G		I	C	E	P	I	C	K
N	E	A	T	E	S	T		L		L		I
A				T				I				C
U		A		I		G	I	M	M	I	C	K
T	O	B	A	C	C	O		I		R		
I		A				B		N		O		A
C	I	T	A	D	E	L		A	N	N	E	X
A		E				I		T		E		E
L	I	D	S		I	N	T	E	N	D	E	D

No. 116

	W		C		B		S	T	E	E	D	S
M	I	S	H	M	A	S	H			N		T
	G		A		N		E			J	O	Y
T	W	I	N		Q	U	A	R	T	O		L
	A		N		U		F			Y		E
I	M	P	E	D	E	D		R	O	S	E	S
			L		T		R		P			
C	O	P	S	E		V	A	M	P	I	R	E
A		R			P		N		O		E	
L		A	R	I	S	E	S		S	O	F	A
L	A	Y			A		A		I		U	
U		E			L	O	C	A	T	I	N	G
S	O	D	I	U	M		K		E		D	

No. 117

No. 118

No. 119

No. 120

No. 121

D	E	M	O	C	R	A	T		I	B	I	S
R		I		O		R		B		A		I
A	R	S	O	N		E	Q	U	A	T	E	D
B		E		T				S		H		E
	F	R	I	E	N	D	L	I	N	E	S	S
S		L		M		R		N				T
C	R	Y		P	R	O	B	E		D	U	E
R				O		L		S		E		P
E	F	F	O	R	T	L	E	S	S	L	Y	
A		U		A				L		A		S
M	O	N	G	R	E	L		I	D	Y	L	L
E		N		Y		A		K		E		A
D	A	Y	S		A	D	D	E	N	D	U	M

No. 122

No. 123

No. 124

No. 125

No. 126

No. 127

S	A	P	P	H	I	R	E		A	T	O	M
A		H		E		E		T		H		A
K	N	O	W	N		V	I	R	T	U	E	S
E		E		C				I		M		T
	I	N	T	E	L	L	I	G	I	B	L	E
S		I		F		A		O				R
T	U	X		O	F	T	E	N		T	E	E
R				R		T		O		E		D
O	V	E	R	W	H	E	L	M	I	N	G	
N		A						E		D		O
G	A	S	T	R	I	C		T	H	R	E	W
E		E		D		H		R		I		L
R	I	D	E		B	I	C	Y	C	L	E	S

No. 128

No. 129

No. 130

No. 131

No. 132

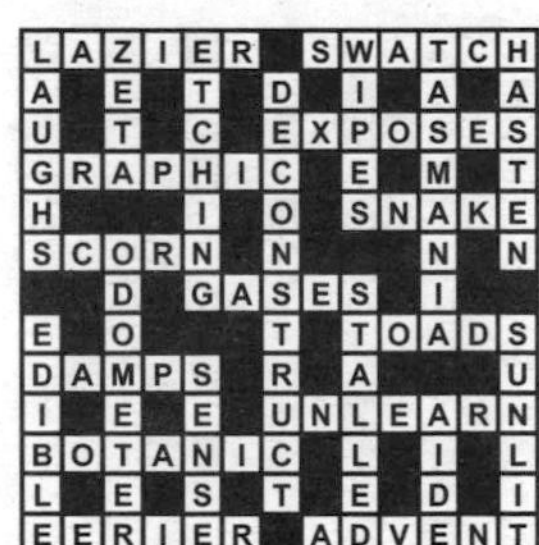

No. 133

C	U	S	P		S	C	U	D	D	I	N	G
R		Q		M		R		I		N		O
E	M	U	L	A	T	E		C	A	G	E	D
S		I		G		A		T		R		S
C	A	B	I	N	E	T	M	A	K	E	R	
E				I		E		T		S		M
N	O	T	I	F	Y		B	O	N	S	A	I
T		O		I		L		R				S
	G	R	A	C	I	O	U	S	N	E	S	S
S		R		E		O		H		I		P
T	I	E	I	N		S	H	I	N	G	L	E
O		N		C		E		P		H		N
P	A	T	T	E	R	N	S		S	T	U	D

No. 134

D	E	C	I	P	H	E	R		D	U	E	L
O		H		R		S		M		R		E
U	S	A	G	E		S	O	A	P	B	O	X
B		G		R		A		T		A		I
L	A	R	G	E	L	Y		T	U	N	I	C
E		I		Q		S		E				O
C	O	N	C	U	R		F	R	Y	I	N	G
R				I		S		O		N		R
O	B	O	E	S		T	A	F	F	E	T	A
S		N		I		R		F		X		P
S	H	I	A	T	S	U		A	W	A	S	H
E		O		E		N		C		C		E
R	U	N	G		A	G	I	T	A	T	O	R

No. 135

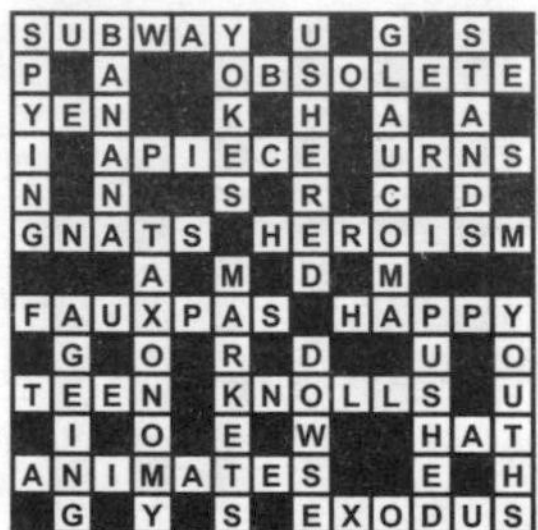

S	U	B	W	A	Y		U		G		S	
P		A			O	B	S	O	L	E	T	E
Y	E	N			K		H		A		A	
I		A	P	I	E	C	E		U	R	N	S
N		N			S		R		C		D	
G	N	A	T	S		H	E	R	O	I	S	M
			A		M		D		M			
F	A	U	X	P	A	S		H	A	P	P	Y
	G		O		R		D			U		O
T	E	E	N		K	N	O	L	L	S		U
	I		O		E		W			H	A	T
A	N	I	M	A	T	E	S			E		H
	G		Y		S		E	X	O	D	U	S

No. 136

S	U	S	T	A	I	N	S		L	O	W	S
P		U		C		E		D		S		T
L	Y	R	I	C		W	A	R	L	I	K	E
E		G		E		E		E		E		P
N	E	E	D	L	E	S		S	Y	R	U	P
D		O		E		T		S				I
I	G	N	O	R	E		A	I	R	M	A	N
F				A		B		N		I		G
E	R	E	C	T		E	N	G	I	N	E	S
R		V		I		F		D		U		T
O	R	I	N	O	C	O		O	U	T	D	O
U		C		N		U		W		I		N
S	I	T	S		E	L	O	N	G	A	T	E

No. 137

A	V	A	I	L	S		A		J		B	
D		R			H	O	S	T	A	G	E	S
D	A	M			E		C		L		E	
E		I	N	S	A	N	E		A	R	T	Y
R		N			R		N		P		L	
S	A	G	E	S		S	T	E	E	P	E	N
			T		S		S		N			
T	R	A	C	H	E	A		B	O	W	E	D
	O		E		R		G			O		E
P	O	U	T		V	I	R	I	L	E		C
	T		E		I		O			F	A	R
R	E	T	R	A	C	T	S			U		E
	D		A		E		S	V	E	L	T	E

No. 138

S	O	N	G		I	N	E	D	I	B	L	E
U		A		D		O		E		E		Z
B	A	S	S	I	S	T		S	I	T	A	R
S		T		S		I		P		W		A
O	L	Y	M	P	I	C	G	A	M	E	S	
N				L		E		I		E		S
I	S	O	B	A	R		B	R	O	N	C	O
C		V		C		A		I				M
	D	E	T	E	R	M	I	N	A	B	L	E
S		R		M		O		G		L		W
W	E	D	G	E		U	N	L	E	A	S	H
A		U		N		R		Y		C		A
T	R	E	A	T	I	S	E		S	K	I	T

No. 139

C	U	B	I	S	M		E		S		B	
A		O			E	S	P	E	C	I	A	L
V	E	X			R		I		E		S	
E		F	J	O	R	D	S		N	E	A	T
A		U			Y		T		A		L	
T	A	L	K	S		C	L	A	R	E	T	S
			E		A		E		I			
S	W	A	Y	I	N	G		J	O	K	E	R
	H	B			T		S			E		A
P	O	L	O		I	N	C	O	M	E		N
	L		A		Q		U			P	E	T
A	L	L	R	O	U	N	D			E		E
	Y		D		E		S	C	O	R	E	D

No. 140

H	E	P	T	A	G	O	N		G	A	L	L
E		U		N		N				F		O
R	O	B	E	S		I	N	S	U	R	E	D
O		L		W		O				I		E
		I		E		N	O	T	I	C	E	S
E	S	C	O	R	T	S		R		A		T
N				I				I				A
T		R		N		A	S	U	N	D	E	R
E	M	E	R	G	E	S		M		R		
R		D				T		P		I		G
I	N	D	E	P	T	H		H	O	V	E	L
N		E				M		E		E		A
G	U	N	K		S	A	D	D	E	N	E	D

No. 141

S	U	P	P	O	R	T	S		B	L	O	C
E		L		B		H		A		A		O
L	E	A	K	S		R	E	U	N	I	O	N
F		T		C		U		T		R		T
C	H	E	R	U	B	S		H	A	S	T	E
O		A		R		H		E				N
N	O	U	G	A	T		E	N	R	O	O	T
T				N		C		T		M		E
A	D	A	P	T		R	E	I	G	N	E	D
I		I		I		U		C		I		N
N	E	M	E	S	I	S		A	M	B	L	E
E		E		M		T		T		U		S
D	A	D	S		A	S	S	E	S	S	E	S

No. 142

D	A	T	A	B	A	S	E		J	A	V	A
I		U		R		K				K		N
C	A	N	O	E		I	T	A	L	I	C	S
E		D		A		R				M		W
		R		K		T	E	N	A	B	L	E
P	L	A	Y	E	R	S		I		O		R
A				V				G				E
M		S		E		S	C	H	O	L	A	R
P	E	T	U	N	I	A		T		A		
H		A				I		C		G		D
L	I	T	E	R	A	L		L	O	O	S	E
E		I				O		U		O		A
T	A	C	T		T	R	I	B	U	N	A	L

No. 143

F	O	R	E	S	T		E	S	T	H	E	R
O		O		O		C		P		A		A
S		A		L		O	B	E	L	I	S	K
S	I	R	L	O	I	N		C		R		I
I				I		S		K	I	L	N	S
L	A	C	E	S		C				E		H
		O		T	O	I	L	S		S		
D		M				O		P	E	S	K	Y
A	M	B	I	T		U		U				E
N		I		E		S	Y	R	I	A	N	A
C	O	N	C	E	A	L		R		L		R
E		E		N		Y		E		T		N
R	A	D	I	S	H		I	D	I	O	M	S

No. 144

	O	V	E	R	B	E	A	R	I	N	G	
S		O		E		N		E		U		E
P	E	W		T	U	R	F	S		L		V
E		E		R		I		P	U	L	S	E
C	A	D	D	Y		C		O		I		R
T					T	H	A	N	K	F	U	L
A		S		T				D		Y		A
C	O	H	E	R	E	N	T					S
U		A		E		E		C	O	M	E	T
L	A	M	B	S		B		A		A		I
A		P		T	A	U	N	T		K	E	N
R		O		L		L		C		E		G
	F	O	R	E	F	A	T	H	E	R	S	

No. 145

P	I	P	E		A	S	P	I	R	I	N	G
R		E		U		T		L		N		O
E	S	T	O	N	I	A		L	E	V	E	L
M		A		A		D		U		O		D
E	E	L		C		I		S	O	L	V	E
D				C	O	A	S	T		V		N
I		P		U				R		E		J
T		R		S	O	F	I	A				U
A	G	E	N	T		L		T		W	E	B
T		V		O		A		I		A		I
I	D	I	O	M		S	N	O	R	K	E	L
O		E		E		H		N		E		E
N	O	W	A	D	A	Y	S		O	N	C	E

No. 146

A	C	H	I	N	G		S		C		C	
D		U			I	M	P	R	O	V	E	D
D	I	D			V		O		C		L	
L		D	E	M	E	A	N		K	I	L	T
E		L			R		G		A		A	
D	W	E	L	L		J	E	S	T	E	R	S
			A		C		S		O			
B	R	A	V	E	L	Y		P	O	S	E	S
	O		E		O		A			W		T
T	U	R	N		S	A	T	I	R	E		A
	T		D		U		O			D	O	G
C	E	R	E	B	R	U	M			E		E
	R		R		E		S	T	I	N	T	S

No. 147

C	O	L	L	I	E	R	Y		A	G	A	R
A		O		N		A		E		R		E
F	L	O	O	D		N	O	X	I	O	U	S
E		S		E				H		W		I
	B	E	S	P	E	C	T	A	C	L	E	D
S		L		E		I		U				I
T	R	Y		N	O	R	M	S		S	O	N
O				D		C		T		E		G
M	A	T	H	E	M	A	T	I	C	A	L	
A		O		N				V		G		G
C	O	P	Y	C	A	T		E	Q	U	A	L
H		I		E		O		L		L		U
S	A	C	K		P	O	L	Y	G	L	O	T

No. 148

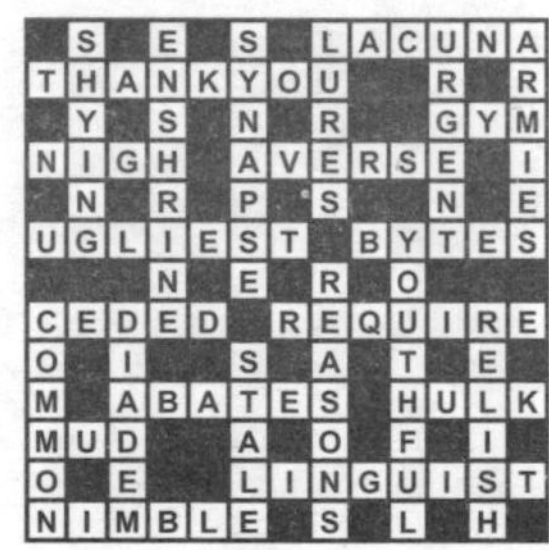

	S		E		S		L	A	C	U	N	A
T	H	A	N	K	Y	O	U			R		R
	Y		S		N		R			G	Y	M
N	I	G	H		A	V	E	R	S	E		I
	N		R		P		S			N		E
U	G	L	I	E	S	T		B	Y	T	E	S
			N		E		R		O			
C	E	D	E	D		R	E	Q	U	I	R	E
O		I			S		A		T		E	
M		A	B	A	T	E	S		H	U	L	K
M	U	D			A		O		F		I	
O		E			L	I	N	G	U	I	S	T
N	I	M	B	L	E		S		L		H	

No. 149

	E	L	E	P	H	A	N	T	I	N	E	
H		I		A		L		A		O		C
O	A	K		N	O	U	N	S		V		A
M		E		E		M		T	H	E	I	R
E	A	S	E	L		N		E		L		D
O					L	I	B	R	E	T	T	I
S		B		A				S		Y		O
T	H	U	R	S	D	A	Y					G
A		R		E		V		B	I	T	E	R
S	T	R	I	P		O		O		A		A
I		I		T	W	I	N	S		C	A	P
S		T		I		D		O		K		H
	C	O	N	C	I	S	E	N	E	S	S	

No. 150

C	O	P	Y		B	E	R	I	B	E	R	I
O		R		A		X		N		N		N
S	T	O	P	G	A	P		C	O	M	I	C
T		S		R		O		O		A		O
E	V	E		I		S		M	A	S	O	N
F				C	H	E	E	P		S		V
F		T		U				A		E		E
E		R		L	E	V	E	R				N
C	H	A	R	T		E		A		P	H	I
T		F		U		L		B		E		E
I	N	F	E	R		V	I	L	L	A	I	N
V		I		A		E		E		K		C
E	S	C	A	L	A	T	E		I	S	L	E

No. 151

	A	P	P	L	I	C	A	T	I	O	N	
A		I		A		L		A		S		R
L	A	X		R	O	O	K	S		T		E
L		E		K		U		S	A	R	I	S
P	I	L	L	S		D		E		I		P
O					C	Y	C	L	I	C	A	L
W		S		A				S		H		E
E	X	H	I	B	I	T	S					N
R		I		Y		E		B	A	S	E	D
F	U	M	E	S		D		I		E		E
U		M		S	H	I	P	S		W	I	N
L		E		A		U		O		E		T
	P	R	E	L	I	M	I	N	A	R	Y	

No. 152

S	I	F	T		A	I	R	B	R	U	S	H
P		E		U		C		L		P		A
R	O	M	A	N	C	E		A	N	G	E	L
I		U		E		B		B		R		F
N	O	R		M		O		B	R	A	S	H
G				P	I	X	I	E		D		E
C		S		L				R		E		A
H		O		O	D	I	U	M				R
I	M	P	L	Y		S		O		H	O	T
C		R		M		S		U		U		E
K	N	A	V	E		U	N	T	A	M	E	D
E		N		N		E		H		A		L
N	O	O	N	T	I	D	E		E	N	V	Y

No. 153

R	I	P	E	N	S		B		M		P	
H		O			T	H	E	M	A	T	I	C
Y	A	W			U		R		C		N	
M		D	I	F	F	E	R		H	I	N	T
E		E			F		I		I		E	
D	A	R	E	S		B	E	D	S	I	D	E
			S		P		S		M			
K	E	T	C	H	U	P		W	O	R	L	D
	L		A		L		F			O		E
H	A	R	P		S	C	A	R	A	B		B
	T		E		A		U			B	I	T
P	E	D	E	S	T	A	L			E		O
	D		S		E		T	I	N	D	E	R

No. 154

T	R	E	S	P	A	S	S		T	U	N	A
A		A		R		C				N		R
B	A	S	T	E		A	B	A	T	I	N	G
S		T		V		L				O		U
		E		A		A	D	D	E	N	D	A
W	A	R	B	L	E	R		E		S		B
O				E				C				L
O		W		N		D	I	E	T	A	R	Y
D	R	I	F	T	E	R		I		B		
W		N				U		T		J		B
O	R	D	E	R	E	D		F	L	U	K	E
R		O				G		U		R		S
M	O	W	N		H	E	L	L	B	E	N	T

No. 155

S	L	A	B		E	T	H	I	O	P	I	A
T		S		D		H		N		R		R
O	U	T	S	I	D	E		T	R	I	C	K
P		I		S		S		E		E		S
P	A	R	O	C	H	I	A	L	I	S	M	
A				O		S		L		T		S
G	Y	P	S	U	M		K	I	R	S	C	H
E		Y		R		S		G				O
	B	R	O	T	H	E	R	I	N	L	A	W
S		A		E		A		B		E		C
C	A	M	E	O		D	I	L	E	M	M	A
A		I		U		O		Y		O		S
R	E	D	E	S	I	G	N		A	N	T	E

No. 156

	F	L	A	B	B	E	R	G	A	S	T	
A		I		U		V		U		C		I
B	O	B		S	H	O	W	N		H		M
R		E		H		L		B	R	O	O	M
A	L	L	A	Y		V		O		O		O
C					R	E	T	A	I	L	E	R
A		A		T				T		S		T
D	U	C	K	W	E	E	D					A
A		T		O		A		B	A	S	I	L
B	L	U	R	S		S		U		U		I
R		A		T	R	I	E	R		P	A	T
A		T		E		E		S		E		Y
	T	E	M	P	E	R	A	T	U	R	E	

No. 157

S	A	I	L		O	P	E	R	E	T	T	A
T		B		L		I		E		E		N
E	P	I	T	O	M	E		M	E	R	I	T
R		Z		S		R		O		M		I
E	X	A	L	T		C	A	R	D	I	A	C
O				P		E		S		N		L
T	A	P	E	R	S		G	E	M	I	N	I
Y		R		O		C		F				M
P	R	O	S	P	E	R		U	L	T	R	A
I		V		E		O		L		H		C
C	L	E	A	R		W	I	L	D	E	S	T
A		R		T		D		Y		T		I
L	O	B	B	Y	I	S	T		T	A	L	C

No. 158

D	I	S	M	A	L	L	Y		S	E	A	R
O		I		C		A		C		L		E
T	O	X	I	C		B	E	I	J	I	N	G
E		T		I				R		T		I
	H	E	A	D	Q	U	A	R	T	E	R	S
S		E		E		P		O				T
C	A	N		N	E	S	T	S		T	I	E
R				T		E		T		E		R
U	N	F	L	A	T	T	E	R	I	N	G	
B		A		L				A		U		T
B	A	C	K	L	O	G		T	H	R	O	W
E		T		Y		O		U		E		O
D	E	S	K		C	O	N	S	I	S	T	S

No. 159

No. 160

No. 161

No. 162

No. 163

	C		F		K		A	R	M	F	U	L
N	O	T	I	O	N	A	L			I		I
	L		R		O		L			A	S	K
L	U	R	E		C	R	E	E	P	S		I
	M		W		K		Y			C		N
A	N	N	O	Y	E	D		A	L	O	N	G
			O		R		S		E			
G	I	D	D	Y		S	C	R	A	P	P	Y
U		I			S		R		R		L	
E		M	A	G	P	I	E		N	E	A	R
S	O	P			U		A		I		I	
T		L			R	U	M	I	N	A	N	T
S	I	E	G	E	S		S		G		S	

No. 164

O	P	A	L		D	O	R	M	O	U	S	E
C		T		I		U		E		N		U
C	R	O	O	N	E	R		A	M	B	E	R
U		N		S				S		O		O
P	R	E	S	U	M	P	T	U	O	U	S	
A				F		L		R		N		P
N	E	W		F	R	A	M	E		D	U	O
T		H		I		I		M				N
	D	I	S	C	O	N	T	E	N	T	E	D
O		T		I				N		U		E
B	R	E	V	E		B	A	T	T	L	E	R
O		S		N		E		S		I		E
E	N	T	I	T	L	E	S		S	P	A	R

No. 165

No. 166

No. 167

No. 168

No. 169

HOMILY STRONG
O E I B O U A
T S Z EQUATES
DISDAIN T G K
O R E STOLE
GORED F I T
E STAMP N
I P C RIGHT
SCUFF T E O
L B O INSULIN
ALLEGRO A U G
N I G N G R U
DACTYL HECKLE

No. 170

No. 171

No. 172

No. 173

No. 174

No. 175

E	M	B	O	S	S		S		A		U	
N		O			H	O	M	E	L	E	S	S
F	O	X			O		U		T		A	
O		E	X	C	E	E	D		R	O	B	E
L		R			S		G		U		L	
D	U	S	T	S		D	E	S	I	R	E	S
			H		M		S		S			
G	H	E	R	K	I	N		S	T	R	A	P
	E		A		M		L			A		U
M	A	T	S		I	R	O	N	I	C		D
	V		H		C		C			K	I	D
R	E	S	E	A	R	C	H			E		L
	N		D		Y		S	O	O	T	H	E

No. 176

D	E	V	E	L	O	P	S		T	O	L	L
A		O		I		A				R		A
F	E	I	G	N		S	N	U	B	B	E	D
T		C		G		T				I		Y
		E		E		R	E	C	I	T	A	L
O	R	D	E	R	L	Y		O		S		I
U				I				N				K
T		D		N		T	R	U	N	D	L	E
S	T	A	G	G	E	R		N		R		
M		R				A		D		I		I
A	W	K	W	A	R	D		R	I	V	E	N
R		E				E		U		E		K
T	E	N	S		G	R	U	M	B	L	E	S

No. 177

No. 178

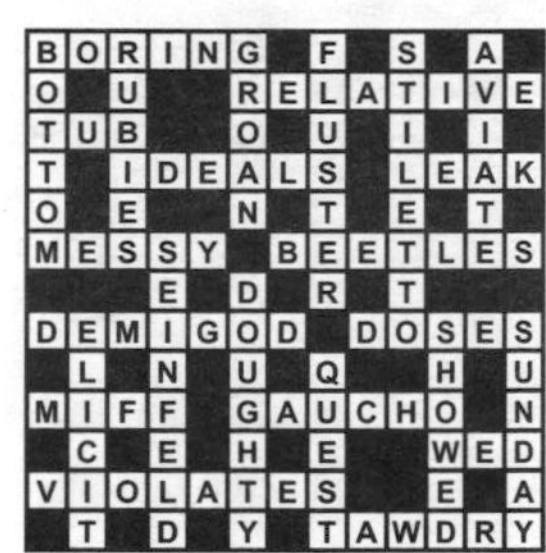

No. 179

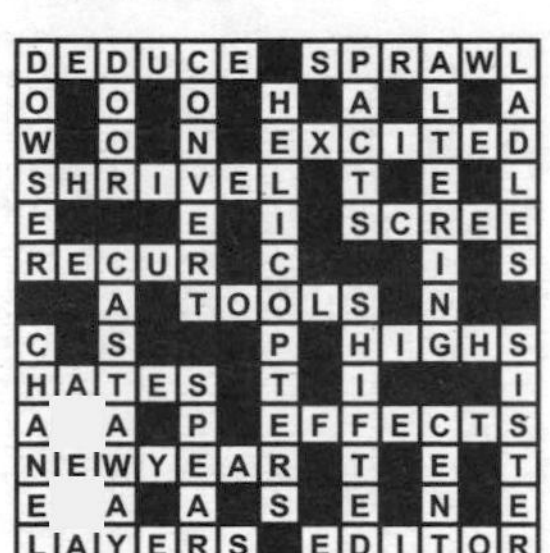

No. 180

No. 181

	T	R	A	N	S	F	I	G	U	R	E	
R		A		U		R		R		A		C
U		M		C	H	I	V	E		Z	O	O
L	A	B	E	L		N		E		O		M
E		L		E		G		D	U	R	U	M
O	V	E	R	U	S	E	S					A
F		R		S				D		A		N
T					I	M	P	E	L	L	E	D
H	A	B	I	T		O		E		C		M
U		O		H		D		P	R	O	V	E
M	E	W		O	P	E	N	S		H		N
B		L		S		S		E		O		T
	E	S	S	E	N	T	I	A	L	L	Y	

No. 182

W	A	S	H	E	R		P	L	A	C	E	D
A		O		N		R		I		R		E
L		U		D		E	X	C	L	U	D	E
L	E	P	T	O	N	S		K		C		P
O				W		P		S	E	I	Z	E
P	U	R	G	E		E				B		R
		E		D	O	C	K	S		L		
S		Q				T		C	R	E	P	T
C	O	U	T	H		A		E				U
R		I		A		B	E	N	E	F	I	T
U	N	R	A	V	E	L		T		L		O
F		E		E		E		E		O		R
F	A	D	I	N	G		A	D	O	P	T	S

No. 183

B	O	L	T		D	E	E	P	N	E	S	S
O		A		R		X		E		M		I
U	P	S	T	A	R	T		R	E	B	E	L
N		E		B		R		S		R		V
T	H	R	O	B		A	W	E	S	O	M	E
I				L		S		V		I		R
F	E	T	T	E	R		B	E	L	L	O	W
U		A		R		L		R				E
L	I	M	P	O	P	O		A	I	D	E	D
N		A		U		G		N		O		D
E	A	R	N	S		J	A	C	U	Z	Z	I
S		I		E		A		E		E		N
S	Y	N	D	R	O	M	E		S	N	A	G

No. 184

No. 185

No. 186

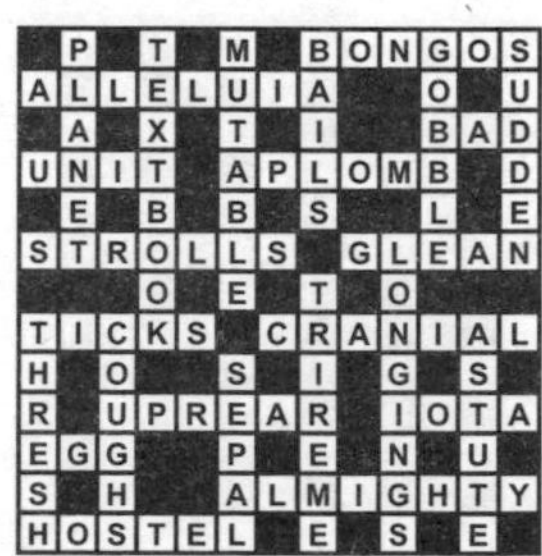

No. 187

S	L	I	G	H	T	L	Y		S	U	R	F
P		L		Y		A		A		N		E
O	X	L	I	P		G	A	B	R	I	E	L
N		N		O		G		S		O		I
T	R	E	A	C	L	E		T	O	N	I	C
A		S		H		D		E				I
N	O	S	H	O	W		A	M	I	D	S	T
E				N		S		I		I		A
O	I	L	E	D		T	H	O	U	G	H	T
U		O		R		R		U		I		I
S	A	S	H	I	M	I		S	E	T	T	O
L		E		A		F		L		A		N
Y	A	R	D		R	E	C	Y	C	L	E	S

No. 188

D	E	R	M	I	S		C		M		B	
A		O			T	E	R	T	I	A	R	Y
H	O	W			E		I		S		O	
L		I	N	G	E	S	T		S	A	G	O
I		N			D		I		O		U	
A	E	G	I	S		A	C	C	U	S	E	D
			N		A		S		R			
P	A	R	T	I	E	S		B	I	P	E	D
	M		E		R		F			U		O
P	U	R	R		O	N	E	O	F	F		T
	L		V		B		A			F	I	T
C	E	R	A	M	I	C	S			I		E
	T		L		C		T	W	I	N	E	D

No. 189

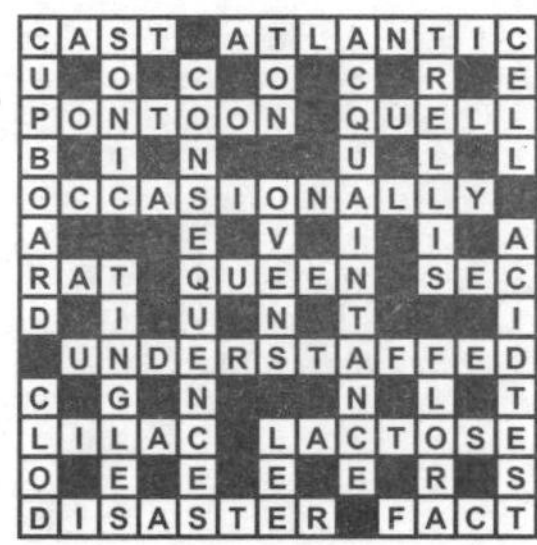

No. 190

No. 191

No. 192

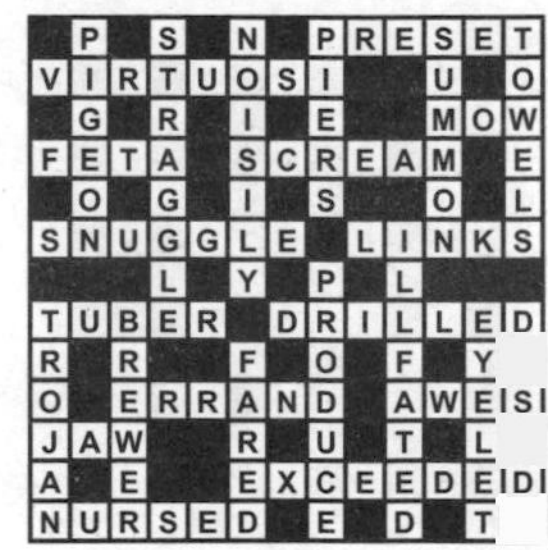

No. 193

E	N	S	E	M	B	L	E		Y	E	T	I
X		E		U		U		E		X		N
A	P	R	I	L		M	I	L	I	T	I	A
G		V		T		B		E		R		P
G	R	A	N	I	T	E		C	L	A	S	P
E		N		L		R		T				R
R	I	T	U	A	L		G	R	O	T	T	O
A				T		H		O		R		P
T	A	S	T	E		A	P	P	L	I	E	R
E		T		R		W		L		P		I
D	I	O	R	A	M	A		A	R	O	M	A
L		M		L		I		T		D		T
Y	U	A	N		L	I	C	E	N	S	E	E

No. 194

C	O	W	A	R	D	L	Y		D	I	S	H
A		A		E		E				N		E
B	I	T	E	S		N	A	M	I	B	I	A
S		E		U		T				O		D
		R		R		I	N	S	U	R	E	R
R	E	S	T	F	U	L		T		N		E
E				A				A				S
P		Z		C		U	P	T	I	G	H	T
R	I	O	T	E	R	S		U		N		
O		D				A		S		E		P
A	B	I	D	I	N	G		Q	U	I	T	E
C		A				E		U		S		E
H	A	C	K		E	S	P	O	U	S	A	L

No. 195

No. 196

No. 197

No. 198

No. 199

	O	V	E	R	A	C	H	I	E	V	E	
A		E		U		A		N		O		F
R	I	G		L	U	N	G	S		Y		U
I		A		E		A		T	R	A	I	N
S	O	N	G	S		D		E		G		C
T					P	A	R	A	K	E	E	T
O		A		D				D		S		I
C	O	N	V	E	R	S	E					O
R		N		V		I		W	O	M	A	N
A	M	U	S	E		N		R		A		A
C		L		L	A	N	C	E		J	A	R
Y		A		O		E		S		O		Y
	P	R	E	P	A	R	A	T	O	R	Y	

No. 200

	D	I	A	G	N	O	S	T	I	C	S	
G		N		E		S		E		O		U
R		T		S	P	I	E	S		P	I	N
A	V	E	R	T		E		T		R		D
N		N		U		R		S	P	A	D	E
D	I	S	T	R	E	S	S					R
F		E		E				B		I		S
A					C	L	A	R	I	N	E	T
T	O	W	N	S		I		O		G		A
H		A		P		N		W	O	R	S	T
E	N	D		O	V	E	R	S		A		E
R		E		O		U		E		I		D
	T	R	A	N	S	P	A	R	E	N	T	

No. 201

No. 202

No. 203

No. 204

No. 205

[illegible]	S		B		S		A	T	R	I	U	M
A	T	L	A	N	T	I	S			N		O
[illegible]	E		C		R		K			H	I	D
T	R	E	K		A	G	E	N	D	A		E
[illegible]	E		F		N		W			L		L
C	O	L	L	I	D	E		F	E	E	D	S
			I		S		P		N			
B	U	M	P	Y		R	E	S	O	L	V	E
L		O			M		P		R		A	
O		R	E	S	E	N	T		M	I	L	D
W	E	T			R		A		O		U	
U		A			C	U	L	T	U	R	E	D
P	A	R	O	D	Y		K		S		D	

No. 206

T	O	T	S		A	C	A	D	E	M	I	C
H		O		I		U		I		A	[illegible]	A
U	N	K	E	M	P	T		S	A	C	K	S
M		Y		P				A		B	[illegible]	E
P	H	O	T	O	G	R	A	P	H	E	R	
I				V		I		P		T	[illegible]	U
N	I	B		E	A	G	L	E		H	O	P
G		L		R		I		A				S
	B	E	W	I	L	D	E	R	M	E	N	T
S		N		S				I		X	[illegible]	R
W	I	D	T	H		C	O	N	S	U	M	E
A		E		E		O		G		L	[illegible]	A
M	A	R	K	D	O	W	N		I	T	E	M

No. 207

No. 208

No. 209

No. 210

No. 211

WHIPPING ZINC
O N Y E N L O
RISER UTOPIAN
D T O T N A S
PRATTLE FUDGE
R N E R L C
OPTICS GATEAU
C H A M L T
EATEN ZAMBEZI
S H I A A G V
STENCIL BRAKE
O M S E L N L
REEF TAPESTRY

No. 212

DIGITS SLIGHT
E U O P U I
A L N ROTTING
REPLICA E L E
L G C STEER
YOUTH T F S
N TRIAD U
G S C RILED
RATES A U R
A E L LUMBAGO
PEAFOWL M I O
E D T Y E M P
SCYTHE CRISPY

No. 213

No. 214

No. 215

No. 216

No. 217

■	L	A	U	G	H	I	N	G	G	A	S	■
U	■	R	■	Y	■	D	■	L	■	S	■	E
N	■	T	■	M	E	L	E	E	■	S	U	M
D	E	I	G	N	■	I	■	A	■	A	■	B
E	■	S	■	A	■	N	■	M	A	Y	O	R
S	T	A	R	S	I	G	N	■	■	■	■	O
I	■	N	■	T	■	■	■	G	■	B	■	I
R	■	■	■	■	W	E	L	L	R	E	A	D
A	W	A	R	D	■	M	■	I	■	D	■	E
B	■	N	■	R	■	B	■	S	O	B	E	R
L	O	G	■	A	L	L	O	T	■	U	■	E
E	■	L	■	P	■	E	■	E	■	G	■	R
■	D	E	T	E	R	M	I	N	I	S	M	■

No. 218

O	P	P	O	S	I	N	G	■	S	T	U	B
U	■	O	■	U	■	U	■	U	■	H	■	E
S	A	T	Y	R	■	T	A	N	K	E	R	S
T	■	E	■	P	■	■	■	D	■	S	■	O
■	I	N	F	R	I	N	G	E	M	E	N	T
O	■	C	■	I	■	A	■	T	■	■	■	T
B	U	Y	■	S	M	I	L	E	■	E	Y	E
E	■	■	■	I	■	V	■	C	■	G	■	D
D	I	S	I	N	F	E	C	T	I	O	N	■
I	■	H	■	G	■	■	■	A	■	T	■	F
E	N	A	B	L	E	S	■	B	R	I	N	E
N	■	R	■	Y	■	U	■	L	■	S	■	U
T	I	D	Y	■	D	E	S	E	R	T	E	D

No. 219

I	N	C	H	■	L	U	K	E	W	A	R	M
M	■	E	■	I	■	P	■	X	■	R	■	I
P	E	D	A	N	T	S	■	T	A	M	E	S
R	■	A	■	T	■	E	■	O	■	F	■	C
E	R	R	O	R	■	T	H	R	O	U	G	H
S	■	■	■	A	■	S	■	T	■	L	■	I
S	U	P	I	N	E	■	T	I	S	S	U	E
I	■	L	■	S	■	C	■	O	■	■	■	V
O	P	A	C	I	T	Y	■	N	A	C	H	O
N	■	C	■	G	■	G	■	A	■	E	■	U
I	N	A	N	E	■	N	E	T	T	L	E	S
S	■	R	■	N	■	E	■	E	■	L	■	L
M	E	D	I	T	A	T	E	■	R	O	S	Y

No. 220

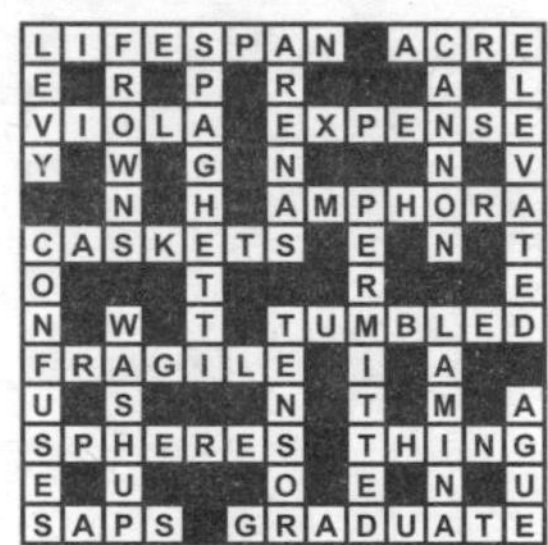

L	I	F	E	S	P	A	N	■	A	C	R	E
E	■	R	■	P	■	R	■	■	■	A	■	L
V	I	O	L	A	■	E	X	P	E	N	S	E
Y	■	W	■	G	■	N	■	■	■	N	■	V
■	■	N	■	H	■	A	M	P	H	O	R	A
C	A	S	K	E	T	S	■	E	■	N	■	T
O	■	■	■	T	■	■	■	R	■	■	■	E
N	■	W	■	T	■	T	U	M	B	L	E	D
F	R	A	G	I	L	E	■	I	■	A	■	■
U	■	S	■	■	■	N	■	T	■	M	■	A
S	P	H	E	R	E	S	■	T	H	I	N	G
E	■	U	■	■	■	O	■	E	■	N	■	U
S	A	P	S	■	G	R	A	D	U	A	T	E

No. 221

C	U	T	E	■	S	P	E	C	I	F	I	C
H	■	I	■	N	■	O	■	R	■	I	■	R
A	G	R	O	U	N	D	■	Y	U	C	C	A
R	■	E	■	R	■	I	■	P	■	T	■	F
A	N	D	E	S	■	U	N	T	W	I	S	T
C	■	■	■	E	■	M	■	O	■	V	■	S
T	A	K	E	R	S	■	A	G	L	E	A	M
E	■	I	■	Y	■	A	■	R	■	■	■	A
R	E	C	O	R	D	S	■	A	S	H	E	N
L	■	K	■	H	■	S	■	P	■	O	■	S
E	P	O	X	Y	■	U	N	H	I	T	C	H
S	■	F	■	M	■	R	■	Y	■	E	■	I
S	U	F	F	E	R	E	D	■	F	L	A	P

No. 222

U	P	H	E	A	V	A	L	■	D	A	S	H
G	■	I	■	L	■	S	■	A	■	C	■	E
L	E	T	U	P	■	S	A	N	G	R	I	A
Y	■	T	■	H	■	E	■	N	■	E	■	V
■	D	I	S	A	S	T	R	O	U	S	L	Y
F	■	N	■	B	■	S	■	U	■	■	■	S
A	R	G	U	E	D	■	E	N	G	I	N	E
R	■	■	■	T	■	G	■	C	■	N	■	T
R	E	Q	U	I	R	E	M	E	N	T	S	■
I	■	U	■	C	■	N	■	M	■	E	■	E
E	M	A	N	A	T	E	■	E	R	R	E	D
R	■	R	■	L	■	V	■	N	■	I	■	E
S	E	T	S	■	M	A	N	T	O	M	A	N

No. 223

P	E	R	S	P	I	R	E		Y	E	L	L
U		E		R		A		C		V		I
S	U	S	H	I		P	R	O	R	A	T	A
H		T		D				N		D		I
	C	A	R	E	L	E	S	S	N	E	S	S
C		T		O		X		I				O
O	R	E		F	I	E	L	D		G	I	N
S				P		R		E		R		S
T	O	T	A	L	I	T	A	R	I	A	N	
U		H		A				A		N		B
M	O	R	O	C	C	O		B	A	D	G	E
E		E		E		I		L		P		A
S	E	E	S		P	L	A	Y	B	A	C	K

No. 224

L	I	T	E	R	A	R	Y		S	C	A	M
O		W		E		E		A		H		I
C	H	I	E	F		N	U	P	T	I	A	L
H		T		R		O		P		L		K
	O	T	H	E	R	W	O	R	L	D	L	Y
M		E		S		N		E				W
E	A	R	T	H	S		A	C	A	C	I	A
R				I		C		I		E		Y
I	N	C	O	N	S	O	L	A	B	L	E	
N		H		G		R		T		S		H
G	R	E	M	L	I	N		I	C	I	L	Y
U		E		Y		E		O		U		M
E	A	R	S		G	R	A	N	D	S	O	N

No. 225

C	A	U	L	D	R	O	N		D	O	E	R
O		N		I		B		A		C		E
N	O	D	E	S		S	T	R	A	T	U	M
D		E		H		E		I		E		O
E	A	R	N	E	R	S		T	U	T	O	R
S		G		A		S		H				S
C	H	O	I	R	S		S	M	U	D	G	E
E				T		P		E		O		L
N	O	I	S	E		L	E	T	T	U	C	E
S		R		N		A		I		B		S
I	N	A	N	E	L	Y		C	A	L	M	S
O		T		D		E		A		E		L
N	E	E	D		I	D	O	L	A	T	R	Y

No. 226

A	U	T	O	C	R	A	T		O	S	L	O
L		Y		H		W		T		C		U
L	A	P	S	E		A	T	H	I	R	S	T
Y		H		E		R		O		U		W
	C	O	N	S	I	D	E	R	A	B	L	E
E		O		E		S		O				I
D	A	N	U	B	E		R	U	L	I	N	G
U				U		M		G		T		H
C	L	E	A	R	S	I	G	H	T	E	D	
A		N		G		S		F		R		O
T	A	T	T	E	R	S		A	B	A	S	H
E		R		R		A		R		T		I
S	A	Y	S		A	L	T	E	R	E	G	O

No. 227

H	I	P	S		P	L	E	A	S	A	N	T
I		L		I		E		R		R		U
S	W	A	R	M	E	D		C	A	S	E	S
T		Y		P				H		E		K
O	B	S	E	R	V	A	T	I	O	N	S	
R				O		C		T		I		P
I	C	E		V	E	R	S	E		C	U	R
C		A		E		I		C				E
	P	R	E	M	E	D	I	T	A	T	E	D
C		D		E				U		R		A
H	E	R	O	N		V	E	R	M	O	N	T
E		U		T		I		E		U		O
F	A	M	I	S	H	E	D		S	T	I	R

No. 228

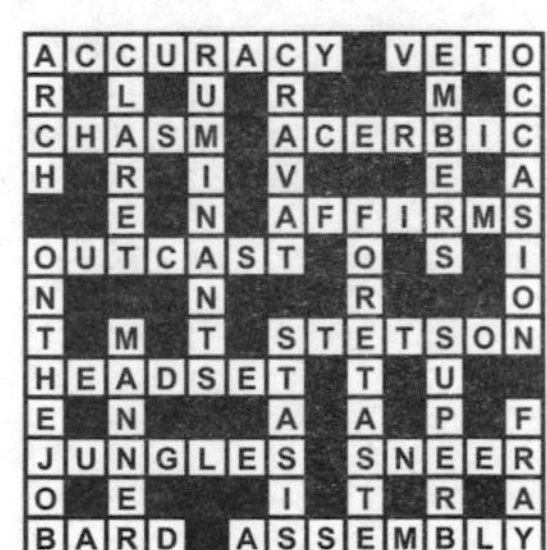

A	C	C	U	R	A	C	Y		V	E	T	O
R		L		U		R				M		C
C	H	A	S	M		A	C	E	R	B	I	C
H		R		I		V				E		A
		E		N		A	F	F	I	R	M	S
O	U	T	C	A	S	T		O		S		I
N				N				R				O
T		M		T		S	T	E	T	S	O	N
H	E	A	D	S	E	T		T		U		
E		N				A		A		P		F
J	U	N	G	L	E	S		S	N	E	E	R
O		E				I		T		R		A
B	A	R	D		A	S	S	E	M	B	L	Y

No. 229

I	M	P	I	S	H		A		P		P	
N		A			E	M	P	E	R	O	R	S
J	E	T			R		O		E		E	
U		I	N	G	O	T	S		A	I	L	S
R		N			D		T		C		I	
Y	E	A	S	T		A	L	C	H	E	M	Y
			W		D		E		E			
S	O	M	E	H	O	W		B	R	O	A	D
	R		E		O		F			O		R
W	A	T	T		R	O	L	L	E	D		O
	T		E		W		U			L	O	W
C	O	X	S	W	A	I	N			E		S
	R		T		Y		G	L	O	S	S	Y

No. 230

B	U	D	S		I	N	T	A	G	L	I	O
R		A		T		E		U		A	[illegible]	V
O	R	I	F	I	C	E		T	E	N	S	E
K		S		T		D		H		T	[illegible]	R
E	G	Y	P	T		E	Y	E	L	E	T	S
N				L		D		N		R	[illegible]	T
H	I	D	D	E	N		S	T	A	N	Z	A
E		E		T		J		I				T
A	S	S	U	A	G	E		C	H	O	R	E
R		E		T		W		I		W	[illegible]	M
T	A	R	O	T		E	N	T	E	N	T	E
E		T		L		L		Y		E	[illegible]	N
D	I	S	P	E	R	S	E		E	D	I	T

No. 231

No. 232

No. 233

No. 234

No. 235

W	O	B	B	L	Y		P		A		S	
I		E			E	N	L	A	R	G	E	S
S	K	Y			L		A		B		I	
D		O	R	A	L	L	Y		O	O	Z	E
O		N			S		P		R		E	
M	O	D	E	L		D	E	P	E	N	D	S
			N		P		N		A			
S	E	T	F	R	E	E		C	L	A	I	M
	N		E		R		B			B		A
B	I	L	E		F	I	E	S	T	A		R
	G		B		E		R			C	A	B
I	M	P	L	I	C	I	T			U		L
	A		E		T		H	A	S	S	L	E

No. 236

	D		P		S		C	U	P	O	L	A
L	I	B	R	E	T	T	O			B		S
	P		I		U		P			J	O	T
P	O	E	M		C	R	E	C	H	E		R
	L		R		K		D			C		A
D	E	C	O	R	U	M		A	P	T	L	Y
			S		P		C		L			
M	I	X	E	D		R	O	T	A	T	E	D
O		E			B		G		T		X	
R		R	A	V	A	G	E		O	N	U	S
S	I	X			N		N		N		D	
E		E			D	E	C	E	I	V	E	R
L	O	S	E	R	S		Y		C		D	

No. 237

N	Y	M	P	H	S		O		A		F	
I		A			C	I	V	I	L	I	A	N
C	U	D			A		E		F		R	
K		C	O	L	L	A	R		R	A	M	S
E		A			D		R		E		E	
D	E	P	T	H		B	U	R	S	A	R	Y
			E		I		N		C			
S	C	O	R	I	N	G		M	O	W	E	R
	L		R		H		C			A		I
P	U	M	A		E	C	H	O	E	S		P
	T		P		R		I			H	I	P
A	C	T	I	N	I	U	M			E		E
	H		N		T		P	A	S	S	E	D

No. 238

No. 239

No. 240

T	A	P	S		M	E	N	I	S	C	U	S
E		U		U		N		N		Y		O
C	H	R	O	N	I	C		V	I	P	E	R
T		S		D		O		U		R		E
O	V	E	R	I	N	D	U	L	G	E	D	
N				S		E		N		S		P
I	N	T	A	C	T		G	E	Y	S	E	R
C		W		O		C		R				U
	H	E	A	V	Y	H	E	A	R	T	E	D
T		E		E		O		B		A		E
U	T	T	E	R		O	I	L	S	K	I	N
G		E		E		S		E		E		C
S	H	R	E	D	D	E	D		B	R	I	E

No. 241

	B		A		N		A	B	O	A	R	D
H	O	G	S	H	E	A	D			D		I
	N		S		R		O			J	U	G
G	O	B	I		V	I	R	A	G	O		G
	B		G		O		N			I		E
R	O	U	N	D	U	P		D	I	N	E	R
			E		S		L		N			
R	U	D	D	Y		S	I	G	H	T	L	Y
A		A			F		G		U		U	
B		W	R	E	A	T	H		M	U	L	E
B	U	D			N		T		A		L	
L		L			C	O	L	A	N	D	E	R
E	N	E	R	G	Y		Y		E		D	

No. 242

	S	E	R	E	N	D	I	P	I	T	Y	
R		N		A		R		O		I		I
E		D		S	N	O	O	P		R	U	M
S	I	G	H	T		P		U		E		M
E		A		E		I		P	A	S	S	E
M	E	M	B	R	A	N	E					D
B		E		N				M		C		I
L					P	A	R	A	B	O	L	A
A	L	L	O	Y		B		N		L		T
N		E		A		L		A	B	O	D	E
C	O	G		C	L	O	U	T		G		L
E		A		H		O		E		N		Y
	I	L	L	T	E	M	P	E	R	E	D	

No. 243

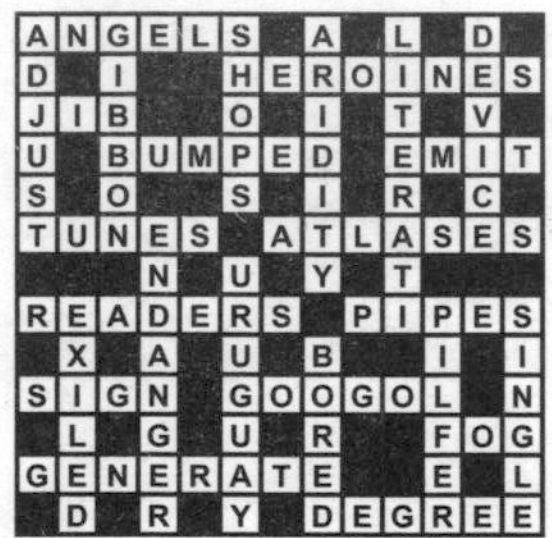

No. 244

No. 245

No. 246

No. 247

	O	B	S	T	R	U	C	T	I	V	E	
A		U		E		P		O		I		O
P	E	G		P	A	R	I	S		R		U
O		L		I		O		S	T	U	N	T
C	R	E	E	D		A		I		S		S
A					T	R	A	N	S	E	C	T
L		D		A				G		S		A
Y	O	U	N	G	E	S	T					N
P		T		I		T		C	O	W	E	D
T	W	I	S	T		R		A		A		I
I		F		A	C	O	R	N		S	U	N
C		U		T		L		D		T		G
	B	L	U	E	B	L	O	O	D	E	D	

No. 248

	P	R	O	S	P	E	C	T	I	V	E	
A		E		E		U		O		O		C
C		C		S	T	R	E	W		W	O	O
K	N	O	T	S		O		E		E		N
N		I		I		P		R	E	L	I	C
O	N	L	O	O	K	E	R					O
W		S		N				C		S		R
L					H	A	L	L	O	W	E	D
E	N	V	O	Y		U		A		A		A
D		O		I		G		S	E	D	A	N
G	I	G		E	V	I	L	S		D		C
E		U		L		T		I		L		E
	H	E	A	D	T	E	A	C	H	E	R	

No. 249

D	I	C	T	A	T	O	R		R	A	I	N
A		A		P		N		P		F		I
B	E	B	O	P		E	M	O	T	I	O	N
S		I		R				S		R		E
	I	N	T	E	R	M	I	T	T	E	N	T
C		E		H		A		G				E
A	P	T		E	A	G	E	R		B	Y	E
L				N		M		A		E		N
L	O	N	G	S	T	A	N	D	I	N	G	
B		E		I				U		E		E
A	R	R	I	V	E	S		A	V	A	I	L
C		V		E		I		T		T		L
K	E	Y	S		S	P	E	E	C	H	E	S

No. 250

B	R	E	A	K	O	U	T		A	F	A	R
O		M		A		P		N		U		A
W	H	E	E	L		L	E	A	R	N	E	R
S		R		E		I		R		G		E
	S	A	T	I	S	F	A	C	T	I	O	N
C		L		D		T		I				E
O	D	D	S	O	N		U	S	U	R	P	S
L				S		R		S		O		S
O	V	E	R	C	A	U	T	I	O	U	S	
S		X		O		S		S		T		P
S	N	I	P	P	E	T		T	W	I	L	L
U		T		E		I		I		N		U
S	A	S	H		I	C	E	C	R	E	A	M

No. 251

D	I	L	E	M	M	A	S		S	C	A	N
A		O		O		L		I		O		E
M	I	D	S	T		L	O	N	G	B	O	W
P		G		H				C		R		L
	D	I	V	E	R	S	I	O	N	A	R	Y
D		N		R		A		M				W
E	R	G		T	H	U	M	P		F	O	E
A				O		C		E		I		D
D	E	C	O	N	G	E	S	T	A	N	T	
L		A		G				E		E		E
I	M	P	O	U	N	D		N	A	S	A	L
N		E		E		U		C		S		K
E	A	S	E		I	D	L	E	N	E	S	S

No. 252

S	E	T	T	E	R		R		B		S	
E		U			O	P	E	R	A	B	L	E
W	A	X			O		A		C		O	
I		E	D	I	T	E	D		T	O	P	S
N		D			S		I		E		E	
G	N	O	M	E		F	L	O	R	I	S	T
			A		S		Y		I			
O	R	A	T	I	O	N		F	A	C	E	S
	E		E		B		A			I		E
F	A	I	R		B	A	C	K	U	P		A
	C		I		I		I			H	E	N
A	T	T	A	I	N	E	D			E		C
	S		L		G		S	O	U	R	C	E

No. 253

M	O	P	E		D	I	S	P	A	T	C	H
E		A		H		N		R		R		I
N	I	T	P	I	C	K		E	L	A	N	D
A		I		G				P		N		E
C	L	O	T	H	E	S	H	O	R	S	E	
I				S		P		N		O		S
N	O	T		P	A	R	E	D		M	A	T
G		E		I		I		E				A
	R	E	F	R	I	G	E	R	A	T	O	R
T		M		I				A		E		G
H	O	I	S	T		C	A	N	A	S	T	A
O		N		E		A		T		T		Z
R	I	G	I	D	I	T	Y		B	Y	T	E

No. 254

E	X	E	M	P	L	A	R		E	T	C	H
N		S		R		R		C		R		E
D	I	S	C	O		R	I	O	T	O	U	S
S		E		P		I		U		P		I
	I	N	C	O	N	V	E	N	I	E	N	T
T		C		R		E		T				A
E	R	E	C	T	S		B	E	A	C	O	N
A				I		P		R		H		T
C	A	R	T	O	G	R	A	P	H	E	R	
H		I		N		O		O		A		P
I	N	D	R	A	W	N		I	M	P	E	L
N		E		L		T		N		E		U
G	U	S	T		F	O	R	T	U	N	E	S

No. 255

U	N	B	U	C	K	L	E		D	R	U	M
N		A		U		O		C		E		E
A	X	I	O	M		C	R	O	Q	U	E	T
C		L		U		A		U		S		A
C	H	I	L	L		T		N		E	L	M
O		F		O	V	E	R	T				O
U		F		N				R		T		R
N				I	T	A	L	Y		R		P
T	O	R		M		R		W	E	I	G	H
A		O		B		C		O		U		O
B	O	U	Q	U	E	T		M	I	M	E	S
L		T		S		I		A		P		I
E	V	E	S		A	C	A	N	T	H	U	S

No. 256

L	I	G	H	T	S		A	V	E	N	G	E
A		I		A		D		I		O		J
N		L		X		O	N	E	T	I	M	E
C	A	L	C	I	U	M		W		S		C
E				I		E		S	A	I	N	T
T	O	K	E	N		S				E		S
		I		G	A	T	E	S		S		
A		N				I		M	E	T	E	S
S	A	G	A	S		C		A				T
C		S		K		A	B	S	E	N	C	E
E	X	H	A	U	S	T		H		I		E
N		I		L		E		E		N		P
D	A	P	P	L	E		E	S	T	E	R	S

No. 257

	S	M	A	L	L	C	H	A	N	G	E	
D		O		A		O		U		E		O
E		R		Y	O	U	N	G		T	A	P
R	A	T	E	D		S		E		U		E
M		A		O		I		R	I	P	E	N
A	L	L	O	W	I	N	G					A
T		S		N				S		G		N
O					P	A	M	P	E	R	E	D
L	O	C	A	L		C		O		E		S
O		I		O		E		N	I	N	T	H
G	A	D		V	O	T	E	S		A		U
Y		E		E		I		O		D		T
	P	R	E	R	E	C	O	R	D	E	D	

No. 258

	A	P	P	R	O	B	A	T	I	O	N	
I		A		O		U		H		U		I
N	I	P		U	N	C	L	E		T		N
F		E		G		K		R	A	G	E	S
L	A	R	C	H		E		E		R		I
A					S	T	U	B	B	O	R	N
M		M		U				Y		W		U
M	E	A	L	T	I	M	E					A
A		J		E		I		F	I	R	S	T
B	L	O	W	N		L		E		A		I
L		R		S	T	I	L	L		F	I	N
E		C		I		E		O		T		G
	C	A	L	L	O	U	S	N	E	S	S	

No. 259

C	O	M	M	I	T		U	P	K	E	E	P
A		I		S		I		U		L		L
R		N		L		N	U	R	S	E	R	Y
V	A	G	R	A	N	T		R		M		I
E				N		E		S	K	E	I	N
R	A	P	I	D		R				N		G
		R		S	H	R	E	D		T		
A		E				O		R	A	S	P	Y
D	I	C	E	D		G		E				O
O		E		E		A	N	D	R	O	I	D
R	A	D	I	A	N	T		G		W		E
E		E		R		E		E		E		L
D	I	S	U	S	E		P	R	I	D	E	S

No. 260

No. 261

No. 262

No. 263

No. 264

No. 265

E	G	G	S		T	H	U	M	B	S	U	P
M		L		C		A		A		E		A
B	O	U	D	O	I	R		N	I	C	E	R
E		E		I		D		U		L		A
L	I	D		N		E		F	L	U	M	P
L				C	O	N	G	A		D		H
I		G		I				C		E		E
S		A		D	R	I	F	T				R
H	O	R	D	E		N		U		D	O	N
M		M		N		T		R		R		A
E	J	E	C	T		E	Y	E	B	A	L	L
N		N		A		N		R		N		I
T	O	T	A	L	I	T	Y		S	K	U	A

No. 266

No. 267

No. 268

No. 269

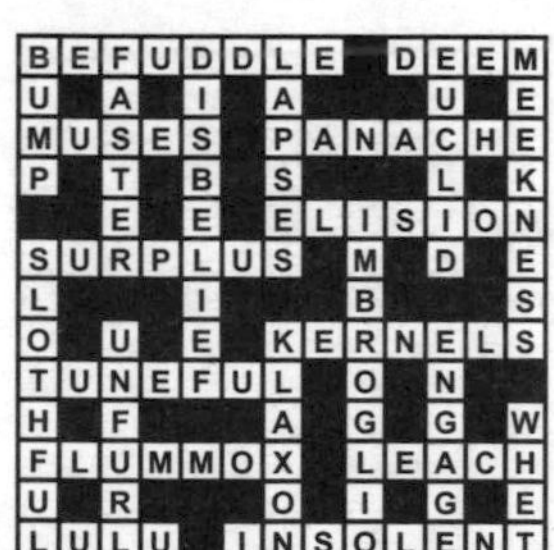

No. 270

No. 271

	A		C		B		S	P	I	R	A	L
O	V	E	R	D	R	A	W			E		O
	O		E		A		A			F	E	W
A	W	E	D		K	U	N	G	F	U		E
	A		I		I		S			T		S
P	L	A	T	I	N	G		C	H	E	A	T
			O		G		D		E			
S	H	A	R	P		D	E	B	R	I	E	F
O		I			G		C		A		I	
F		R	E	P	U	T	E		L	A	T	E
F	I	B			A		N		D		H	
I		U			R	E	C	O	R	D	E	D
T	O	S	S	E	D		Y		Y		R	

No. 272

U	N	D	O		A	R	G	U	M	E	N	T
N		O		I		O		N		X		R
D	E	M	O	N	I	C		A	C	C	R	A
E		E		D		O		T		L		N
R	A	D	I	O		C	U	T	L	A	S	S
S				C		O		R		I		G
T	W	E	N	T	Y		H	A	M	M	E	R
A		C		R		C		C				E
N	O	U	R	I	S	H		T	R	E	S	S
D		A		N		A		I		R		S
I	N	D	I	A		R	A	V	I	O	L	I
N		O		T		G		E		D		O
G	A	R	N	E	R	E	D		R	E	I	N

No. 273

No. 274

No. 275

No. 276

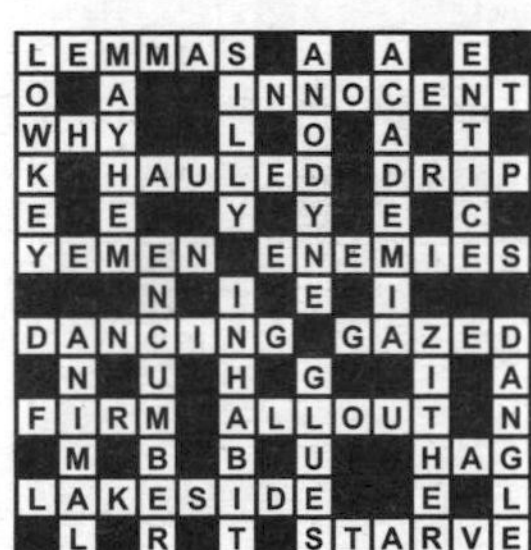

No. 277

M	A	S	T	E	R	L	Y		S	P	A	N
A		T		N		E		S		R		O
G	R	A	N	T		P	O	P	C	O	R	N
N		T		R		T		R		N		A
E	T	U	D	E		O		E		G	A	P
T		R		P	A	N	D	A				P
I		E		R				D		A		E
C				E	L	A	T	E		N		A
N	U	N		N		T		A	S	T	E	R
O		I		E		H		G		E		A
R	E	C	L	U	S	E		L	I	N	E	N
T		H		R		N		E		N		C
H	O	E	S		H	A	N	D	M	A	D	E

No. 278

No. 279

	S		T		M		B	E	I	R	U	T
M	E	M	O	R	I	A	L			E		O
	L		M		S		O			S	A	W
B	E	T	A		F	I	B	U	L	A		E
	N		H		I		S			L		R
D	E	C	A	N	T	S		S	P	E	C	S
			W		S		B		E			
C	O	C	K	Y		B	A	D	D	E	B	T
H		R			S		B		A		Y	
E		A	I	R	W	A	Y		G	L	E	N
W	I	G			I		I		O		B	
E		G			N	O	S	E	G	A	Y	S
D	R	Y	I	N	G		H		Y		E	

No. 280

No. 281

R	E	F	U	G	E		S	P	E	N	D	S
O		A		R		H		E		U		A
B		N		A		E	N	C	O	R	E	S
B	E	G	O	N	I	A		K		T		H
E				O		V		S	P	U	M	E
R	I	V	A	L		Y				R		S
		O		A	C	H	E	D		E		
D		C				A		W	A	D	E	S
A	P	A	R	T		N		I				T
P		L		R		D	E	N	S	I	T	Y
P	R	I	V	A	T	E		D		R		L
E		S		C		D		L		A		E
R	E	T	A	K	E		L	E	A	N	E	D

No. 282

No. 283

	A		A		A		C	O	B	W	E	B
P	R	I	S	O	N	E	R			O		E
	M		P		T		I			B	O	W
N	A	M	E		H	U	B	B	U	B		A
	D		R		I		S			L		I
R	A	D	I	C	L	E		S	M	E	L	L
			T		L		S		A			
D	R	A	Y	S		S	T	A	R	L	E	T
I		D			A		I		A		X	
B		A	I	R	B	A	G		T	A	P	E
B	A	G			U		M		H		E	
L		E			Z	E	A	L	O	T	R	Y
E	R	S	A	T	Z		S		N		T	

No. 284

No. 285

S	E	W	N		U	N	D	E	R	P	I	N
O		H		T		O		V		E		E
L	E	A	T	H	E	R		O	X	B	O	W
D		R		I		D		L		B		T
I	N	F	E	C	T	I	O	U	S	L	Y	
E				K		C		T		E		C
R	E	S	I	S	T		T	I	N	S	E	L
S		H		K		I		O				U
	D	I	S	I	N	G	E	N	U	O	U	S
S		R		N		U		A		W		T
T	A	K	E	N		A	I	R	L	I	N	E
E		E		E		N		Y		N		R
M	E	R	I	D	I	A	N		A	G	E	S

No. 286

F	L	A	P	P	I	N	G		E	W	E	S
L		L		R		A		D		I		O
I	M	A	G	E		S	T	I	R	R	U	P
R		R		D		S		S		E		H
T	E	M	P	E	R	A		C	O	R	G	I
A		E		C		U		O				S
T	I	D	I	E	S		I	N	D	U	C	T
I				S		O		S		N		I
O	G	L	E	S		P	R	O	S	A	I	C
U		E		O		T		L		W		A
S	A	M	U	R	A	I		A	W	A	I	T
L		U		S		M		T		R		E
Y	A	R	N		T	A	K	E	H	E	E	D

No. 287

S	T	A	D	I	U	M	S		A	C	E	S
E		N		N		A		G		R		L
M	U	S	I	C		D	I	O	C	E	S	E
I		W		O		E		L		S		I
C	R	E	A	M		U		D		S	A	G
O		R		P	U	P	A	E				H
N		S		A				N		C		T
S				T	E	R	S	E		R		O
C	O	Y		I		E		A	L	O	O	F
I		A		B		L		G		W		H
O	P	H	E	L	I	A		L	I	B	R	A
U		O		E		T		E		A		N
S	H	O	P		M	E	A	S	U	R	E	D

No. 288

M	I	G	R	A	T	E	S		F	L	E	A
I		A		S		L				E		S
T	O	R	U	S		I	M	P	U	G	N	S
E		A		E		X				A		I
		G		R		I	M	P	A	C	T	S
C	R	E	A	T	O	R		T		Y		T
O				I				A				E
U		S		V		G	U	R	G	L	E	D
G	E	N	T	E	E	L		M		I		
H		I				I		I		Z		F
I	N	V	O	K	E	D		G	R	A	P	E
N		E				E		A		R		E
G	O	L	D		G	R	E	N	A	D	E	S

No. 289

	E		C		C		A	F	F	O	R	D
A	N	C	H	O	R	E	D			U		E
	T		I		A		M			T	O	P
L	I	S	P		V	O	I	C	E	S		U
	R		M		I		X			E		T
G	E	N	U	I	N	E		W	I	T	T	Y
			N		G		O		N			
W	I	N	K	S		A	B	S	C	O	N	D
A		E			F		E		L		O	
F		I	C	A	R	U	S		I	C	O	N
F	I	G			E		I		N		S	
L		H			E	S	T	E	E	M	E	D
E	N	S	U	E	S		Y		S		S	

No. 290

C	A	M	S		Q	U	A	C	K	I	N	G
O		E		T		M		H		C		O
M	I	N	E	R	A	L		A	M	I	N	O
P		S		A		A		M		N		D
L	E	A	R	N		U	M	P	T	E	E	N
I				S		T		I		S		A
M	E	N	A	C	E		C	O	R	S	E	T
E		U		E		G		N				U
N	O	M	I	N	A	L		S	T	A	I	R
T		E		D		O		H		L		E
A	G	R	E	E		W	H	I	R	L	E	D
R		A		N		E		P		O		L
Y	U	L	E	T	I	D	E		A	W	A	Y

No. 291

	A	C	U	P	U	N	C	T	U	R	E	
F		H		A		E		A		E		C
A		A		P	A	G	E	S		B	A	A
M	I	L	K	Y		A		K		U		N
I		I		R		T		S	A	T	E	D
L	E	C	T	U	R	E	S					L
I		E		S				R		T		E
A					F	R	E	E	W	I	L	L
R	U	L	E	D		O		I		T		I
I		U		R		T		S	L	A	N	G
T	I	N		O	A	T	H	S		N		H
Y		G		O		E		U		I		T
	D	E	S	P	O	N	D	E	N	C	Y	

No. 292

S	A	T	U	R	A	T	E		W	A	R	M
I		R		E		R		C		N		A
D	R	I	L	L		A	M	O	U	N	T	S
E		D		E		U		S		U		S
S	T	E	R	N	U	M		M	A	L	T	A
P		N		T		A		O				C
L	I	T	T	L	E		S	P	E	E	C	H
I				E		C		O		G		U
T	R	A	Y	S		H	O	L	L	O	W	S
T		B		S		E		I		T		E
I	D	Y	L	L	I	C		T	A	I	N	T
N		S		Y		K		A		S		T
G	A	S	H		T	S	U	N	A	M	I	S

No. 293

	C		P		E		C	O	H	O	R	T
M	Y	T	H	I	C	A	L			F		H
	C		O		H		E			F	L	Y
E	L	A	N		E	V	A	D	E	S		M
	E		E		L		T			E		U
E	D	I	T	I	O	N		L	O	T	U	S
			I		N		I		U			
S	H	A	C	K		S	M	I	T	T	E	N
E		N			S		M		D		X	
A		S	P	O	U	S	E		A	C	I	D
M	A	W			L		R		T		L	
A		E			L	I	S	T	E	N	E	R
N	O	R	W	A	Y		E		D		S	

No. 294

H	I	G	H	S	E	A	S		O	G	L	E
U		A		E		U				R		X
S	P	U	R	N		T	U	R	N	O	U	T
H		G		S		H				O		E
		E		A		O	A	R	S	M	A	N
A	U	D	I	T	O	R		E		S		D
T				I				M				E
T		S		O		S	T	I	R	R	E	D
A	T	L	A	N	T	A		N		E		
C		I				D		I		B		W
K	I	N	D	L	E	D		S	H	O	V	E
E		G				E		C		R		L
R	A	S	P		I	N	F	E	R	N	A	L

No. 295

	A	C	C	O	M	P	A	N	I	E	D	
A		H		R		A		O		A		A
P		I		C	A	R	E	T		R	O	B
P	U	N	C	H		S		E		L		A
R		E		A		E		D	O	Y	E	N
O	B	S	T	R	U	C	T					D
X		E		D				W		S		O
I					A	M	E	R	I	C	A	N
M	A	N	N	A		A		I		R		M
A		E		L		N		T	E	A	S	E
T	O	W		B	E	F	I	T		W		N
E		E		U		U		E		L		T
	C	R	U	M	B	L	I	N	E	S	S	

No. 296

A	M	B	L	E	D		S		M		K	
P		A			E	N	C	L	O	S	E	S
P	L	Y			V		H		N		N	
L		I	N	S	I	D	E		R	A	N	T
E		N			L		M		O		E	
S	E	G	U	E		H	E	A	V	I	L	Y
			N		B		S		I			
S	T	A	D	I	U	M		P	A	C	K	S
	H		E		F		B			A		P
T	E	A	R		F	R	O	Z	E	N		O
	O		A		O		O			Y	A	K
G	R	A	C	I	O	U	S			O		E
	Y		T		N		T	A	N	N	I	N

No. 297

	V		S		C		D	E	A	R	T	H
D	A	I	Q	U	I	R	I			E		A
	C		U		R		T			W	O	W
D	A	T	A		C	U	C	K	O	O		K
	T		N		L		H			R		E
N	E	E	D	L	E	D		A	D	D	E	D
			E		D		S		I			
P	E	A	R	L		S	A	M	P	L	E	D
R		V			S		W		L		M	
A		O	U	T	C	R	Y		O	V	I	D
Y	E	W			A		E		M		N	
E		E			N	A	R	R	A	T	E	S
R	I	D	G	E	S		S		T		M	

No. 298

	R	O	C	K	T	H	E	B	O	A	T	
C		R		I		A		Y		S		I
O		I		T	R	I	L	L		H	A	M
M	A	G	I	C		L		A		E		P
M		I		H		E		W	I	S	E	R
I	N	N	U	E	N	D	O					E
N		S		N				S		G		S
G					T	R	O	U	B	L	E	S
L	A	C	E	D		A		B		I		I
I		O		R		D		J	U	M	B	O
N	O	W		A	G	I	L	E		P		N
G		E		I		U		C		S		S
	G	R	A	N	D	M	O	T	H	E	R	

No. 299

B	Y	P	A	S	S		L		A		A	
U		A			K	N	E	A	D	I	N	G
Z	A	P			U		A		V		T	
Z		A	R	R	A	Y	S		O	I	L	S
E		Y			S		H		C		E	
R	E	A	D	Y		R	E	P	A	I	R	S
			R		T		D		T			
D	E	P	O	S	E	D		D	E	B	T	S
	S		W		A		G			A		Y
A	C	T	S		S	C	R	E	W	S		M
	O		I		I		E			H	O	B
S	R	I	L	A	N	K	A			E		O
	T		Y		G		T	A	S	S	E	L

No. 300

O	U	T	B	U	R	S	T		A	G	E	D
P		A		N		O		I		A		I
P	O	L	K	A		N	O	N	P	L	U	S
O		K		S		N		V		E		T
R	A	I	N	S		E		E		S	P	A
T		N		A	L	T	E	R				S
U		G		I				T		F		T
N				L	I	T	H	E		L		E
I	L	K		A		U		B	L	U	F	F
T		N		B		S		R		V		U
I	C	I	C	L	E	S		A	R	I	E	L
E		F		E		L		T		A		L
S	E	E	N		R	E	D	E	P	L	O	Y